THE PHYSICALLY AND SEXUALLY ABUSED CHILD
Evaluation and Treatment

Pergamon Titles of Related Interest

Brassard/Germain/Hart PSYCHOLOGICAL MALTREATMENT OF CHILDREN AND YOUTH

Mrazek/Kempe SEXUALLY ABUSED CHILDREN AND THEIR FAMILIES

Plas SYSTEMS PSYCHOLOGY IN THE SCHOOLS

Roberts PEDIATRIC PSYCHOLOGY: Psychological Interventions and Strategies for Pediatric Problems

Santostefano COGNITIVE CONTROL THERAPY WITH CHILDREN AND ADOLESCENTS

Wielkiewicz BEHAVIOR MANAGEMENT IN THE SCHOOLS: Principles and Procedures

Related Journals*

CHILD ABUSE AND NEGLECT: An International Journal

CHILDREN AND YOUTH SERVICES REVIEW

CLINICAL PSYCHOLOGY REVIEW

JOURNAL OF CHILD PSYCHOLOGY AND PSYCHIATRY AND ALLIED DISCIPLINES

*Free sample copies available upon request

PSYCHOLOGY PRACTITIONER GUIDEBOOKS

EDITORS
Arnold P. Goldstein, Syracuse University
Leonard Krasner, Stanford University & SUNY at Stony Brook
Sol L. Garfield, Washington University

THE PHYSICALLY AND SEXUALLY ABUSED CHILD
Evaluation and Treatment

C. EUGENE WALKER
BARBARA L. BONNER
University of Oklahoma Health Sciences Center

KEITH L. KAUFMAN
The Ohio State University

PERGAMON PRESS
New York · Oxford · Beijing · Frankfurt
São Paulo · Sydney · Tokyo · Toronto

U.S.A.	Pergamon Press, Maxwell House, Fairview Park, Elmsford, New York 10523, U.S.A.
U.K.	Pergamon Press, Headington Hill Hall, Oxford OX3 0BW, England
PEOPLE'S REPUBLIC OF CHINA	Pergamon Press, Room 4037, Qianmen Hotel, Beijing, People's Republic of China
FEDERAL REPUBLIC OF GERMANY	Pergamon Press, Hammerweg 6, D-6242 Kronberg, Federal Republic of Germany
BRAZIL	Pergamon Editora, Rua Eca de Queiros, 346, CEP 04011, Paraiso, São Paulo, Brazil
AUSTRALIA	Pergamon Press Australia, P.O. Box 544, Potts Point, N.S.W. 2011, Australia
JAPAN	Pergamon Press, 8th Floor, Matsuoka Central Building, 1-7-1 Nishishinjuku, Shinjuku-ku, Tokyo 160, Japan
CANADA	Pergamon Press Canada, Suite No. 271, 253 College Street, Toronto, Ontario, Canada M5T 1R5

First edition 1988

Library of Congress Cataloging-in-Publication Data

Walker, C. Eugene (Clarence Eugene), 1939–
The physically and sexually abused child.

(Psychology practitioner guidebooks)
Bibliography: p.
Includes index.
1. Child abuse.   2. Child molesting.   3. Abused children—Medical care.   4. Abused children—Mental health services. I. Bonner, Barbara L.   II. Kaufman, Keith L.
III. Title. IV. Series.   [DNLM: 1. Child Abuse—prevention & control.   2. Child Abuse, Sexual—prevention & control.   WA 320 W177p]
RC569.5.C55W35–1987   362.7′044   87-8245

British Library Cataloguing in Publication Data

Walker, C. Eugene
The physically and sexually abused child :
evaluation and treatment.—(Psychology
practitioner guidebooks).
1. Abused children—Medical care   2. Child abuse
I. Title   II. Bonner, Barbara L.
III. Kaufman, Keith L.   IV. Series
618.92   RJ507.A2

ISBN 0-08-032769-9 Hardcover
ISBN 0-08-032768-0 Flexicover

*Printed in Great Britain by Hazell Watson & Viney Limited
Member of BPCC plc, Aylesbury, Bucks*

This book is dedicated to our children, Chad, Kyle and Cass (CEW),
Susan (BLB), and Benjamin Ryan (KLK).

Contents

Preface

The intent of this book is to provide parallel coverage of the topics of physical abuse and sexual abuse of children. It was our desire to review the literature and present a model for the assessment and treatment of children involved in such circumstances. We felt a need to present an overall strategy for clinicians that would emphasize the similarities and point out the differences between the two forms of abuse. The literature in the two areas is at different levels of development. Therefore, some chapters are closely parallel while others show considerable diversion. This is not simply an idiosyncrasy of the present text but an accurate reflection of the literature in the area. Thus, while it is possible to present detailed instructions for parent training in the chapters dealing with physical abuse of children, such detail is not possible for the sexually abused child. In this area, we have only sketchy beginnings of useful treatment approaches. While all three authors participated in the preparation of this manuscript, the major effort for each chapter was assumed by one of the authors. Chapters 1, 2, 3, 7, and 8 were prepared by C. Eugene Walker, Chapters 4, 5, and 6 by Keith Kaufman, and 9, 10, and 11 by Barbara Bonner. Chapter 12 was a joint effort of Keith Kaufman and Barbara Bonner. We sincerely hope that the present volume will aid clinicians in developing an effective treatment strategy that can be used in cases of physical and sexual abuse.

Part I
Introduction

Chapter 1
Introduction and History of Abuse

EARLY HISTORY

This manuscript could not have been written 100 years ago. Indeed, most of it could not have been written 20 years ago. The reason is not that child abuse is a recent phenomenon. The most ancient writings contain frequent accounts of severe child abuse. From ancient times to the present, many societies have practiced infanticide for population control and for the elimination of children with birth defects. Such children often were abandoned to die, drowned, or smothered. In numerous societies throughout recorded history, it was the custom to offer children as sacrifices to gods. Political motivation also resulted in a great deal of child abuse. Kings and king makers seldom hesitated to eliminate newborn heirs who might be unwanted contenders for the throne. There are also numerous accounts in the Bible of mass slaughter of children. Best known among these are the order by Pharaoh that all newborn Jewish males be executed (Exodus 1:15–22) and the decree of Herod, who feared the coming of the Messiah, that all children in Bethlehem be killed (Matthew 2:16).

Although killing may be the most extreme form of abuse of children, it is by no means the only form. Numerous societies prescribed body mutilation as a standard part of the child rearing process. The binding of the feet of females in China is a well-known example. Many primitive groups practiced various forms of tattooing and exaggeration of parts of the body as well as piercing parts of the body with sharp objects. Furthermore, the genitals were mutilated in ceremonies in various societies. The subincision practice of the Arunta, an Australian aboriginal tribe, is an example of this. In this ritual the urethra is ceremonially cut open along the length of the penis of young boys (Lazarus, Speisman, Mordkof, and Davison, 1962). In gentler civilizations such practices would be out of the question; however, it has been customary in such societies to subject children to severe beatings and deprivations as a part of child

3

rearing. Parents, priests, and schoolmasters from ancient times regarded it as a sacred duty to severely chastise children, literally to "beat the devil out of them" so that they would grow up as responsible adults (Bakan, 1971).

It was long considered acceptable to severely punish or even kill a disobedient or "wicked" child. For example, in the early 1600s, Massachusetts adopted the "stubborn child act" which permitted parents to put a child to death if the child was rebellious and disobedient (Bremner, 1970).

Children were also commonly treated as slaves by the adults in their family, sold into slavery, or hired out as workers in factories to exploit them for their labor potential. The history of the labor movement and industrialization in modern Western cultures contains many discussions of the abusive use of children in the labor force. Children were often involved in dangerous occupations for long hours (10 to 14 hours) per day with the result that many of them died (Bakan, 1971).

Sexual exploitation of children likewise has a long and ancient history. Many religious ceremonies and initiation rights in ancient civilizations involved sexual activity between adults and children. Children have been bought and sold as prostitutes since time began. Pedophilia and incest have been common practices in many cultures by large numbers of people (De Mause, 1974).

Lest we think that all of this refers only to ancient and more primitive cultures, it should be pointed out that virtually all of these practices existed in one form or another in the civilized world barely 100 years ago and most persist even to the present time. In the 18th and 19th centuries abandonment of children was common, leading to the need for foundling homes and orphanages. In London in the 19th century, 80% of illegitimate children who were put in the care of foster nurses died. These nurses accepted the infants, collected the fees for their care, and then killed the babies (Kempe and Kempe, 1978). During this period, child prostitution in the streets of London was rampant, and it was common to mutilate children to make them cripples so that they would be more effective as beggars. Although the more flagrant forms of abuse are no longer legally sanctioned, especially in Western civilization, it is clear from the data to be presented in this chapter that much abuse is still occurring to children.

One of the most astonishing features of child abuse is that it has only been recognized as a *problem* in very recent times. There are many reasons for this. One is that children have always been regarded as the property of their parents and parents were given a wide latitude in how they treated their children, much as would be the case with other personal possessions. Even Aristotle, who was a champion of rather enlightened views of democracy and political control, stated, "Now a slave, or a child before it has reached a certain age and acquired an independent status, is in a manner of speaking a part of oneself. Since nobody deliberately injures himself, he cannot be guilty of injustice towards them. This means that there can be nothing in their relations which is politically just or unjust" (Thomson, 1953). It should be noted that Aristotle did not condone or encourage child abuse, but the concept of justice that saw children as having no independent status or rights contributed to a climate that failed to prevent child abuse. Second, religious and legal systems have supported this view of children as property to the extent that no one even questioned its advisability or concerned himself or herself about such matters as the rights of children. Third, in times when birth control was inadequate, children were often seen as liabilities in terms of their economic drain on the family. Resources such as food, shelter, heat, and clothing were very scarce. Under such difficult circumstances, some forms of child abuse (e.g., exploitation as laborers or prostitutes) were often practiced as acceptable means of enhancing the survival of the family. Finally, in times when large families that were frequently decimated by disease were the norm, the bond of affection and concern for one's children was greatly diminished. The result was that children were regarded as fair game for use and abuse by parents much as livestock might be today. As De Mause (1974) pointed out, ". . . there would be a point back in history where most children were what we would now consider abused."

Consideration of the foregoing answers a commonly asked question regarding child abuse. With all of the attention in professional literature and popular media given to the problem of child abuse, many wonder if there has been an increase in this problem in recent years. The answer is probably much to the contrary. There is probably less child abuse currently than in the past. However, we are more aware of it and recognize it as a problem that must be dealt with. Therefore, what would have been considered normal child rearing in the past is currently perceived as the social problem of child abuse for which remedies are sought.

RECENT HISTORY

The development of our current sensitivity to child abuse is an interesting story. The story begins in 1874 with the case of Mary Ellen Wilson, an 8-year-old illegitimate child in the care of foster parents. The foster mother was the former wife of Mary Ellen's natural father. The natural father had died after bringing the child to live with him and his wife because her real mother was a "good for nothing" (Bremner, 1971). A woman visiting a dying person in an adjoining house discovered that this child was being starved and beaten on a daily basis. The woman sought help from several sources without success. Finally, she approached Henry Bergh who had earlier founded the Society for Prevention of Cruelty to Animals. Although it has often been stated that Bergh and the attorneys involved argued that Mary Ellen was an animal and, therefore, entitled to protection, this was not the case (Bremner, 1971). Bergh became involved as a citizen and appealed to the court to protect the child because she deserved it, not because she was an animal and he was the founder of the Society for Prevention of Cruelty to Animals. Mary Ellen was removed from the custody of her foster parents and placed in an orphanage. The foster mother was found guilty of assault and battery and sent to prison for 1 year. Eight months later, in December 1874, the Society for Prevention of Cruelty to Children was formed largely through the efforts of Elbridge Gerry, the attorney hired by Henry Bergh to handle the Mary Ellen case (Bremner, 1971). This movement spread throughout the United States and other countries with many local societies being formed. However, as late as 1970, the Society for Prevention of Cruelty to Animals in New York City had more money in contributions than did the Society for Prevention of Cruelty to Children (Light, 1973). Nevertheless, during the 19th and 20th centuries, much legislation was passed for the protection of children. There were child labor laws as well as legislation providing for financial support of children and their families who were in need and for education of all children.

Despite these developments, the medical recognition of child abuse was slow to develop. One of the earliest medical books printed in the English language was a book of pediatrics by Thomas Phaire in 1545. In this volume, Phaire commented on one of the problems of children that was common during his time. This involved neglecting children during cold weather, which led to "Stifnes of limmes . . . which thyng procedeth many tymes of cold, as when a chylde is found in the frost, or in the strete, cast away by a wycked mother!" (Smith, 1975). In 1860, Ambroise Tardieu, a Professor of Legal Medicine in Paris, wrote a paper based on autopsy findings of 32 children who were killed by whipping and burning. This may well be the first description of the battered-child syndrome (Kempe & Kempe, 1978). Despite this, John Caffey, a specialist in pediatric radiology, wrote an article in 1946 in which he discussed certain unexplainable injuries observed in young children. The injuries that he noted were multiple fractures of long bones of several infants found to be in various stages of healing, and these were associated with subdural hematomas. Although Caffey suspected that these conditions were traumatic in origin, he was mystified as to the cause. In a later article, Silverman (1953) presented the idea that they were due to negligence on the part of caretakers for the children, but cautioned physicians to be careful not to induce excessive guilt in the caretakers about these lesions and even commented on the "accident proneness" of one of his patients because new injuries kept occurring. In 1955, Woolley and Evans (1955) were the first physicians to attribute the skeletal lesions noted by Caffey, Silverman, and others to intentional acts of parents or others caring for the children. In 1957, Caffey reexamined his earlier observations and reached the same conclusion. In 1961, Kempe, a pediatrician, had become concerned about the abuse of children and arranged an interdisciplinary presentation at the annual meeting of the American Academy of Pediatrics on the subject of what he termed the battered-child syndrome. His description of this syndrome was published the following year in the *Journal of the American Medical Association* and has become a classic in the area (Kempe, Silverman, Steele, Droegemuller, & Silver, 1962). Since that time, thousands of articles and books have been written on the topic. Major research funds have been provided by governmental as well as private foundations to investigate the recognition, treatment, and prevention of abuse to children. All of the states have passed laws regarding mandatory reporting of child abuse and have moved to provide services to children and families in which abuse has occurred.

During the time that physical abuse was being recognized among professionals, the problem of sexual abuse was largely ignored. It was known that children were sexually abused, but the incidence was greatly underestimated. For example, it is well known that Freud, after hearing many of his patients report such incidents, concluded that these were fantasies. A part of the person's "sickness" was that he or she had such fantasies (Jones, 1953). Most professionals felt that actual sexual abuse was a rare and extreme situation that occurred only in very disturbed families. As had been the case with physical abuse, when unusual circumstances having to do with sexual behaviour were observed, the professional frequently discretely failed to pursue the details and preferred to pretend that nothing had happened. However, by the mid 1970s sensitivity to the problem of sexual abuse of children had greatly increased and professionals began to be equally concerned about this problem. Since that time, much research has been done, programs have been developed, and efforts are beginning in the area of prevention.

DEFINITION OF ABUSE

Child maltreatment is considered to involve physical abuse, emotional abuse, sexual abuse, and neglect. These aspects are often thought of as being the same and are generally covered in the same legal statutes. However, they are different. Although they may overlap in some cases, they generally are separate and distinct. Physical abuse is generally defined as inflicting injury such as bruises, burns, head injuries, fractures, internal injuries, lacerations, or any other form of physical harm lasting at least 48 hours (National Center on Child Abuse & Neglect, 1981). This category may also include excessive corporal punishment and close confinement such as tying or binding the child and locking him or her in a closet.

A rare, although important, form of physical child abuse has recently been identified. This is the Munchausen by proxy syndrome in which parents subject children to medications, surgery, and other medical procedures for which there is no reason (Liston, Levine, & Anderson, 1983; Meadow, 1985; Paperney, Hicks, & Hammar, 1980; Shnaps, Frand, Rotem, et al., 1981; Woollcott, Aceto, Rutt, et al., 1982). The original description of the Baron Von Munchausen syndrome referred to adults who repeatedly sought medical treatment, especially surgery, despite the fact that such treatment was unnecessary (Asher, 1951). The clinician working in a medical setting should be alert to the possibility that children presented for treatment may not be ill but may be victims of the Munchausen by proxy syndrome.

Emotional abuse is more difficult to define, but it involves the use of excessive verbal threats, ridicule, personally demeaning comments, derogatory statements, and threats against the young person to the extent that the child's emotional and mental well-being is jeopardized.

Sexual abuse is often defined as "the involvement of dependent, developmentally immature children and adolescents in sexual activities they do not fully comprehend, are unable to give informed consent to and that violate the social taboos of family roles" (Helfer & Kempe, 1976). This definition includes a wide range of activities such as an adult exhibiting his or her genitalia to the child, forcing the child to exhibit himself or herself to the adult, fondling of genitals, manual or oral stimulation of the genitals, vaginal or anal intercourse, and involving the child in prostitution or in the making or use of pornography.

Neglect refers to acts of omission in which the child is not properly cared for physically (nutrition, safety, education, medical care, etc.) or emotionally (failure to bond, lack of affection, love, support, nurturing, or concern). This may include expulsion from the home, refusal to accept a runaway child back home, and similar circumstances.

FREQUENCY OF ABUSE

Over the years, the statistics on the frequency with which children are abused have varied remarkably. Estimates have varied from a few thousand to the millions. The figures vary for a number of reasons, one having to do with the definition of abuse. If a conservative definition of abuse is used, for example, only cases in which actual trauma requiring emergency medical treatment was required, one figure will be obtained. However, if this definition is expanded to include overly severe corporal punishment and similar events, a greater figure will be obtained. If to that are added cases of emotional abuse, a still greater figure will be obtained.

The same point could be made for sexual abuse. A substantial number of cases involve repeated intercourse. However, if fondling and other kinds of sexual behaviour are included, a much larger figure is obtained. If such things as exhibitionism and harassment involving verbal comments and suggestions of a sexual nature are added, a still higher figure would be obtained.

Beyond the definitional problems that account for many variations in statistics are the tendencies of various organizations to combine cases in different categories. Some associations, such as the American Humane Association, combine all incidents of physical abuse, sexual abuse, emotional abuse, and neglect into one figure, resulting in a great number of what they term *maltreated* children. However, other reporting agencies combine these categories differently, resulting in different statistics. In addition, some statistics deal with the number of abusive incidents whereas others deal with the number of children abused. The former figure is much higher, because many children are repeatedly abused. Likewise, many children are maltreated in more than one way, for example physically and sexually abused.

An additional distinction in statistical reporting of pathological conditions involves incidence versus prevalence. Incidence refers to the number of new cases reported within a specific time period. Prevalence, in the present situation, refers to all living persons at a given time that were victims of child abuse. Therefore, if January 1, 1987 were chosen as the specified time, all living adults who were abused as children and all children who had been victimized to that date would constitute the prevalence. The situation is further complicated by the fact that these kinds of incidents are known to be greatly underreported. If we were literally aware of every time a child was abused or neglected in any way, these statistics would be overwhelming.

One final complication is that the statistics vary considerably depending on their source. For example, some statistics are based on cases reported to child protective services in various states; however, not all cases are reported to these agencies. In addition, once a report is made, these agencies attempt to validate whether or not abuse has actually occurred. If statistics are based on reported cases, they are high; if based only on validated cases, they are much lower. Nationwide, approximately 40% of cases reported are actually validated (Department of Health and Human

Services, 1981). This by no means indicates that the other 60% are necessarily false reports. The staggering case loads and limited staff time available for investigation make it impossible to validate many reported cases even though abuse has actually occurred. There are many cases in which there is a strong suspicion, but it is impossible to collect convincing evidence. At any rate, different statistics are obtained when reported cases are tallied as opposed to validated cases.

Police reports are a second source of statistics, but because only a selected minority of cases are reported to the police, these are heavily biased. Likewise, the records of hospitals, clinics, and emergency rooms can be examined. Again, not all cases are taken to these facilities. Therefore, statistics that have been published from these sources are biased and incomplete. There have also been studies of perpetrators of physical and sexual abuse. However, these studies have of necessity been done with those who have been caught and are under some legal or criminal authority. Statistics gathered from such individuals will only be a partial reflection of the problem and will in no way be complete. Finally, some of the best data have been gathered from surveys of college students or large numbers of individuals in the community. These statistics come closer to the actual figures than do any of the other sources, although they too generally suffer from sampling biases and errors.

It does not take much perspicacity to recognize that no matter how the statistics are computed, the problem of child abuse has considerable magnitude. For some years, the American Humane Association has collected and combined statistics from child protective services in all of the states. The most recent figures available are those from 1983. The American Humane Association estimates from the reports received that approximately 1.5 million children were maltreated (physical abuse, sexual abuse, emotional abuse, and neglect) during this year (Russell & Trainor, 1984). The rate of reporting has increased each year within the last decade. In 1976, 10.1 children per thousand were reported. By 1983, 23.6 children per thousand were reported. Most persons familiar with the area are certain that even with these increases only the tip of the iceberg is visible at present.

Reported statistics further indicate that approximately 60% of maltreated children are neglected rather than abused. Because cases of abuse tend to be more dramatic, they have received more attention in terms of research and treatment. However, the statistics clearly indicate that the next effort must be directed at working with the neglected child and his or her family. Table 1.1 presents data on the relationship of the perpetrator to the child for several types of maltreatment.

These data have been compiled using only perpetrators who were caretakers for the children. Cases involving strangers or outsiders (a small

Table 1.1. Type of Maltreatment and Child Relationship to Perpetrator—Caretakers
(N = 85,039 Children)

Child Perpetrator Relationship	Major or Major with Minor Physical Injury (N = 1,356)	Minor or Unspecified Physical Injury (N = 15,339)	Sexual Maltreatment (N = 3,683)	Deprivation of Necessities (N = 44,591)	Emotional Maltreatment (N = 6,311)	Other Maltreatment (N = 1,424)	Multiple Maltreatment (N = 12,335)	Percentage of All Relationships
Natural parent	81.5%	76.1%	58.9%	90.7%	80.0%	91.5%	80.8%	84.3
Other parent†	9.1%	13.5%	30.8%	1.2%	6.7%	2.4%	5.8%	5.9
Natural and other parent	4.7%	5.7%	4.4%	4.8%	10.0	4.8%	8.9%	5.9
Other relative	1.8%	2.3%	3.0%	2.1%	2.1%	0.9%	2.1%	2.1
Nonrelative	1.6%	1.4%	2.3%	0.1%	0.5%	0.1%	0.4%	0.5
Other perpetrator Combinations	1.2%	1.1%	0.7%	1.1%	0.7%	0.3%	2.1%	1.2
Total	100%	100%	100%	100%	100%	100%	100%	100

* Refers to relationships in which a child has more than one type of maltreatment indicated and "Major or Major with Minor Physical Injury" or "Minor or Unspecified Physical Injury" does not apply.

† "Other parent" refers to adoptive, step-parents and foster parents.

From the American Association for Protecting Children, Inc. (1985).

minority of the cases) are not included. Examination of this table indicates that the natural parent generally is the one most likely to abuse the child in each category.

Table 1.2 presents data on the age of children who are maltreated. Examination of this table indicates that maltreatment generally decreases with age. Some categories such as minor physical injury or emotional maltreatment remain the same, but the majority of categories decrease with age. The most impressive finding in this table is that children aged 5 years and younger are generally at the greatest risk. This is the time they are least able to protect themselves and are least likely to be observed by outsiders such as school teachers who may note that abuse is taking place. Therefore it is especially important for individuals who do have contact with very young children to be aware that much abuse takes place during these early years. Significantly, the only category of abuse that increases with age is sexual abuse.

Many children die as a result of abuse. It has been estimated that between 1,000 and 5,000 children per year suffer such a fate (American Medical Association, 1985). In the American Humane Association (American Association for Protecting Children, 1985) data, the average age of children who died as a result of abuse was 2.61 years versus an overall average of 7.14 years for children maltreated.

Because the incidence of abuse is greatly underreported, data presented by Gelles (1978) are of particular interest. Gelles has reported the results of a 1976 interview survey of a representative sample of 2,143 American families. Interviews were conducted with 960 men and 1,183 women. Gelles presents data for each family in which there was a child between the ages of 3 and 17 living in the home. It should be recalled that much abuse takes place between the ages of 1 and 3. However, the present data are reported only for families who have children between the ages of 3 and 17. It is also important to note that this was a *self report* study based on interviews with caretakers of the child. This would also result in some degree of underreporting. Gelles used a very broad definition of abuse involving any act of violence toward the child. In defense of this position, he points out that if such actions were taken by persons outside the family, they would be regarded as assaults. The fact that they occurred at the hands of a family member is regarded by Gelles as flimsy justification for such acts of violence against children. He reports that 73% of the reporting sample admitted at least one violent act in the course of rearing their children. An earlier study by Korsch, Christin, Gozzi, & Carlson (1965) indicated that one fourth of young mothers admitted to beating their child before the age of 6 months and one half had beaten the child by age 12 months. Table 1.3 presents the Gelles statistics for parent-to-child violence according to sex of the parent. In all categories ,

Table 1.2. Type of Maltreatment and Age of Involved Child
(N = 381,168 Children)

Age (yr)	Major or Major with Minor Physical Injury (N = 8,800)	Minor or Unspecified Physical Injury (N = 71,884)	Sexual Maltreatment (N = 27,714)	Deprivation of Necessities (N = 192,223)	Emotional Maltreatment (N = 24,808)	Other Maltreatment (N = 15,917)	Multiple Maltreatment (N = 39,822)	Percentage of All Involved Children (N = 717,315)	Percentage of All U.S. Children (N = 62,580,000)
0-5	64.1%	37.3%	24.8%	48.6%	34.0%	47.0%	41.5%	43.3%	34.5%
6-11	19.8%	32.6%	34.3%	34.2%	34.2%	26.8%	31.7%	32.5%	30.7%
12-17	15.9%	30.0%	40.6%	18.2%	31.9%	26.2%	27.0%	24.1%	34.7%
Total	100%	100%	100%	100%	100%	100%	100%	100%	100%

From the American Association for Protecting Children, Inc. (1985).

except those involving weapons, mothers were responsible for more violence against children than were fathers. Data from the American

Table 1.3. Parent-to-child Violence by Sex of Parent*

Incident	Time			
	In Past Year		Ever	
	Father	Mother	Father	Mother
Threw something	3.6%	6.8%	7.5%	11.3%
Pushed, grabbed, shoved	29.8	33.4	35.6	39.5
Slapped or spanked	53.3	62.5†	67.7	73.6‡
Kicked, bit, or hit with fist	2.5	4.0	6.7	8.7
Hit with something	9.4	16.7†	15.7	23.6‡
Beat up	0.6	1.8	4.0	4.2
Threatened with knife or gun	0.2	0.0	3.1	2.6
Used knife or gun	0.2	0.0	3.1	2.7

* Reports of 523 fathers and 623 mothers; figures for all incidents represent at least 520 fathers and 619 mothers.

‡ $\chi^2 \leqslant 0.05$.

† $\chi^2 \leqslant 0.01$.

From Gelles (1978).

Humane Association indicate a similar trend and indicate that mothers are also more likely to neglect their children (Russell & Trainor, 1984). Table 1.4 presents the data broken down as to whether the abuse involved a son or a daughter. It can be seen from this table that boys are more likely to be subjected to violence than are girls. One further point in considering these statistics is that the sample included only families in which two caretakers were present. These consisted of couples who were married or living together as a conjugal unit. Because some researchers (American Humane Association, 1985) have reported that abuse and neglect occur at a higher rate in *single-parent* families in proportion to their percentage of the total population, these statistics would again be a low estimate. The fact that mothers are more likely to use violence on their children and are more likely to use it on boys can be accounted for by a variety of factors such as the longer period of time mothers are with the children and their feeling of weakness or powerlessness in their inability to control the children, especially boys. Nevertheless, the amount of violence toward children voluntarily reported by parents is staggering. Even if we take only the lower half of the table beginning with the use of the fist and progressing through the use of a knife or gun many children were reported to have been abused in this manner by their parents. The parents who reported voluntarily without doubt under-reported their acts of violence, and many exceedingly violent families were probably unavailable for interview or declined to be interviewed. Gelles' data certainly underline the widespread nature of the problem.

Table 1.4. Parent-to-child Violence by Sex of child*

| | Time | | | |
| | In Past Year | | Ever | |
Incident	Sons	Daughters	Sons	Daughters
Threw something	5.9%	4.4%	10.1%	8.8%
Pushed, grabbed or shoved	38.1	24.9†	43.9	30.7†
Slapped or spanked	60.1	56.1	73.9	67.8‡
Kicked, bit, or hit with fist	3.8	2.6	8.0	7.3
Hit with something	14.9	11.2	21.5	18.1
Beat up	1.6	0.7	4.2	4.0
Threatened with knife or gun	0.2	0.0	2.4	3.3
Used knife or gun	0.2	0.0	2.6	3.3

*Reports on 578 sons (responses reported for at least 574) and 547 daughters (responses for at least 545).

† $\chi^2 \leqslant 0.01$.

‡ $\chi^2 \leqslant 0.05$.

From Gelles (1978).

Turning to sexual abuse, the statistics are equally overwhelming. Table 1.5 presents the characteristics of children reported to have been sexually abused between 1976 and 1982.This table indicates that the number of reports has grown steadily over the years. Females are overwhelmingly more likely to be sexually abused than are males. Moreover, although much abuse occurs among younger children (even infants) and adolescents, the average age is about 10.

Table 1.5. Child Characteristics by Year: Sexual Abuse Only

| | Year | | | | | | |
	1976	1977	1978	1979	1980	1981	1982
Average	(N = 2,105)	(N = 4,354)	(N = 6,713)	(N = 14,777)	(N = 10,729)	(N = 27,672)	(N = 32,048)
Age							
(yr)	10.76	10.94	10.70	10.61	10.60	10.23	9.97
Sex (%)	(N = 2,122)	(N = 4,371)	(N = 6,869)	(N = 14,432)	(N = 21,384)	(N = 26,086)	(N = 30,990)
Male	15.4	14.2	13.3	14.4	15.7	16.4	16.8
Female	84.6	85.8	86.7	85.6	84.3	83.6	83.2
Race (%)	(N = 2,086)	(N = 4,184)	(N = 5,059)	(N = 10,662)	(N = 15,839)	(N = 19,555)	(N = 23,131)
White	74.4	78.0	75.8	71.9	74.8	74.6	73.7
Black	16.1	13.3	14.6	17.8	15.2	15.7	14.7
Other	9.5	8.7	9.6	10.3	10.0	9.7	11.6

From Russell & Trainor (1984).

Table 1.6 presents the characteristics of the perpetrator of sexual abuse. The main perpetrator in cases of sexual abuse clearly is a male usually

Table 1.6. Perpetrator Characteristics: Sexual Abuse

Average Age	(N = 1,665)	(N = 3,606)	(N = 4,336)	(N = 7,700)	(N = 12,200)	(N = 16,595)	(N = 20,178)
(yr)	35.65	35.60	35.57	36.18	35.17	35.42	33.66
Sex (%)	(N = 1,949)	(N = 4,145)	(N = 5,648)	(N = 9,772)	(N = 15,340)	(N = 20,557)	(N = 24,488)
Male	78.7	80.5	79.0	78.5	80.5	78.3	77.7
Female	21.3	19.5	21.0	21.5	19.5	21.7	22.3
Relationship to Involved Children	(0)	(0)	(0)	(N = 3,700)	(N = 6,140)	(N = 6,701)	(N = 8,015)
Parent (all) (%)	—*	—*	—*	80.6	75.5	77.4	76.0
Natural (%)	—*	—*	—*	51.1	58.3	57.7	59.0
Step (%)	—*	—*	—*	22.4	10.5	15.0	13.6
Other relative (%)	—*	—*	—*	16.3	18.2	15.0	15.7
Other (%)	—*	—*	—*	3.1	6.3	7.5	8.2

*Data not compatible for years before 1979.

From Russell & Trainor (1984).

Table 1.7. National incidence Estimates by Major Form of Maltreatment and by Severity of Maltreatment-related Injury or Impairment: Estimated Number of Recognized In-scope Children per 1,000 per Year

Form of Maltreatment and Severity of Injury/Impairment	No. of In-scope Children	Incidence rate* (per 1,000)
Form of maltreatment†		
Total, all maltreated children	652,000	10.5
Total, all abused children	351,100	5.7
Physical assault	207,600	3.4
Sexual exploitation	44,700	0.7
Emotional abuse	138,400	2.2
Total, all neglected children	329,000	5.3
Physical neglect	108,000	1.7
Educational neglect	181,500	2.9
Emotional neglect	59,400	1.0
Severity of child's injury/impairment		
Fatal	1,000	0.02
Serious	137,400	2.2
Moderate	411,600	6.6
Probable	102,000	1.6

*Numerator = estimated number of recognized in-scope children; denominator = 61,900, the estimated total number (in thousands) of children under 18 in the United States in December 1979.

†Totals may be lower than the sum of the categories, because a child may have experienced more than one in-scope category of maltreatment.

From the National Center on Child Abuse and Neglect (1981).

middle-aged (average age approximately 35 years). In a well-done study of college students in New England, Finkelhor (1979) reported that 19.2% of the women and 8.6% of the men indicated that they had been sexually abused as children. Using college students in New England universities would tend to give a low estimate. When combining these data with other findings, most researchers suspect that 20 to 25% of females and approximately 10% of males are sexually abused as children. Finkelhor's data further indicate that 43% of the girls were abused by family members, and only 24% by strangers. The other 33% were abused by acquaintances. With respect to boys, the trend is slightly different. Only 17% are abused by family members, with 30% by strangers and 53% by acquaintances. His data also indicate that 60% of the cases of abuse were single occurrences. Therefore, the most common situation is one in which the child is victimized only once. However, cases of repeated abuse are more serious in terms of consequences. In the Finkelhor study the mean age at which children reported abuse was 10.2 for girls and 11.2 for boys.

Table 1.8. Form of Maltreatment by Child Demographic Characteristics: Percentage of Estimated Total Number of In-scope Maltreated Children

| Child characteristic | Form of maltreatment | | | | | | | | Total |
| | Abuse | | | | Neglect | | | | |
	Physical	Sexual	Emo-tional	Total	Physical	Educa-tional	Emo-tional	Total	
Estimated no. children (1,000)	207.6	44.7	138.4	351.1	108.0	181.5	59.4	329.0	652.0
Age of child (% known)	(99)	(99)	(100)	(99)	(100)	(99)	(100)	(99)	(99)
0–2	11	2	3	7	23	0	6	9	8
3–5	17	6	9	12	9	3	5	5	9
6–8	17	11	17	17	20	18	13	18	17
9–11	16	21	19	18	18	19	16	18	19
12–14	19	28	20	21	14	29	20	22	21
15–17	20	32	32	25	16	31	40	28	26
Total	100	100	100	100	100	100	100	100	100
Sex of child (% known)	(99)	(99)	(100)	(99)	(100)	(99)	(100)	(100)	(100)
Boys	47	17	43	43	53	63	72	61	52
Girls	53	83	57	57	47	37	28	39	48
Total	100	100	100	100	100	100	100	100	100
Child's ethnic group* (% known)	(99)	(99)	(99)	(99)	(99)	(99)	(99)	(99)	(99)
White	86	88	92	89	84	72	89	77	82
Black	13	11	7	10	15	27	11	22	16
Other	1	1	1	1	2	1	1	1	1
Total	100	100	100	100	100	100	100	100	100

*For comparison with Census data, "White" includes "White, not of Hispanic origin" and "Hispanic."

From the National Center on Child Abuse and Neglect (1981).

In closing, it is instructive to examine some interesting summary data presented in the findings of the national study of the incidence and severity of child abuse and neglect. Table 1.7 presents the number of children this study uncovered as having been victimized in various ways and its estimate of the number per thousand who are likely to be abused in that manner during a given year. Table 1.8 presents data with respect to age, sex, and ethnic group for incidence of maltreatment. Anyway one looks at it, child maltreatment is a major social problem.

REPORTING OF CHILD ABUSE

Because of the seriousness of the problem of child abuse, all states have enacted child protection and reporting statutes. Athough the language employed varies from state to state, the general provisions of these laws are highly similar. Basically, any individual who has reason to *suspect* that a child is being maltreated is required to report this to the proper authorities. Individuals who in good faith make such a report are specifically protected from any legal liability as a result of making the report. It is incumbent upon every practicing clinician to be aware of the law in his or her state and to have at hand the phone number of the agency to which cases of maltreatment are to be reported. These are readily available from the state health department.

Clear understanding of the intent and implications of these laws is extremely important for the practicing professional. First, it must be emphasized that reporting of cases of *suspected* child abuse is *required*. It is not merely an option for the clinician to consider. If the clinician has good reason to suspect that a child is being maltreated, a report must be made. The American Medical Association has recently prepared an excellent guide for physicians that lists the signs and symptoms that would lead one to a reasonable supposition that abuse has taken place and provides information about how to make reports (American Medical Association, 1985). It should be emphasized that the clinician needs only to suspect that abuse is occurring to report. He or she need not be certain of the facts. As will be discussed in this volume, child protective service workers have the task of investigating the circumstances and validating whether abuse is actually occurring. If abuse is occurring, they will take steps to protect the child. If such is not the case, no harm will come to the family or child. In most states, individuals who fail to report suspected child abuse may suffer criminal or civil penalties.

In determining the necessity for making a report, the clinician should keep in mind that the purpose of the law is to protect children, not to apprehend criminals. The crucial question is whether the particular child or other children may be at risk for ongoing abuse. Therefore, if an adult patient mentions that as a child he or she was abused by a parent a report is not necessary because the adult is no longer under the care of these individuals and no longer at risk. However, if there are younger children in the care of those same parents or grandparents, it would be necessary to inquire about the possibility that they are being abused. If significant information is uncovered, this would result in a report. The usual strictures regarding confidentiality of patient communications are specifically overruled in such situations.

When the problem of possible abuse arises, the professional should pursue the matter until it is clear that a report should or should not be filed. Discretely avoiding the topic is not appropriate. If a report is to be made, the clinician should indicate to the family that he or she is required to report cases of child abuse or maltreatment. The clinician can further indicate that this is the law and that he or she has no choice in the matter. Following this, some reassurance can be offerred to the effect that if no evidence of maltreatment is found, nothing will come of it. However, if there is reason to do so, steps will be taken to protect the child.

If the child is at significant immediate risk, or if the parents will likely leave the city or state to avoid investigation, the clinician is required to keep the child on the premises while the report is being made and until a child protection worker arrives to take charge.

In a high percentage of cases, the parents are cooperative and often relieved that invervention will put a stop to the abuse. The abuse generally takes place impulsively in times of stress and turmoil. When the parents are in the clinician's office, they are generally calmer and more aware that something should be done. However, the clinician should be prepared for the occasional parents who become hostile or aggressive.

It is wise for all agencies and even solo practitioners to have a step-by-step policy on how to handle cases of suspected abuse. This policy should outline the various signs and symptoms that indicate possible abuse. It should contain a provision for on-the-spot consultation with peers (in person or by phone) or with child protection workers. For example, if a clinician has reason to believe that child abuse has occurred and should be reported, he or she may request a quick consultation with another colleague to review the details and circumstances or the clinician may call a child protection worker and briefly discuss the situation. The next step is to inform the parents of the necessity for reporting the abuse and call the appropriate agency. Provision will then be made for the safety of the child, and initial efforts may be made to engage the family in treatment. Such a step-by-step policy relieves the clinician of the pressure of decision making when an actual crisis arises. The structure of the set policy will enable the clinician to go through the process efficiently and responsibly.

Surveys indicate that professionals frequently do not report child maltreatment (e.g., National Center on Child Abuse & Neglect, 1981; Finkelhor, 1984). It should be emphasized that this policy is against the law and contrary to the best interests of the child and family. Although all persons, especially mental health workers, find the role of reporter to be unpleasant, it is absolutely essential that we face up to our responsibility and fulfill the professional requirements with which we are entrusted by society. Reporting of child maltreatment is mandatory. There are no reasons or excuses that justify failure to do so.

Part II
Physical Abuse

Chapter 2
Understanding Physical Abuse

When confronted with the stark realities of child abuse, even the experienced clinician is often horrified and begins to wonder how such terrible things could happen. Familiarity with the circumstances and causes of abuse is essential to proper analysis and appropriate treatment. To that end, hundreds of investigations in the last two decades have attempted to identify the crucial factors involved. Unfortunately, at this point it is impossible to specify the exact circumstances that lead to child abuse for several reasons. The sensitive nature of the area makes it difficult to perform carefully controlled research. Experimental studies generally are impossible for the obvious reason that abuse cannot be permitted to occur just so it can be studied. Prospective studies in the literature are few because they are expensive and time consuming. As a result, most studies are retrospective and the data are gathered after the abuse, which introduces unknown biases. Ethical issues having to do with patient rights also result in only biased samples being available for study. The mechanics of such research require that the investigator have access to cases, and the agency or setting chosen as the source of cases results in biases related to the particular population that the agency serves. In addition to being biased, many sample sizes employed in studies have been unusually small. The definition of what constitutes abuse and the thoroughness with which abuse is validated often vary from one study to another. Many subjects involved in the research projects, for both realistic and unrealistic reasons, are less than cooperative and have good reason to dissimulate. The victims are often very young as well as fearful and intimidated by the adults involved; therefore, they do not make reliable reporters of the events. As noted, it is impossible to directly observe abuse or to manipulate independent variables to study the process. As a result, interviews, psychological testing, and simulated child-rearing situations have been used to gather data. Because this is a new area, few psychological instruments are available that have been specifically designed for the task, and the uncertainties of the area make it unclear even what questions should be asked in an interview or what sort of behaviors ought to be observed in a structured observation. Finally, child abuse does not appear to be a unitary phenomenon. Many diverse factors and circumstances can result in child abuse. The end result is that no statement can be made with respect to child abuse that would hold for all or even most cases and for which the data would be consistently supportive. There are several excellent and comprehensive reviews of the literature in the area of child abuse that examine each possible variable with respect to the available data pro and con (Berger, 1985; Wolfe, 1985; Spinetta & Rigler, 1972; Gelles, 1973). The interested reader may want to examine some of these reviews for additional information. In the present chapter, we will refer to the studies selectively in an effort to give the reader an understanding of the typical findings and to provide information useful in understanding the phenomenon of child abuse to the extent that it is possible based on the available literature.

MODELS OF CHILD ABUSE

Three general conceptual frameworks may be employed to understand child abuse. One, called the psychiatric model, assumes that the causes of abuse are to be found in the personality characteristics and/or psychopathology of the parents or children involved. A second model, the sociological model, assumes that the causes are to be found in societal conditions such as poverty and unemployment. A third model, which might be termed an interactional model, assumes that variables in both of the first two may be involved and that they interact within a social-situational context which results in abuse. We shall briefly discuss the first two models and then present a composite interaction model that has proved helpful in evaluating and analyzing child abuse cases in our work.

Psychiatric Model

In its earliest and boldest form, the psychiatric model asserted that child abusers were obviously seriously disturbed individuals with significant psychopathology that resulted in their abusing children. The two major types of pathology generally mentioned in this context were psychotic disorders (with the attendant loss of contact with reality) and severe psychopathic character disorders (with sadistic features). Individuals with serious alcohol and drug abuse problems have been similarly implicated. Although it is true that such individuals abuse children and that children in their care are at great risk, only a small number of all reported abuse cases can be attributed to such individuals (Berger, 1985; Wolfe, 1985). It is generally accepted that less than 10% of cases of abused children result from seriously disturbed parents (Kempe & Helfer, 1972). However, in a much larger number of cases the parental/family problems are severe enough that the child must be removed from the home for adequate protection, and many of these children may never be able to return safely to the care of their parents.

A wide variety of less severe forms of psychopathology have been described in connection with abusive parents such as immaturity (Cohen, Raphling, & Green, 1966), impulsivity (Elmer, 1965), low frustration tolerance (Heins, 1969), difficulty expressing anger appropriately and/or controlling anger (Spinetta, 1978), rigidity and inflexibility (Milner & Wimberley, 1980; Fontana & Bernard, 1971), dependent and narcissistic (Young, 1964), depressed (Milner & Wimberley, 1980; Lahey, Conger, Atkeson, & Treiber, 1984), of low intelligence (Fisher, 1958; Simpson, 1967), unable to form attachments because of a lack of basic trust (Pollock & Steele, 1972), being low in empathy (Steele, 1980), having feelings of loneliness, futility, and apathy (Simpson, 1967; Hunter, Kilstrom, Kraybill, & Loda, 1978), having low self-esteem and feelings of insufficiency (Disbrow, Doerr, & Caulfield, 1977; Melnick & Hurley, 1969), having unrealistic expectations of children (Spinetta, 1978; Dubanoski, Evans, & Higuchi, 1978; Elmer, 1977; Smith & Hanson, 1975; Steele, 1970), being unaware of the developmental level of their child (Galdston, 1965; Helfer, 1980; Steele & Pollock, 1974; Wasserman, 1968), having negative expectations for their child (Larrance & Twentyman, 1983), being deficient in child management skills (Bousha & Twentyman, 1984; Burgess & Conger, 1978; Burgess, 1979; Burgess & Conger, 1977), being overly reactive emotionally to both normal and noxious stimuli (Frodi & Lamb, 1980; Wolfe, Fairbanks, Kelly & Bradlyn, 1983; Knutson, 1978), being under a high degree of stress (Conger, Burgess, & Barrett, 1979; Milner & Wimberley, 1980), finding the parenting role stressful (Mash, Johnston, & Kovitz, 1983), having numerous physical or health problems (Conger, Burgess, & Barrett, 1979), being involved in marital conflict and family discord (Reid, Taplin, & Lorber, 1981; Lorber, Felton, & Reid, 1984), and having a history of abuse in their own childhood (Gelles, 1973; Gil, 1970; Helfer, 1980; Paulson & Chaleff, 1973; Scott, 1980; Smith, 1975; Spinetta & Rigler, 1972; Steele, 1970, 1976, 1980).

In an effort to organize the data, various typologies of child abuse have been proposed. One of the oldest and most widely cited attempts at typology was developed by Merrill (1962). In his first category the parent has considerable personal hostility and aggression that may be triggered by the ordinary difficulties and frustrations of childrearing. A second in his system is the parent who is characterized by excessive rigidity, compulsiveness, and a lack of warmth toward the child with leads to punitive control of the child. Finally, in his third category is the parent who may abuse the child through passivity, dependence, and immaturity. The problem with this typology as well as with the others that have been suggested is that they tend to reduce the possible pathways to abuse to a limited number and the categories selected are based on the clinical experiences and impressions of the author rather than on data. Such typologies tend to focus on only one or two of the many aspects of a situation that may eventually result in abuse. The model proposed later in this chapter can readily accommodate other typologies, but it has the advantage of including a wide range of possibilities in several different categories, all of which may interact to produce abuse.

Because the psychiatric or psychopathologic model generally assumes that the causes of abuse lie in the personality of the parent or abuser, many investigations have concentrated on that dimension. However, some investigators have noted that the characteristics of the child may also be an important factor. Athough it is true that in many families all of the children are abused at one time or another, there are many instances in which one child is singled out for abuse. Characteristics that have been implicated in precipitating abuse are a child's discipline or management problems (Green, 1976; McRae, Ferguson, & Lederman, 1973; Helfer, 1973), hyperactivity (Baldwin & Oliver, 1975; Friedrich & Boriskin, 1976), irritability and colic (Baldwin & Oliver, 1975), coordination problems or physical handicaps (Friedrich & Boriskin, 1976; Johnson & Morse, 1968), prematurity at birth (Baldwin & Oliver, 1975; Elmer & Gregg, 1967; Faranoff, Kennel, & Klaus, 1972; Fomufod, Sinkford, & Louy, 1975; Friedrich & Boriskin, 1976; Frodi, 1981; Herrenkohl & Herrenkohl, 1979; Hunter, Kilstrom, Kraybill, & Loda, 1978; Kenel, Voos, & Klaus, 1976; Klein & Stern, 1971; Lynch & Roberts, 1977; Martin, 1976; McRae, Ferguson, & Lederman, 1973; Smith, 1975), and low intellectual ability or retardation (Friedrich & Boriskin, 1976; Gil, 1970). Some of these obviously might be the result of abuse rather than the cause. However, a central characteristic of all of the foregoing is that they result in a situation in which the care of the child is more demanding and difficult than that if those factors were not present. Therefore, if there is a predisposition on the part of the parent to be abusive, characteristics such as the aforementioned ones might elicit that abuse. It is also clear that in a family situation, family members other than the abuser and victim may be participants in the process that leads to abuse. Very little research has focused on this aspect, but some have speculated that the nonabusive parent (when both are not involved) may be overly passive, dependent, depressed, or incapacitated in some other manner. Virtually nothing is known about the siblings of abused children (Berger, 1985).

Sociological Model

Turning to the sociological model to account for child abuse, a number of general factors as well as some specific situational factors are mentioned. For example, among the general factors are such factors as low socioeconomic status or poverty (Gelles, 1973; Giovannoni & Billingsley, 1970), single parent families (Gil, 1970; Smith, Hanson, & Noble, 1974), unemployment (Gelles, 1973), social isolation of the family and a lack of an extended family or peer support network (Gil, 1970, 1975), large families (Light, 1973), and role reversal in which the parent looks to the child for support and satisfaction of needs (Blumberg, 1974; Green, Gaines, & Sandgrund, 1974). When the child disappoints the parent in fulfilling such needs, the parent may strike out in a hostile manner. For example, the present author has seen numerous cases of child abuse by teenage mothers who became pregnant while unmarried. Often, they decided to have the child and rear it themselves even though the father had withdrawn from the situation. In many cases, these mothers had rather unrealistic expectations about how much enjoyment would be derived from caring for a baby and having a child that would love and adore them. When they were confronted with the harsh realities of the limits that rearing an infant placed on their personal and social life as well as the physical work demands of caring for the infant (such as changing diapers, feeding, and comforting the child), the situation became overwhelming and abuse occurred.

Some of the more specific situational sociological variables that have been implicated are high levels of stress from work-related problems, marital discord, conflicts over school performance, illness and crying of the child, and similar circumstances that create severe distress in the parent (Gelles, 1973). Although many of these sociological factors are found in abusive families, they do not sufficiently explain the problem. Many families experience the same degree of stress and do not abuse children. Also, many children are abused in situations that have relatively small amounts of these stressors.

Interactive Model of Child Abuse

Although it is true, as pointed out earlier in this chapter, that there are insufficient data to make a definitive statment on any etiologic factor in child abuse and that child abuse is not a unitary phenomenon caused by the same factors or mix of factors in every case, it is possible to make some generalizations from the literature available and organize them in a way that provides a model for understanding the process by which abuse might occur. Let us review some of the generalizations that do emerge from the literature. First, there are factors in the parents such as psychopathology or personality characteristics that appear to predispose some individuals toward abusive behavior. Most notable among these is a personal history of a childhood that was lacking in nurturance and that provided punitive or violent models. Therefore, some studies have shown a lack of nurturance or support in the childrearing methods employed with the parent who becomes an abuser (Spinetta & Rigler, 1972). Many studies have emphasized that a significant percentage of these individuals were abused themselves (Baldwin & Oliver, 1975; Blumberg, 1974; Cohen, Raphling, & Green, 1966; Fontana & Bernard, 1971; Gelles, 1973; Gil, 1970; Green, Gaines, & Sandgrund, 1974; Helfer, 1980; Hunter, Kilstrom, Kraybill, & Loda, 1978; Johnson & Morse, 1968; Justice & Justice, 1976; Kempe & Helfer, 1972; Nurse, 1964; Oliver & Taylor, 1971; Paulson & Chaleff, 1973; Scott, 1980; Silver, Dublin, & Lourie, 1969; Smith, 1975; Spinetta & Rigler, 1972; Steele, 1970, 1976, 1980; Steele & Pollock, 1974; Van Stolk, 1972; Walters, 1975; Young, 1964; Zalba, 1967; Green, 1979). In addition, a rather provocative finding in one study indicated that although the child may not have been personally abused, the often considerable marital discord and spouse abuse that they witnessed (Gelles, 1980) may have played a modeling role in their later behavior.

Second, as a result of these factors, such parents appear to have a disturbed relationship with their child, which may take the form of being low in empathy, having unrealistic attitudes and expectations, or being inept or inconsistent in child management techniques.

Third, there is evidence that factors within the child such as unusual handicaps or behaviors that are difficult to manage contribute to an abusive situation.

Fourth, various factors of a sociological nature (e.g., poverty and unemployment) provide a social context that sets the stage for abuse. These major categories of variables appear to interact in a complex manner, the end result of which may be abuse. We may combine all of these plus other possible factors in a conceptual model as in Figure 2.1. In this model, all of the characteristics discussed so far can be placed in a sequence that eventually results in abuse. Although too complicated to show in the figure, all of the factors in the model are thought to interact with each other in complex combinations. It should be emphasized that this is a conceptual model based on the available literature and understanding of the problem. The model does not have empirical validity and has not been tested. This conceptual model currently is useful to the clinician in that it insures that the clinician will look at all possible variables in a systematic way and will consider their interactions in terms of how abuse may be produced. This will help the clinician organize rel-

Figure 2.1

PHYSICAL ABUSE ASSESSMENT:

MODEL

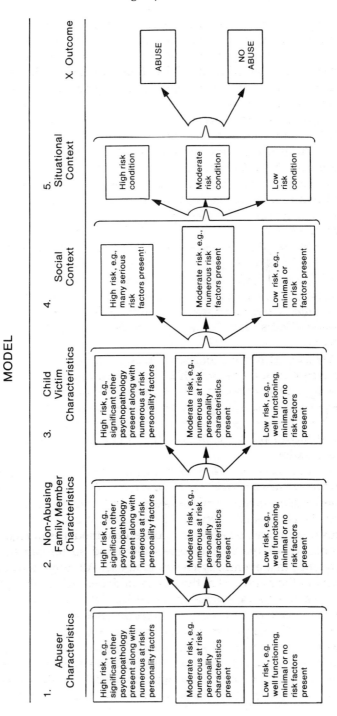

evant data and reduce the likelihood that important information will be overlooked or that idiosyncratic biases will have an undue influence on the clinical assessment of a given case.

Examination of the model in Figure 2.1 indicates that five major factors are implicated in the process that may result in abuse. These have been identified from a logical analysis of the extant literature. Three levels are indicated for each of the factors; however, it is essential that the reader understand that these factors are viewed as representing a continuum. We have identified a low, middle and extreme range of the continuum to facilitate discussion. Therefore, the boxes do not imply discrete categories, but rather they are intended to communicate points on a continuum. The two final outcomes indicated are *abuse* or *no abuse*. The model is intended to be descriptive and to facilitate assessment and effective treatment planning.

The model is designed to assess a family at a given time and to determine the likelihood that abuse will occur in the near future for a child in that family. In some cases, abuse may not yet have occurred, and the model might be used to assess the danger that the first instance of abuse may be imminent. In other cases, abuse may already have occurred, and the model would then be applied to evaluate the possibility of additional abuse occurring in the near future.

The factors of the model are shown linearly and a progression is indicated from the left hand to the right hand outcome side of the figure. However, the reader should understand that this is a schematic model presented in a linear fashion strictly for convenience. If the total model were to be represented, it would require an elaborate system showing interactions between all of the factors in a variety of combinations and loops. However, attempting to present that complexity in a figure would confuse rather than clarify the process. Therefore, an overly simplistic linear presentation was selected. As the model implies, the more a given family can be characterized by the top end of the continuum rather than the bottom, the more likely it is that abuse will occur. Likewise, the more factors in which the family can be classified at the minimal risk or well-functioning end of the continuum, the more likely it becomes that abuse may be prevented even though the risk element in other factors may be high.

Perhaps some examples will clarify the use of the model. If we consider the abuser characteristics, it is obvious that some individuals evaluated as possible abusers may appear to be well functioning in all major realms of their life, and there may be few of the characteristics present that are generally associated with an abuser. Conversely, as we move up the scale, the mid-range is represented by an individual who has some of the personality characteristics of an abuser, but who is generally able to control these. Finally, as we move to the top most extreme of the scale, we are confronted by individuals who have numerous personality characteristics of individuals who might be abusive to children and who, in addition, have significant other psychopathology that makes it highly unlikely that they would be able to control their behavior or function effectively if entrusted with the care of children. We could similarly examine each of the other four factors and note that a continuum exists, with the degree of risk increasing as the top part of the scale is approached. To further amplify this process a few vignettes may be useful. A man who is exceptionally strong and may be easily aroused to anger could well represent a well-functioning minimal or no-risk factor type individual because he is generally capable of controlling himself around children and does not have the classic characteristics of a potentially abusing parent. Likewise, the other family members and the child in this case may be well functioning and normal (second and third factors). In addition, the man may be gainfully employed at a job that he enjoys and may seldom be at home with the children except when his spouse is also present to assist in their care (fourth and fifth factors). This pattern would be highly unlikely to lead to abuse. However, it would be possible for this individual in a moment of anger to accidently bruise or even break a bone of one of the children because of his excessive strength and strong anger, although there was no malicious intent to abuse the child. Conversely take this same situation and change the social context and situational context factors so that the male spouse in this case loses his job, which makes it necessary for him to remain home all day with the children. In addition, as a result of his loss of employment, the mother is forced out of the home to find a job to help support the family. This might well result in a situation in which this individual would be at home with a number of new and difficult tasks without the support of his wife, and he may well strike out abusively at the children. Suppose further that one of the children is hyperactive or retarded or has some significant pathology. This combination might indeed make such striking out at that child even more likely, with the result that abuse might occur. Therefore, it can be seen that factors may interact in a variety of ways, with the outcome being either abuse or not abuse depending on the particular levels of the factors involved.

Let us examine a second vignette beginning with a moderate risk situation. We will assume that we have a mother who was abused as a child, who feels inept as a parent, and has a number of other risk factors in terms of personality. She is married to a man who has had a similarly abusive upbringing, they have children who are difficult to manage, and although the father is gainfully employed, he has a relatively low income job, making the provision of the necessities for living a constant struggle.

As a result, they live in a neighborhood where it is unsafe for the children to play outside unsupervised. As a result, the children must be in the house and underfoot most of the time. This type of situation is likely to result in numerous instances of conflict and physical punishment, which may eventually culminate in abuse. Although we will not take time to elaborate all of the possibilities, let us make a few changes in this situation and see their effect. If the potential abuser has numerous personality characteristics consistent with abuse, but there is a well-functioning marital partner who is very capable in child management and the child is well behaved, this may produce a situation in which the likelihood of abuse is greatly reduced. However, if the marital partner is disorganized by alcohol abuse or serious emotional disturbance and the child is a significant management problem, the likelihood of abuse greatly increases.

One final example of the use of the model will suffice. Examining the top end of the continuum represented in this model, we see the possibility that the potential abuser has numerous personality characteristics consistent with abuse as well as serious psychopathology that renders this person out of control a great deal of the time. If this person (1) is paired with a marital partner with similar problems, (2) has a child who is a management problem, and (3) exists in a social and situational context high in abuse potential (e.g., unemployed and isolate), there is a significant probability that serious abuse will occur. However, if the nonabusing family member happens to be a well functioning and capable parent, this person may well protect the children and neutralize the high potential for abuse in the other partner. It is hoped that these illustrations of how the model works will give the reader sufficient information to apply the model to the wide range of possibilities that families in abusive situations present.

Clinical use of this model also will asssist the clinician in considering different forms of intervention for different aspects of the case so that a combined treatment program can be developed that will have the maximum probability of success.

This model could be tested empirically, however. For example, it would be possible to develop checklists and scaling systems whereby the characteristics of the abusing parent(s) could be converted to a 10-point scale. Likewise, the characteristics of the child and other family members as well as the social and situational factors could be scaled on a 10-point system. It would then be possible to evaluate families for their potential to abuse and empirically validate the system both retrospectively and prospectively.

EFFECTS OF ABUSE ON CHILDREN

The effects of abuse on children are many and serious. Certainly, in the most extreme case, abuse results in the death of the child. In addition, many children suffer disfigurement and permanent handicaps as a result of abuse. Child abuse can obviously have a serious and detrimental impact on the physical and emotional development of the child by interfering with socialization, education, and all aspects of normal child development (Williams, 1978). These effects can continue to have an impact in adulthood in terms of disturbed interpersonal relationships, predisposition to emotional disturbance, and increased potential for abusing their own children. A high incidence of brain damage, learning disability, growth retardation as well as failure to thrive, and secondary retardation has been found in abused children (Kempe, Silverman, Steele, Droegemuller, & Silver, 1962; Martin & Rodeheffer, 1976). Furthermore, the increased incidence of antisocial behavior, aggressiveness, and juvenile delinquency as well as adult criminal behavior has been related to abuse (Lewis, Shanok, Pincus, & Glaser, 1979). For example, a recent article has linked being abused as a child with committing murder as an adult (Lewis, Moy, Jackson, Aaronson, Restifo, Serra, & Simos, 1985). In less serious cases, abused children have been characterized by withdrawal, passivity, depression, and apathy (Green, 1978; Galdston, 1965). Therefore, child abuse may have a profound effect on the entire life of the individual who has been abused and may also affect future generations of that family as well as society at large (Martin and Beezley, 1976).

Chapter 3

Assessment of Physical Abuse

There are several components to the assessment of child abuse cases. In a typical case, suspected abuse is reported by an interested party to the office of child protection services, or its equivalent, in the state where the child resides. Social workers trained in child abuse visit the home and investigate the situation (referred to as the process of validating the abuse). If the case worker believes that there is a basis for the complaint, several actions may be taken. For example, the child or the abuser may be removed from the home and the family may be engaged in treatment to prevent further instances of abuse, or both. Foster care may be arranged for the children or termination of parental rights may be sought. Criminal charges may be brought against the parents. Excellent discussions of this process may be found in two books edited by Kempe and Helfer, entitled *The Battered Child* (1968) and *Helping the Battered Child and His Family* (1972). Generally the validation process will include a medical examination. The medical process for evaluating and documenting child abuse has been discussed in the Kempe and Helfer books just noted as well as various articles (Holter & Friedman, 1968; Wilson, 1977; Lauer, Ten Broeck, & Grossman, 1974). Most mental health workers who provide treatment do not become involved in child abuse cases until the process of social work validation, medical documentation, and emergency intervention has been completed. Therefore, this chapter will focus on evaluating the family and child for long-term treatment once abuse has been confirmed.

Occasionally, a practicing mental health professional will be called on by the child protection service agency to assist in validating the abuse and then preparing a case for court. This is an important responsibility, but one that would take us too far afield in the confines of the current chapter to discuss in detail. The interested reader may find information

34

about this process in the chapter on child abuse by Magrab in *Psychological and Behavioral Assessment: Impact on Pediatric Care* (1984).

One efficient strategy for assessing a child-abusing family is to use the model presented in Figure 2.1 along with the worksheet presented in Figure 3.1. Use of this model and worksheet enables the mental health professional to carefully assess all aspects of the situation, weigh each with respect to significance, and choose an intervention strategy for each component of the case that will result in successful treatment. The present authors have employed a problem/asset-oriented strategy in using the model presented. Figure 3.1 indicates how this may be applied to a given case.

Presently, we shall examine the model and discuss ways of proceeding with the assessment. A word of caution is in order regarding the amount of assessment to be accomplished with a particular case. Many techniques and instruments will be presented in this chapter. However, the examiner should choose methods carefully from those listed and avoid over-evaluation. In our discussion, we will assume that all members of the family and the child are available for assessment. Often, the family has been separated, and referrals have been made to different agencies for different components of the treatment process. Although this sometimes may be necessary, it is generally best if one agency and clinician team can serve the entire family.

ABUSER CHARACTERISTICS

Following the model presented, the first task is to assess the characteristics of the abuser that may have played a part in the abusive situation. The intent in this portion of the assessment is to determine whether serious psychopathology is present and which of the significant risk factors identified in the literature are present in the abuser. The mental health professional involved with such patients must often deal with his or her own emotional reactions to the situation. Often the professional has been presented with graphic accounts and photographs of the abuse that took place. These details are often abhorrent and unsettling. However, to be effective in ameliorating the situation, the clinician must control these reactions and approach the case objectively, with the mission clearly in mind of being helpful to all individuals involved. One useful consideration in aiding the clinician to adopt the appropriate stance is to remember that many abusing parents were themselves abused as children. The clinician's task at that point is to deal with *two* individuals who have suffered child abuse (the parent and the child who is the currently identified patient).

Initially, many parents approach the session with the clinician in a

Figure 3.1. Physical abuse process therapy worksheet.

1. Abuser				2. Nonabusing Family Members				3. Child Victim				4. Social Context				5. Situational Context			
a. Identified Problems	b. Planned Intervention	c. Identified Assets	d. Planned Use	a. Identified Problems	b. Planned Intervention	c. Identified Assets	d. Planned Use	a. Identified Problems	b. Planned Intervention	c. Identified Assets	d. Planned Use	a. Identified Problems	b. Planned Intervention	c. Identified Assets	d. Planned Use	a. Identified Problems	b. Planned Intervention	c. Identified Assets	d. Planned Use
1. ___	1. ___	1. ___	1. ___	1. ___	1. ___	1. ___	1. ___	1. ___	1. ___	1. ___	1. ___	1. ___	1. ___	1. ___	1. ___	1. ___	1. ___	1. ___	1. ___
2. ___	2. ___	2. ___	2. ___	2. ___	2. ___	2. ___	2. ___	2. ___	2. ___	2. ___	2. ___	2. ___	2. ___	2. ___	2. ___	2. ___	2. ___	2. ___	2. ___
3. ___	3. ___	3. ___	3. ___	3. ___	3. ___	3. ___	3. ___	3. ___	3. ___	3. ___	3. ___	3. ___	3. ___	3. ___	3. ___	3. ___	3. ___	3. ___	3. ___
4. ___	4. ___	4. ___	4. ___	4. ___	4. ___	4. ___	4. ___	4. ___	4. ___	4. ___	4. ___	4. ___	4. ___	4. ___	4. ___	4. ___	4. ___	4. ___	4. ___
5. ___	5. ___	5. ___	5. ___	5. ___	5. ___	5. ___	5. ___	5. ___	5. ___	5. ___	5. ___	5. ___	5. ___	5. ___	5. ___	5. ___	5. ___	5. ___	5. ___
6. ___	6. ___	6. ___	6. ___	6. ___	6. ___	6. ___	6. ___	6. ___	6. ___	6. ___	6. ___	6. ___	6. ___	6. ___	6. ___	6. ___	6. ___	6. ___	6. ___

hostile and defensive manner, because of extensive interviews and probing by social workers, physicians, and sometimes police detectives in attempting to validate the extent of the abuse. Although this process is necessary, it is upsetting to the parents, and they tend to view the current assessment as an extension of what has taken place already. It is important that the clinician makes a concerted effort to develop rapport with the patient and establishes a trusting and candid relationship. There are several ways to do this. First, the personnel in the clinic and the clinician should approach the patient with warmth and respect. It is frequently helpful if the clinician can make a positive gesture to the parents as the session begins. For example, the clinician might ask if they had difficulty finding the office, show some concern about seeing that they have a comfortable chair for the interview, offer them a cup of coffee, or some similar gesture. Certainly, a smile and a friendly handshake are in order. Before the assessment begins, the clinician must establish the limits of confidentiality that the family can expect. In most cases, there is a legal process involved and the clinician will be required to report to a child protection agency, the district attorney, a particular judge, or some other individual who is responsible for seeing that the case is handled properly. This information should be made clear to the family in advance.

When a parent is aware that the clinician will be reporting to a child protection worker or law enforcement official, the parent certainly may choose not to reveal certain information. This will interfere with the clinical process to some extent, but it is essential, in terms of professional ethics, that the patient be aware of the contingencies involved. If the clinician is sufficiently sensitive and establishes good rapport with the patient, it will generally not be an insurmountable obstacle.

The clinician should not insist that the parents immediately admit to the abuse. Some will readily admit to it, whereas others will not. It serves no purpose to begin the assessment by arguing with the patient. The clinician should simply indicate his awareness that protective services workers are convinced that abuse has occurred. As rapport is established and the evaluation progresses, the parents will generally cease to be defensive and assent to their role in the abuse. At the end of the assessment, a gentle but firm confrontation may be necessary for treatment to commence, but by then the relationship with the parents should be strong enough to sustain the confrontation. Moreover, the clinician will have the added credibility of speaking from first-hand knowledge of the case rather than depending on reports of others as is the situation at the start of the process. One way to handle this confrontation is to say something like, "I understand that things can get out of hand when you are very frustrated in trying to control your children. At times like that you may go too far and do something harmful to them . . . but we can help you to learn to handle things better so that will not happen. Are you willing to try?"

To begin the assessment itself, many clinicians find some general questions on how the parent is feeling to be very helpful. For example, the clinician might simply say that he or she realizes that the situation has been very stressful and wonders how the parent is feeling. A question such as, "I guess you have been going through some pretty rough times lately," is often a good opening. Other questions may be asked about how this is affecting them physically, emotionally, and in their relationships with others, their job, and so forth. During this opening phase of the interview, it is helpful if the clinician indicates to the parent that he or she understands his or her feelings, does not intend to be judgmental, and is optimistic that some things can be done to help straighten things out. This attitude communicates to the parent that the clinician cares about her or him and is interested in helping. It also frequently helps if the clinician gives the parent license to express certain feelings. A statement such as, "Often people in a situation such as yours feel that . . .," is a useful technique. Following such initial rapport building, a variety of structured assessment techniques may be used to take some pressure off the parents to express themselves when they are upset and confused. Because many individuals lack the ability to clearly articulate their feelings and thoughts, structured tests make it easier for them to respond.

Among the structured techniques that may be used is a structured mental status interview (Johnson, 1981). Psychological testing may include any of the standard testing instruments for evaluating psychopathology such as the Minnesota Multiphasic Personality Inventory (Dahlstrom, Welsh, & Dahlstrom, 1972) and the Rorschach (Exner, 1986) tests. Numerous studies have employed these instruments in evaluating child-abusing parents. Although none have been found to successfully predict or identify abuse (Wolfe, 1985), they are useful in identifying the presence of psychopathology and risk factors especially anger and impulse control. The Novaco Anger Inventory (Novaco, 1978) is also useful in evaluating a parent's responses to stressful and anger-provoking situations.

Because child abuse frequently results from frustration over the parent's inability to successfully manage the child, some assessment of the parents' intellectual and abstract reasoning ability as well as their ability to generate suitable management alternatives and to change their own behavior may be necessary. The Wechsler Adult Intelligence Scale-Revised (Wechsler, 1981) or other tests of intelligence may provide information on these points.

The parents' knowledge of the appropriate behavior for children of different ages and their expectations about their child's behavior must be explored. Some instruments are available to help evaluate parenting skills and parent-child relationships. A few of the more useful inventories will be described here.

The Eyberg Child Behavioral Inventory (Eyberg & Ross, 1978) lists 36 common behavioral problems of children and asks the parent to indicate how often each behavior occurs as well as whether the parent finds the behavior to be a problem. Helfer and his colleagues have developed the Michigan Screening Profile of Parenting out of their research with abusing parents (Helfer, Hoffmeister, & Schneider, 1978). This instrument is useful in evaluating parents' ability to cope with the stresses of child rearing. The Parenting Stress Index by Abidin (1983) consists of 120 items that yield scores on total stress, child-domain stress, and parent domain stress as well as life stress. The child domain is further broken down into adaptability, acceptability, "demandingness", mood, distraction-hyperactivity, and reinforces parents. The parent domain score is subdivided according to depression, attachment, restriction of role, sense of competence, social isolation, relationship to the spouse, and parent health. The Knowledge of Behavioral Principles as Applied to Children (O'Dell, Tarler-Benlolo, & Flynn, 1979) is an inventory that assesses the parent's knowledge of behavioral principles as they apply to child management. The parents respond by identifying what they consider to be the correct way to handle various problems exhibited by children. The score reflects the degree to which the parents identify the correct approach to child management according to child behavior experts. The Child Abuse Potential Inventory (Milner, 1986) is a 160-item inventory constructed to identify individuals who have many characteristics of parents who might be expected to abuse a child. Finally, the 77-item Parent Attitude Survey (Hereford, 1963), developed by Carl Hereford at the University of Texas, assesses parental attitudes in five areas: confidence, causation, acceptance, understanding, and trust. As indicated, the aforementioned instruments are useful in providing parents with a structured format in which to express their attitudes, opinions, and problems. The scores obtained can then be compared with those of various normative and reference groups to get some indication of the significance of the results. In addition, specific items can be discussed with the parents. By endorsing a particular item, the parent may indicate a problem area that can be followed up with additional probes on interview to obtain a complete picture. This gradual progression from structured answers to a more general discussion is often very helpful in obtaining complete information from parents.

Interviews following the structured assessment should explore the manner in which the parents were reared, how they felt about it, how much it carries over into the way they are rearing their children, the ways in which their methods are different, the main areas in which they feel they have difficulty in managing their child, and the methods they have found to be successful or unsuccessful. Interview information should also be obtained about how they view their child and if they feel that their relationship with the child is such that it can change for the better. Magrab (1984) and Kelly (1983) have presented useful interview guides for this phase of the assessment.

In completing the psychological assessment and gathering information, it is generally wise to have several short sessions rather than prolonged sessions. With each contact the parents tend to feel more relaxed and respond better. Prolonged contacts often exhaust them and result in diminishing clinical returns. It is often useful to ask the parents to monitor and record certain behaviors between sessions which can then be discussed. Also, they can be encouraged to make lists of things they want to discuss or to keep a diary. All of these facilitate the process of obtaining complete information. Each parent should be afforded the opportunity to speak with the examiner alone, so they can express themselves without fear of retaliation from the other and can express personal concerns they may not want to reveal to the other. Likewise, they should be seen together to observe their interactions and how they handle situations. The nature of their relationship to each other should be explored in terms of marital conflicts, sources of mutual support, sexual difficulties, disagreements about money matters, and related issues.

Finally, it is very useful to observe parents' behavior. Many useful and enlightening observations can be made from the waiting room. When possible, it is helpful to visit the home and observe the family members in their normal environment. If certain times are noted by the parents as being especially difficult (e.g., getting the children off to school, mealtime, and bedtime), it may be possible to schedule a visit for one of those crucial times. Wolfe and his colleagues (Wolfe, Sandler, & Kaufman, 1981) have developed procedures and a worksheet for conducting structured home observations that have been used successfully with child-abusing families. If home visits are not possible, a more practical alternative is to have the parents simulate interactions in the clinic setting. For example, they can bring a lunch to the clinic and have a meal, with the staff observing. They may bring children's homework or some other task and be observed while they interact with the children around the task. The clinician may structure a decision-making or task completion project (e.g., planning a family outing or vacation) for the family and observe how they handle this situation. All of these procedures provide important information toward understanding the difficulties in the family.

The general procedure in filling out the worksheet in Figure 3.1 is to identify from all of the aforementioned sources the specific problems and assets present. Interventions can then be identified for the problems and uses planned for the assets.

NONABUSING FAMILY MEMBERS

Because little research has considered the nonabusing family members and no specialized scales are available for assessing them, only standard instruments of the type mentioned in the preceding section and observation/interview methods may be employed. However, a full understanding of the problem requires careful analysis of the strengths and weaknesses of the other family members. Specific interventions may be called for when weaknesses are noted. The strengths may be used as part of the overall treatment plan.

CHILD VICTIM

The next component of the model concerns the characteristics of the child. As was the case with the parents, the child should be approached in a warm, supportive manner. The child will sometimes discuss the abuse. At other times, the child may fear retribution or not want to get his or her parents in trouble. If the child does not volunteer information, it is wise not to press for it. This information will surface later in the security of treatment and can be dealt with then. The clinician making the assessment may want to consult the medical report as well as the social history for details of the abuse and to note any physical, handicapping, or early developmental characteristics that may have predisposed the child to abuse. Those involved in the validation process for abuse should be encouraged to record their sessions with the child on videotape or audiotape. The clinician can then observe or listen to the tape and will not have to probe the child for details. Having the child continually recount the experiences is upsetting and may cause iatrogenic difficulties that would be avoided if the situation were handled more skillfully.

A careful program of observation, interview, and psychological testing of the child should be accomplished. Any of the standard psychological instruments available for children can be used. The assessment should include a basic developmental, intellectual, and academic assessment to determine the child's status. If signs of organicity, learning disability, or related problems are noted, a careful evaluation should be made with the many available appropriate educational diagnostic instruments and neuropsychological techniques such as the Halstead-Reitan (Reitan & Davison, 1974) or the Luria (Luria, 1966). If hyperactivity is suspected, the Conners' scales (Conners, 1970, 1969) can be used by having the parents and teachers provide the needed ratings. An emotional-mental status examination of the child should be included. Numerous interview formats and standard psychological testing instruments are available for this purpose that apply to children of different ages. The interested reader might want to consult Magrab's *Psychological and Behavioral Assessment: Impact on Pediatric Care* (1984), Goldstein & Herson's *Handbook of Psychological Assessment* (1984), or Karoly's *Handbook of Child Health Assessment* (in press) for details.

In addition to general assessment instruments there are specific tests for anxiety such as the State-Trait Anxiety Inventory for Children (Spielberger, Gorsuch, & Lushene, 1970) and for depression such as the *Children's Depression Inventory* (Kovacs, 1981), which are helpful. Several fear surveys have also been developed (e.g., Ollendick, 1983; Walker, 1979) that are useful in assessing the child's emotional status, feelings of safety, and stress.

Finally, observations should be made of the child as he or she relates to the parents, to siblings, and to the examiner. These relationships can be observed in the home, at school, and in simulated situations in the office. Some clinicians are puzzled that the child often clings to and expresses love for the abusive parent. Such behavior often occurs and has been learned through negative reinforcement, in that, this behavior successfully averted some attacks in the past.

Ultimately, assessment of the child should involve an overall assessment of physical and emotional health, developmental progress, academic achievement, and behavioral appropriateness. Following this, the child's section of the worksheet can be completed.

One final point worth noting before closing this section is that the clinician should be careful not to be misled by some statements the child may make during the assessment. Children, in the midst of an assessment involving child abuse, frequently recant their story and say they just want the family to be left alone. This results from a number of factors. Often parents and relatives attempt to make the child feel guilty for what has happened. They point out that the family has been torn apart, and that the offending parent might be sent to jail, with the child living in foster homes separated from the family for the rest of his or her life. In addition, they sometimes convince the child that he or she really was bad and needed that kind of punishment, that the parents were right and that all of the trouble was caused by the child who is wrong. This certainly can be upsetting to the child, who often decides that things were not so bad at home, with the subsequent request that everything return to the way it was before. Needless to say, if the case is abandoned at this time, the child will be a victim of further abuse and will be extremely fearful of making a second report. Therefore, the clinician should offer the child reassurance but must continue with the assessment to see that treatment is provided.

SOCIAL CONTEXT

Proceeding to the next component of the model, assessment of the social context of the family is in order. Some information on this variable is available from the psychological testing and interviews conducted with parents and family members. Likewise, the social work history obtained in the validation process will often contain considerable information on employment, living conditions, socioeconomic level, and family circumstances. Additional information can be obtained by a careful interview regarding family, relatives, church, and other social network supports available. The Social Readjustment Scale (Holmes & Rahe, 1967) is useful in evaluating the degree of stress that the family is experiencing as a result of changes in the last few months. The Hassles Scale (Kanner, Coyne, Schaefer, & Lazarus, 1981) assesses the daily problems that create stress.

Careful evaluation of all of this information will enable the clinician to delineate specific problems and strengths in the social context. An intervention strategy can be developed for each problem. For example, it may be possible to assist one or both parents in obtaining employment or making suitable child care arrangements, to encourage involvement with a church group that can lend support, or to apply for welfare benefits that can be of assistance in dealing with the problems involved. Existing assets such as relatives or friends who live nearby can also be programmed for use as appropriate.

SITUATIONAL CONTEXT

Evaluation of the situational context is relatively simple if the model under discussion has been followed. Considerable information obtained from the history, observations, and psychological testing will be useful in filling in the details of the specific situations under which the abuse occurred. Depending on the situation, interventions can be planned. For example, it may be possible to place the child in a nursery school setting during the day so that the mother has more time away from the child, or to arrange for transportation and supervision at an emergency nursery center when the mother feels that she is reaching a point where she can no longer control herself. In addition, various support networks can be enlisted to assure that high stress situations do not occur frequently and are successfully dealt with when they do.

CONCLUSION

Examination of the model reveals that several components interact to eventually produce abuse. Careful evaluation of each component and a multifaceted intervention program that attempts to reduce all these components to a low risk level may produce a situation in which the outcome of the process is *no abuse* rather than *abuse*. Careful evaluation of the progress of the family must be made during treatment, and it is crucial that there be a regular follow-up after treatment ends, by either the clinician or social agencies, to insure that the abusive pattern does not return. Treatment generally must be long term, involving a year or two, although some cases can be handled in less time.

Effective treatment will make it possible, in many cases, to reunite the family and have the parents rear their children much more effectively, with no further abuse. However, in some cases the problems and deficits are such that they cannot be changed sufficiently for the child to ever be safe. At these times, decisions must be made on the future care and safety of the child, involving terminating the custody of the parents and placing the child in an adoptive or foster home. Although this drastic step should be avoided when possible, clinicians need to be realistic and make this very tough decision when it is called for. The important principle in all of the assessment and treatment process is the safety and well-being of the child throughout his or her developmental years. Preservation of the family is an important but secondary goal.

Chapter 4
Treatment of the Physical Abuser of Children

As noted in Chapter 2, only a small portion of abusive parents exhibit severe pathology. This finding, however, does not preclude their presentation for treatment, or negate the potential for multiple problems to assume overwhelming proportions. The box in the upper left-hand corner of Figure 2.1 (column 1) identifies a group of parents who, based on assessment, can be characterized as exhibiting severe psychopathology associated with their abusive acts. Pathology may manifest in different forms.

Severe marital discord also represents a problem that may necessitate immediate intervention. Stabilizing the marital relationship can facilitate the parents' cooperation and reduce the probability that the frustration and anger from marital discord will be directed towards the children. Alcohol and drug addiction has frequently been associated with physical abuse (Mayer & Black, 1977; Tinklenberg, 1973). When substance abuse/addiction is severe, it is often best to provide appropriate drug or alcohol dependency treatment as an initial step in the intervention process. Referral to a specialized program (e.g., inpatient alcohol treatment) may be necessary before a parent can benefit from other types of treatment. For example, an intoxicated parent is unlikely to make use of parenting skills taught in typical child abuse treatment programs.

When the parents are psychotic or schizophrenic, the clinician has few options other than to help the parent secure appropriate intensive psychiatric treatment. Once such a person is stabilized on psychotropic medication, he or she can often then benefit from other treatment modalities.

In fatal abuse (Jason & Andereck, 1983; Jason, Carpenter and Tyler, 1983), the mental health professional's role may be limited to psychological assessment of the parents or consultation regarding surviving siblings. In this capacity, court testimony may also be required to clarify the existence or severity of the parents' pathology or to recommend placement for the remaining children. (See Shapiro, 1984, for an extended discussion of expert testimony.)

In many cases of the type just described, circumstances may dictate working with an abusive parent who is concurrently attending some other treatment program. This need not be seen as a treatment barrier and can be successful if communication lines between therapists are adequately maintained. It is often helpful for both therapists and patients to meet and develop a written agreement specifying therapists' and patients' responsibilities.

Typically, many parents that therapists are asked to see fall into the moderate- or low-risk categories indicated in the lower two squares of the first column in Figure 2.1. These parents will differ primarily in the number and severity of problems they have in a variety of key areas (e.g., child management skills, realistic developmental expectations, and anger/impulse control). Frequently, low-risk parents are self-referred or were reported for an isolated incident of abuse or both.

The parent may have had a series of stressful life events such as divorce, unemployment, financial difficulties, and health problems culminating in the parent's lateness for a job interview because his or her 4-year-old son spilled a grape soda on him or her as he or she was about to leave. Although this parent would not normally lash out on the child, he or she did in this case and the bruises might be noted at a child care center and reported. This parent's situation may be much different from that of a parent or parents who have repeatedly used excessive force with their children. Such parents would more likely fall into the moderate category, requiring more intensive treatment.

Completed assessments of these parents will serve as the basis for developing an individualized treatment protocol. Because the areas are relatively discrete and measurable, treatment can be criterion based, and parents can be reassessed after receiving basic training in a particular skill. If the skill has been mastered, that part of the training can be terminated. Conversely, continuing areas of weakness can be focused upon and reviewed. In this way, parents are always aware of treatment goals and expectations. The responsibility then becomes theirs, with the duration of treatment dependent upon their motivation and performance.

A broad range of treatment approaches for physically abusive parents, as discussed in the literature, are psychodynamically oriented (see Steele & Pollack (1974) for a discussion of a representative approach.) Although there have been anecdotal reports of success with psychoanalytic approaches, there is a paucity of empirical literature supporting its efficacy. In contrast, a large body of literature exists that empirically supports the effectiveness of behavioral approaches with child management difficulties in general (Berkowitz & Graziano, 1972; Patterson, Reid, Jones, & Conger, 1975; O'Dell, 1974; Forehand & King, 1977; O'Dell, Blackwell, Larcen, & Hogan, 1977; Johnson & Christensen, 1975; Roberts, McMahon, Forehand, & Humphreys, 1978; Sandler, Van Dercar, & Milhoan, 1978) and more specifically in the treatment of physically abusive parents. (See Isaacs, 1982 for review.) As a result, this chapter will emphasize intervention elements from treatment programs with demonstrated effectiveness (e.g., Lutzker, Welsch, & Rice, 1984; Wolfe, Sandler, & Kaufman, 1981). In fact, Fantuzzo & Twentyman (1986), in a recent review, suggest that Wolfe et al.'s (1981) study represents one of only a few outcome studies that meet acceptable methodological standards. This further highlights the effectiveness of the skills-based behavioral approach and supports our emphasis on such techniques.

Treatment will be examined in relation to problem areas commonly identified in the literature. Child management skills, anger and impulse control, attitudes/expectations, and problem solving reflect the treatment techniques that will be discussed. An attempt has been made to avoid duplicating treatment guidelines that have been well articulated elsewhere. However, enough detail is provided to allow the clinician to use the chapter as a primary guide for treating abusive parents.

CHILD MANAGEMENT SKILLS

A particular focus of research in the area of physical abuse has been the identification of skills deficits that differentiate abusive from nonabusive parents. (See Wolfe, 1985, for a review.) Child management deficits have been a major thrust of these investigations. Findings indicate that abusive parents are less likely to provide tactile and auditory stimulation (Dietrich, Starr, & Kaplan, 1980); therefore, they avoid touching their children in a positive manner or engaging in positive behaviors directed toward their children (Bousha & Twentyman, 1984; Burgess & Conger, 1978), and they communicate less frequently with their children and are less likely to exhibit facilitative behavior (Disbrow, Doerr, & Caulfield, 1977). Furthermore, they are inconsistent in their discipline (Young, 1964; Elmer, 1967), a situation that has been related to less effective parenting (Parke & Deur, 1972). When abusive parents do direct attention toward their children, it is often coercive (Reid, Taplin, & Lorber, 1981) or physically negative and aggressive (Bousha & Twentyman, 1984; Lahey et al., 1984). In response, abused children direct much aversive behavior towards their parents (Reid et al. 1981) and are more likely to be noncompliant than are nonabused children (Bousha & Twentyman, 1984). Parke and Collmer (1975) suggest that the abusive parents' inability to terminate their children's aversive behavior is directly related to levels of punishment that become abusive.

When parenting deficits of the preceding type are present, child management skills development should be a priority. A brief survey of methods to accomplish this is presented.

Recording Behavior

Parents' perceptions of their child's behaviors, both negative and positive, are often based on subjective generalizations. Rather than reflecting their child's actual behavior, parents' complaints often reflect their mood, unrealistic expectations, developmentally appropriate variations in the child's behavior, or an isolated incident involving the child. If changes in children's behavior are to be used as an indicator of a parent's success in applying child management skills, it is imperative that behavioral reports be as reliable as possible. This end can be achieved by spending a relatively brief period teaching parents to identify, define, and record common classes of behavior. Such skills also serve to reinforce the parents' use of other techniques (i.e., reward and punishment), particularly when they result in observable improvements in their children's behavior.

In introducing the concept of recording behaviors, it is helpful to present a brief explanation of why this practice may be of some value to the parent. The clinician may want to explain to the parents that specifically defining the problem makes it easier to communicate and ensures that all parties involved are talking about the same problem. It also increases the probability of uncovering the causes of the problem and identifying potential solutions.

Recording behaviors entails four major steps: (a) identifying a relevant target behavior; (b) developing a behaviorally specific definition of the target behavior; (c) monitoring the behavior as it occurs; and (d) visually displaying or graphing the target behavior.

Identifying and Defining Target Behaviors

The target behavior can be any behavior of the child that would be desirable to change: it is not unusual for parents to begin by identifying a broad category of behaviors (e.g., being more responsible at home). To be useful, however, such broad categories must be refined into specific behaviors. A well-defined target behavior will be: (a) observable; (b) specifically defined and described; (c) stated as simply as possible; and (d) measurable.

Observable behaviors are those that fall into the realm of public behavior. They can be seen and/or heard by anyone instructed to look for them while observing the child. A behaviorally specific definition should indicate when and where the target behavior occurs, and who is present when it occurs. The target behavior should be a clearly described target in concrete terms. "Terry's hitting his sister Cindy, while at home, after school" is an example of a behavior that is both behaviorally specific and observable.

Care should be taken to insure that the chosen behavior is not too complex. Stating the target behavior in the simplest possible terms helps avoid the possibility of inadvertently combining two or more behaviors into one target statement. Finally, target behaviors should be measurable, that is, they must have a distinct beginning and an endpoint, and it must be possible to express them numerically so that changes in the behavior will be readily observable as changes in the numbers recorded. This factor is very important to help detect early signs of positive results. For example, if hitting one's sister at home after school is the target, a decrease from 12 such incidents per evening to 8 is a 33% reduction and suggests good progress. However, most parents would not subjectively report much difference. They would be likely to say, "He's still hitting his sister after school." Pointing out the real change, objectively measured, can be used to motivate them to continue the program until it becomes subjectively apparent.

Monitoring Target Behaviors. Once a target behavior has been identified and defined, a system for recording it is necessary. The most common target behaviors are recorded in terms of either their frequency or duration of occurrence. In some cases, behaviors can be recorded either way. Typically, however, the recording mode (i.e., frequency versus duration) will be dictated by the definition of the problem. The following list contains examples of how some common behavior problems might be recorded:

Frequency	*Duration*
1. Number of times late from school	1. Number of minutes late from school
2. Number of times a child has to be told to clean his or her room	2. Number of minutes it takes a child to clean his/her room
3. Number of times a child must be reminded to get dressed	3. Number of minutes it takes a child to get dressed
4. Number of times a child does not complete homework	4. Number of minutes it takes a child to complete homework

A variety of methods can be used by parents to record their children's behavior. When frequency counts are appropriate, parents can use a pad and pen, a grocery counter, or a chalk board. Recording the duration of a particular behavior will necessitate the use of a clock, a kitchen timer, or a stopwatch. Recording sheets can be kept simple, including only required information. The example in Figure 4.1 could be used for monitoring the number of times Timmy swears during meals (for a 5-day period). This approach allows the results to be examined for differential patterns of behavior. For example, Timmy's swearing may only be a problem at breakfast. This information could radically affect the design of a behavior change program.

Figure 4.1. Sample Behavior Rating Form.

	Breakfast	Lunch	Dinner
Day of the Week			
Monday	_____	_____	_____
Tuesday	_____	_____	_____
Wednesday	_____	_____	_____
Thursday	_____	_____	_____
Friday	_____	_____	_____

Graphing Target Behaviors. Converting the results of a data recording sheet into a visual representation, such as a graph, offers a number of advantages and is often useful. First, it aids in understanding the relation between the behavior in question and other environmental stimuli (e.g., differing contingencies at breakfast due to time pressure). Graphs also allow a visual comparison of the child's pretreatment (or baseline) behavior with that behavior after an intervention program has been instituted. Finally, graphs allow both parent and child to observe changes in behavior, which may prove to be reinforcing as well as conducive to future goal setting.

Parents have the least difficulty in understanding how to graph behaviors if they are guided through an illustrative problem. Figures 4.2 and 4.3 provide examples of the process of graphing a child's behavior. The parents can then be assigned to record and graph a problem behavior one of their children is currently exhibiting. The behavior should be defined with the therapist's help, and plans for recording and graphing should also be discussed. With two-parent families, each parent may choose a separate problem behavior, they may cooperate on tracking one behavior, or they may keep individual records of the same behavior, which can be compared against each other for accuracy. Parents' initial

Figure 4.2. Data recording example.

Problem: Your 7-year-old son has recently discovered that swearing quickly attracts the attention of others. This has been a particular problem during meals. You are unsure as to how much of a problem it really is and if a certain meal is worse than the others. You decide to begin keeping track of Steven's swearing during breakfast, lunch, and dinner. You have made an appointment with a mental health professional in 6 days and want to bring the information with you.

DATA RECORDING SHEET

Target Behavior: Number of times Steven swears at each meal.

	Day of the Week				
Meal	Wednesday	Thursday	Friday	Saturday	Sunday
Breakfast	3	2	3	1	2
Lunch	1	0	*	0	0
Dinner	7	9	9	8	9

* = Went over a friend's house for lunch; no data recorded.

Figure 4.3. Data graphing example.

GRAPHING FORM

Target Behavior: Number of times Steven swears at each meal.
Range: From a low of zero (0) to a high of nine (9).

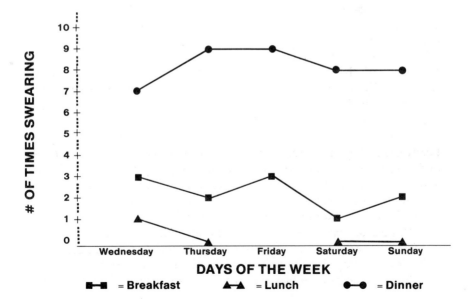

attempts at graphing can be reviewed during the following session. Additional graphing assignments can be used to enhance the parents' competence.

More detailed discussions of graphing and recording have been described by Miller (1980) and Powers & Osborne (1976). A thorough review of such material before teaching parents these skills is recommended.

Structured Approach To Giving Commands

A frequent complaint expressed by parents in treatment is that their children are noncompliant. The noncompliant child is in sharp contrast to most parents' expectation that children should do what they are told when they are told to do it. Within this context, parents will often become frustrated and angry, perceiving their children's noncompliance as hateful, a personal affront or stubbornness. Such feelings can quickly lead to harsh physical discipline as punishment for the child. Yet, if we examine the situation more carefully, it is not unusual for parents to be unaware of the active role they play in eliciting such behavior. In observing parents' use of language when they are attempting to give a command, it frequently becomes apparent that they use interrogatives (e.g., "Why don't you pick up your toys?" or "Don't you think that it's time for you to go to bed?") when they think they are telling their child to do something. In reality the child may be responding to the implied choice in the statement. Naturally, this creates problems.

If parents are asked to recount how they usually let their children know they want them to do something, examples of questions intended as commands will often arise. This offers the opportunity to ask parents what they would do if they were offered a choice with one alternative that was much less desirable (e.g., going to bed now versus staying up later). In this way, parents will discover that many times their children's responses are not intended to be hateful or stubborn. The therapist might suggest that the parents monitor their own use of commands and note the times they ask a question when they mean to give a command. Furthermore, parents can practice giving commands during the session with the therapist present. The therapist can request that they restate questions in command form when they catch themselves or when the therapist points it out.

A second barrier to children's compliance in many households is related to parents' consistency in stating commands and following through on the consequences of noncompliance. In many families a parent saying, "I want you to begin cleaning your room now," may mean anything from (a) you will be punished if I have to ask you again to (c) I am probably going to end up asking you at least five more times before I get angry, to (c) I will probably forget that I asked you. To intervene, the therapist might suggest that parents have a standard framework for giving commands. This framework should be used each time in the same fashion. Here is an example of a useful framework:

1. Ask the child to complete the behavior in a manner in which you would like to be asked ("Donna, we'll be leaving for grandma's house soon. Please start picking your toys up off the living room floor now, so that you'll be done when it's time to leave.").
2. Give the child a couple of minutes to begin. If the child starts cleaning up, reinforce him or her (e.g., "Keep up the good work. I really like it when you do what I ask".)
3. If the child does not comply, remind him or her and state the consequences of noncompliance ("Donna, you need to start cleaning up right now. Remember the rule, if you don't get finished in time, you'll lose ½ hour of your TV time tonight.").
4. Again, allow the child a couple of minutes to comply and reward the effort if he or she begins.
5. If the child still does not comply, follow through on the consequences described (e.g., "I've asked you twice to start cleaning up and you haven't. You've just lost ½ hour of your TV time tonight.").
6. Once the punishment has been administered, the slate is clean and the process begins again with a pleasant request (e.g., "Donna, please get started cleaning . . .").
7. Particularly with younger children, a physical prompt may be necessary (e.g., calmly but firmly lead the child by the hand to the room and have him or her start to clean).
8. Repeat the process as many times as necessary and remember that commands should be clear and specific and arguing should be avoided.

In using this framework for giving commands, it is expedient to have the parents explain the forthcoming change in their behavior before beginning. A family conference is often a useful medium for such a discussion. The explanation should include a review of past approaches that have not worked and a step-by-step presentation of how the new approach will be implemented.

Incompatible Behaviors: A Framework for Change

Most parents are well oriented to the process of attending to their children when they misbehave. They recognize punishment as a necessary means of controlling their children's behavior and often reconcile themselves to the fact that childrearing necessitates a lot of punishing. Often, the same parents rarely reinforce their child's appropriate behavior. They think, "If you spare the rod, you will spoil the child." They also state, "Why should I give my kids something for doing what they're supposed to do?" These predominant cultural attitudes represent a barrier to effective child management and need to be altered. The therapist should help parents understand that parenting involves both reinforcement of appropriate behaviors and punishment of inappropriate behaviors. When parenting becomes truly effective, parents reinforce frequently and punish sparingly. This concept represents the foundation of behavior change in child management.

In presenting these ideas it is helpful to offer supporting arguments. The therapist might ask parents to examine the quality of the time they spend interacting with their children and may suggest that if they are like most parents, much of their time is spend disciplining (yelling, threatening, spanking, etc.). A far smaller percentage of their time is spent positively interacting with their children. Generally if they think about it, parents will admit that they are not satisfied with this distribution of time. However, parents frequently forget that effective punishment should be self-limiting, that is, punishment should result in a decrease in misbehavior over time, thereby reducing the need to use it. Furthermore, parents need to become more familiar with the power of reinforcement as an agent for change. Developing an awareness of children's desire for parental time, attention, and approval will facilitate understanding the importance of reinforcement. In bringing these ideas together the therapist can explain to parents that the only successful way to change their children's behavior is to deal simultaneously with the inappropriate behavior that should be eliminated and its appropriate opposite that should be encouraged. The latter are referred to as incompatible behaviors. The graphic illustration in Figure 4.4 demonstrates why a dual focus is necessary and effective.

Because the amount of behavior that can occur in a given period is limited, the amount (%) of positive behavior affects the amount (%) of negative behavior and vice versa. In the preceding example, Nancy initially (time period A) spent a greater percentage of time engaged in negative behavior. In time period B, an increase in positive behavior necessarily results in a decrease in negative behavior.

Figure 4.4. An illustration of the effects of increasing/decreasing positive and negative child behaviors.

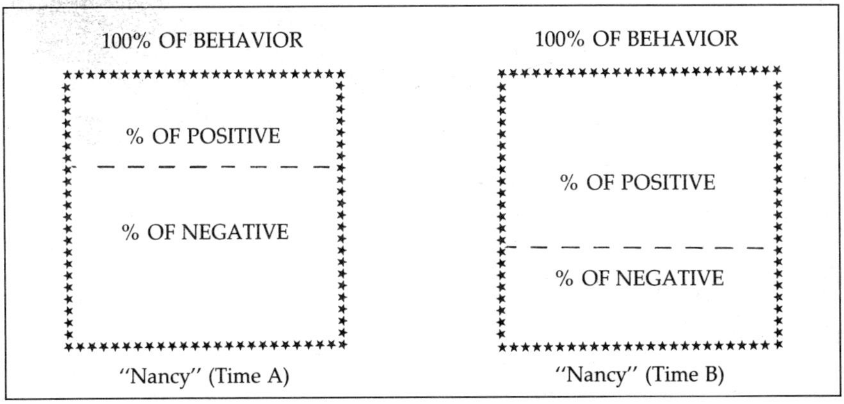

100% OF BEHAVIOR	100% OF BEHAVIOR
% OF POSITIVE	% OF POSITIVE
% OF NEGATIVE	% OF NEGATIVE
"Nancy" (Time A)	"Nancy" (Time B)

Although parents will be tempted to strictly focus on influencing either inappropriate (negative) or appropriate (positive) behavior, this approach is less likely to be successful in the long run than is attending to both. When parents focus more heavily on their child's misbehavior, the child learns that he or she can get more attention from acting out. As a result, inappropriate behavior is accidentally reinforced. When appropriate behavior is exclusively attended to, children may find themselves in control of the household because they are directly reinforced for appropriate behavior but suffer no consequences for inappropriate behavior. In fact, failing to apply negative consequences to inappropriate behavior indirectly reinforces this behavior by condoning its occurrence, while permitting any naturally favorable consequence of the behavior to occur.

Because this is a novel approach for many parents, attention should be given to helping them recognize incompatible behaviors as dual targets for intervention. The therapist might offer a couple of problem behaviors and describe incompatible behaviors. Following this, the parents can be asked to identify a problem that they have at home and a corresponding incompatible behavior.

Increasing Children's Appropriate Behaviors

Parents in our society are far more oriented toward attending to their children's misbehavior than to their appropriate behavior. The watch words in parenting seem to be, "If the kids are being good, don't disturb them . . .". Yet children demand a certain amount of parental attention on a regular basis. If parents do not provide this attention in a positive manner, children often resort to inappropriate behavior to obtain it. This situation is particularly problematic for abusive parents because their children's recurring demands for attention in this manner may play a role in eliciting their use of physical punishment. A major task in teaching parents child management skills is to increase their use of positive teaching and reward-oriented techniques while decreasing their dependence on punishment techniques.

Facilitating a shift in parents' childrearing practices necessitates dispelling two common misconceptions. First, the use of rewards is not synonymous with bribery. In childrearing, if the parent rewards the child for appropriate behavior, this is honest pay for honest work. A bribe, however, is a reward given to someone for doing something they really should not do. With minimal prompting, parents generally recognize that their lives are shaped by the use of rewards and reinforcers and that this is beneficial to survival. A creature that continually engages in behaviors that have no positive consequences would become extinct. The second major barrier occurs as a result of many parents' belief that "catching your kids when they're being good" involves too large a commitment of time. These same parents are usually unaware of the time involved in disciplining their children for misbehavior. A discussion related to how much time they spend interacting with their children in a positive context as opposed to a negative context is often sufficient to change their minds. (See the section on Incompatible Behaviors for a more complete discussion.)

Types of Reinforcers. Parents who are unfamiliar with the use of a reinforcement-oriented approach often have difficulty generating a broad enough spectrum of rewards to keep their children's interest. These parents need to be educated in the various categories of reinforcers, what things are inherently reinforcing, and how to increase the value of a reinforcer. By definition, a reinforcer is any event that follows a response and increases the probability of that response recurring in the future.

Three major categories of reinforcers are material, social, and activity. Social reinforcers reflect consensually accepted cultural acknowledgment. Smiles, verbal praise, a pat on the back, a nod, attention, a kiss, awards, a hug, and a wink are some examples of social reinforcers. Activity reinforcers can include special time with a parent, going to the park, seeing a movie, watching TV, playing outside, staying up later than usual, borrowing the car, and participating in athletics. Material rewards probably represent the most frequently used form of reinforcer. This category is made up of tangible objects (e.g., toys, candy, food, stickers, and comics) and tokens that can be traded for valued objects or activities (e.g., money, points, and stars).

It is important to stress that an item or an act is not automatically reinforcing by virtue of its inclusion in one of these three categories. Rather, a reinforcer is determined empirically by its ability to increase the future occurrence of a particular behavior in a specific child. An event that is reinforcing to one child could actually be punishing to another (e.g., attending dance classes). Reinforcers are defined by their effect on the particular organism in question (i.e., a specific child in the present case).

Although there is no guarantee that a particular object will be reinforcing to a specific child in a certain setting at a particular time, some reinforcers do have inherent value and do not need to be taught. These reinforcers, called primary reinforcers, include such things as air, water, food, and sleep. Things and events that do not fall into this category are called secondary reinforcers. In contrast to primary reinforcers, these items or events have no value until they are paired with something that already has value to the individual (i.e, a primary reinforcer or an established secondary reinforcer). For example, by pairing verbal praise with feeding and holding a child, praise by itself can become reinforcing. Once understood, this process will allow parents to broaden the scope of available reinforcers for use with their children.

Determining What Is Reinforcing. The initial step in using a more positive approach to childrearing is to identify reinforcers that have value for the children. The therapist should caution parents about simply deciding what their children should like. Rather, reinforcers should be selected by: (a) observing each child to see what he or she likes; (b) taking some guesses as to what the child might like; and (c) directly asking the child about their preferences. Reinforcers should be identified in each of the three aforementioned major reinforcement categories: material, social, and activity. A Reinforcement Questionnaire, which is basically a rating sheet for potential reinforcers (e.g., kids rate reinforcers from great to terrible), is often helpful in identifying the most potent reinforcers for each child. The survey can be easily generated by listing a wide variety of reinforcers that would appeal to most children.

How to Reinforce. For reinforcement to be effective it should be implemented in an organized, systematic fashion. The following rules will facilitate success.

1. Reinforce immediately following the target behavior.
2. Reinforce positive behavior consistently.
3. Avoid unintentionally reinforcing undesirable behavior.
4. Reinforce often enough to maintain desirable behaviors and to meet children's attentional needs.

5. Match the intensity (amount) of reinforcement with the difficulty level of the desired behavior.
6. Correctly label the behavior being reinforced (e.g., "I really like the way you got your chores done as soon as you got home from school . . .").
7. Be enthusiastic when reinforcing (e.g., smile to let the child know you are excited).
8. Be sure to use a variety of reinforcers to avoid losing the child's interest.
9. Withhold reinforcers for incorrect responses (e.g., If the child is asked to finish her homework, she should not be reinforced until her homework is complete).
10. Reinforce effort as much as possible to encourage the child to keep trying even if the task is difficult.
11. Control access to reinforcers (i.e., a reinforcer loses its value if the child can have it any time he or she wants).

Parents should also be reminded that:

1. Events that are reinforcing to one child may not be reinforcing to another.
2. Events which are reinforcing to a child at one time may not be reinforcing at another time.
3. The value of a reinforcer can be increased by depriving the child of it for a period of time.
4. A reinforcer may lose its value if used too frequently.
5. Events that have little or no value to a child can be turned into valuable reinforcers by following their presentation with a known reinforcer.
6. To teach a new behavior reinforce successive approximations of the target behavior. As you "shape" the new behavior, require attempts closer to the target behavior being reinforcing.
7. In teaching a new behavior or increasing a low frequency behavior, reinforce it each time it occurs to get it going.
8. To make an established behavior more resistant to extinction, reinforce it intermittently in an unpredictable way.

These rules and reminders can be distributed to parents and then reviewed item by item.

Although few parents have heard of the Premack Principle (sometimes called Grandma's Rule), many are familiar with the idea that children are willing to engage in a less preferred behavior if it is followed by a more preferred behavior. For example, children are willing to wash the dishes if they are allowed to go out and play when they finish. In this example, washing the dishes is the less preferred behavior and it is followed by going out to play, which is the more preferred behavior. Using this principle as a guideline, parents can increase their children's interest in targeted behaviors. However, it is important to note that children will typically want to engage in the more preferred behavior first (e.g., "When I finish playing outside, I'll do the dishes."). Although parents may be tempted to concede to their wishes, it is not a recommended course because children who have completed the preferred activity often have little incentive to actually follow through with the less preferred behavior. It is helpful to have parents practice using the following phrase: "When you've finished . . . (the task to be completed), then you can . . . (the reward)." This will remind them to use this framework with their children and will facilitate successful implementation.

Using a grab bag is an excellent way to get children involved in a reinforcement program. Rewards are written on slips of paper and placed in small grocery bags. The bags can be divided by the value of the rewards available within (e.g., bag 1 contains rewards costing under $1.00, bag 2 contains rewards costing between $1.00 and $2.00, etc.). When a child completes a task, he or she can be rewarded by picking from one of the bags. In this way, rewards may be offered that are of appropriate value for the task completed. A second approach is to vary the value of the rewards offered in a single bag. The element of surprise associated with this approach has the advantage of increasing the child's motivation, as the competition of any task may result in a big prize.

Using Token Reinforcers. In most instances, the need for stronger reinforcers is indicated by either the child's history or the intended type of target behaviors. When children have been reared in an environment devoid of reinforcement, they frequently do not respond positively to many secondary reinforcers. This greatly restricts the selection of reinforcers available to a parent with such a child. Similarly, when parents identify a number of behaviors that they expect their children to complete on a regular basis (e.g., household chores), a restricted number of secondary reinforcers that interest their children can prove to be a particular logistic problem. In both situations, a token reinforcer can provide a convenient means of delivering a reinforcer that is of interest to the child, no matter what his or her preference. This is accomplished by giving the child tokens (e.g., poker chips) or points (e.g., check on a wall chart) that can then be traded in for backup reinforcers of the child's liking.

For most parents, tokens represent one of the most familiar forms of reinforcement available to them. Although some parents may have initial difficulties making the connection, money is an example of a token reinforcer. Yet, almost any object that can be traded for something of value can be used as a token. Although tokens fall into the category of secondary reinforcers, they carry with them a number of distinct advantages: (a) convenience, i.e., they are easily carried and administered; (b) utility, in that they can bridge the time gap between appropriate behavior and reinforcement; and (c) very powerful, that is, they can be traded for a variety of potent reinforcers.

Token reinforcement systems are easily designed and implemented with only a modicum of professional direction. (See Walker, Hedberg, Clement & Wright, 1981 or Christophersen, Barnard, Ford & Wolf, 1976 for a detailed discussion.) The system basically includes: (a) a list of target behaviors (e.g., chores); (b) a reinforcement menu (i.e., a list of available reinforcers); and (c) a recording sheet. Some systems are designed to include both positive and negative behaviors. In this type of system, positive behaviors are rewarded by giving the child a predetermined number of points, and negative behaviors are dealt with by fining the child a predetermined number of points. In using a point/token system, there are a number of guidelines that will prove helpful to parents including:

1. The program should be explained to the child before implementation.
2. Behaviors should be verbally labeled as points are awarded and fines assessed.
3. Points should be given or taken away immediately following the behavior.
4. Fines should be fair but should have enough impact to dissuade the negative behavior.
5. Points should be given or taken away *only* contingent on target behaviors.
6. A variety of back up reinforcers should be available.
7. The target behaviors least preferred by the child should earn more tokens.
8. The most desired reinforcers should cost more tokens or points.
9. Consistency in carrying out the program is important.
10. The value of tasks, fines and reinforcers can all be adjusted if necessary.
11. Millionaires may be a problem. If children accumulate too many points, they often lose their motivation.
12. If accumulation of too many points becomes a problem, only allow a certain number of points to be carried over after a certain date. The child may choose one or two major reinforcers to spend the points on before that date (e.g., a new bike or a trip to an amusement park).
13. There should be no bankruptcy. A child who has a negative point

value should immediately have some consequence to get back to zero (e.g., extra chores or time out).

14. Parents should not nag their child to complete their tasks. Children can be prompted twice, no more. If prompts are needed, the reinforcers are not potent enough and new ones should be selected.

For many parents, not using a token system that includes fines should be a consideration. It is often much wiser to implement a point system that focuses solely on increasing positive behaviors.

Teaching Parents to Reinforce. Simply presenting materials in a didactic fashion is often not enough to ensure parents' mastery of the necessary skills. With each concept, the therapist should model the behavior with the child while the parents observe. The parents may then attempt the technique while the therapist observes. The therapist should then give the parents feedback as well as reinforcement for their effort. This should be followed by additional opportunities for parents to practice the technique, a homework assignment involving its use and follow-up the next session. Particular attention should be given to the subtleties of delivering a reinforcer (i.e., tone of voice, facial expression, and words chosen). Parents should also be warned that their use of reinforcement (particularly social) may feel somewhat awkward initially. With a little practice, they will feel considerably more comfortable.

To get parents into the habit of reinforcing their children, daily prompts may be used. For example, they may place 10 to 15 (e.g., poker chips, match sticks, or pennies) in their pocket each morning. Each time the parent reinforces one child, one token may be placed in a jar. The goal should be an empty pocket by bedtime each evening. A similar effect can be achieved by asking parents to keep a daily frequency count of the number of times they reinforce their children. To facilitate compliance, parents may be told that the assignment will be discussed in the next session. The therapist may begin each session with a review of the assignments.

Decreasing Inappropriate Behavior

For most parents, punishing their child is a routine part of every day living. There is little need to convince parents of its necessity. Punishment, however, remains a concept fraught with misconceptions. Because many parents use less effective forms of punishment or are inconsistent in their use of punishment, their efforts often seem to have little effect on their child, leading some parents to believe that trying to punish their child is a futile waste of energy. Other parents become frustrated with having to continually deal with the same misbehaviors and resort to more punitive forms of punishment to get out their own frustrations or because they fear that the child will get the upper hand if they do not. Most parents, even abusive ones, worry that the use of punishment may adversely affect their relationship with their children, but they are at a loss as to what to do.

The therapist will want to help parents understand that punishment can be an effective way of reducing children's inappropriate behavior. Moreover, if the right techniques are chosen and applied consistently, the need to punish will decrease. In this way, parents can reduce the incidence of recurrent misbehavior and increase the amount of time in which they can interact in a positive manner. When punishment is used in this way, it is easily separated from emotional issues and allows the parents to take full advantage of this technique as a teaching tool.

In teaching parents to decrease their children's inappropriate behavior, a number of goals should be kept in mind. Parents should be taught why physical punishment should be avoided and be given a broader repertoire of alternative punishment techniques, and a knowledge of how to match appropriate forms of punishment to different types of misbehavior.

Dealing with Parents' Reliance on Physical Punishment. It is not unusual to find an almost exclusive reliance on punitive forms of physical discipline in abusive parents. The fact that physical discipline immediately inter-rupts the inappropriate behavior often leads parents to believe that it is effective. However, closer examination reveals that the effects of physical discipline are only temporary. This finding can be verified by asking parents if their children continue to misbehave despite the spankings. The answer is almost always yes. In fact, they probably would not be in treatment if this were not so. Confusion intrudes because the act of hitting a child immediately disrupts the process of misbehaving (e.g., a child drawing on the wall reflexively withdraws the crayon when she or he is hit on the hand or bottom). That is not to say that hitting the child decreases the probability of this behavior (e.g., drawing on the wall) recurring in the future. In fact, because hitting the child may result in increased attention, the misbehavior may actually occur more frequently over time. In teaching abusive parents to decrease their children's misbe-havior, it is almost impossible to avoid the issue of physical discipline. If the therapist takes the position that physical punishment should never be used, the therapist will lose credibility with the parents and no further progress will be made. However, if the therapist states that physical punishment will rarely, if ever, be needed if other more effective tech-niques are used, the parents may show some interest. To this end, it is helpful to discuss some common adverse side effects of relying too heavily on physical discipline. These include: (a) Children learn aggressive forms of problem solving, which get them into trouble in other situations (e.g., school); (b) Children learn to fear their parents and avoid coming to them for help when they are in trouble or have difficulties; (c) Children quickly learn to lie about misbehavior to avoid punishment, (d) Children do not learn about the appropriate way to behave in the problematic situation; and (e) It becomes impractical when children get older (e.g., Imagine trying to put a 6'4", 240-pound, 17-year-old over a parent's knee for a spanking).

A final consideration for parents should be the reason they were referred in the first place—child abuse due to physically punitive punishment. The probability of this recurrence greatly decreases if physical forms of punishment are avoided or used sparingly under very controlled conditions. It is unlikely that using an ineffective form of punishment is worth the possible hassle of dealing with state agencies and being mandated to attend treatment. After the issue has been thoroughly discussed, parents generally agree to avoid physical punishment until they have been in treatment and learned alternatives to physical punishment as well as the proper use of such methods. Whether or not they make such an agreement, the therapist will have to be alert to the possibility that abuse can recur during treatment and should warn the parents of the consequences of that recurrence. Some parents may be sufficiently lacking in control that they may have to agree never to use physical punishment or risk loss of custody of their children. In reality, physical punishment is rarely, if ever, necessary and child abuse is never justified.

How to Punish. As with reinforcement, the first lesson parents must learn is that consistency must form the foundation for punishment. To have punishment work as it should (i.e., progressive improvement in a child's behavior with decreasing need for punishment), children need to be able to anticipate their parents' reactions to a variety of behaviors. They should be able to count on the fact that misbehavior will be met with punishment and appropriate behavior will result in parental approval. In this way children know what boundaries exist to guide their day-to-day activities.

This is not to say that children will welcome these limits. Parents need to be warned that they will be tested frequently in the beginning. Rather than seeing this as a negative process, parents should be told that this is their child's way of checking to see if they mean what they say. The child's testing of the limits is a natural reminder for parents to be consistent.

Punishment should be applied in a well thought out, organized manner. A number of "rules" may be offered to parents as guidelines:

1. Punish immediately after the behavior to be extinguished.

2. Punish each time the target behavior occurs.
3. Correctly label the behavior being punished.
4. Be sure to reinforce an appropriate, incompatible behavior while punishing the inappropriate behavior.
5. Avoid unintentionally rewarding inappropriate behavior (e.g., by arguing with the child or by laughing at misbehavior).
6. Match the intensity of the punishment with the severity of the misbehavior.
7. Have a variety of punishments at your disposal.
8. Carry out punishment calmly and deliberately.
9. Avoid getting involved in an emotional discussion while administering punishment (e.g., whether or not the child is loved). Avoid assaults on the child's character.
10. Ignore attempts to negotiate or play on the parents' emotions.
11. Use a warning signal before actually administering punishment.
12. For effective punishment, include both taking reinforcers away and providing a means for earning part or all of them back.

These guidelines should be presented to parents and then discussed in terms of their practical implementation.

In helping parents to chose potential punishers in this category, the therapist might suggest that they review their list of reinforcers. Each item that can be used as a reinforcer can also be taken away and used as a punishment. Parents can be assured that missing an afternoon of playing outside or an hour of TV will not adversely affect their child's development.

Effective Alternatives to Physical Punishment.

Rules. In many households the implementation of something as simple as an explicit and consistent set of rules will reduce misbehavior. Rules should be a set of basic guidelines intended to curtail frequently occurring inappropriate behaviors. Rules are most effective when they are (a) simply stated, (b) stated in a positive form (the behavior a parent would like to see), (c) easily enforcible, and (d) include consequences for noncompliance. The therapist can help parents and their children develop rules that are then posted in a central location. When rules are broken, parents should ask the child to state the rule that applies and then tell them what would have been a more appropriate response. The parents and child can then follow through with predetermined consequences for that particular infraction. Rules can be discussed and adjusted as necessary.

Extinction. Despite being considered a mild form of punishment, extinction can be effective in certain situations. Extinction refers simply to the process of ensuring that a behavior is not reinforced over a period of time.

Following repeated emissions of the behavior without reinforcement, the behavior will decrease in frequency and eventually be extinguished. Ignoring is a form of extinction that is typically successful in reducing the frequency of such behaviors as interrupting and whining. Ignoring can be followed by stronger forms of punishment and should always be applied in conjunction with reinforcing incompatible behaviors.

Response cost. Response cost is a punishment technique that involves taking away a privilege, object, or activity following a child's misbehavior. This technique is most effective when the reinforcer removed is logically connected to the misbehavior. For example, a child riding a bicycle in the street might lose its use for the rest of the day, siblings fighting over a favorite toy may both lose its use for a specified time. In this way, children quickly learn the connection between the inappropriate behavior and associated consequences. Other reinforcers that can be removed include part or all of an allowance, time watching TV, and play time. Whatever the reinforcer, care should be taken in deciding the amount to be removed. The punishment needs to be stronger than the payoff the child gets from the misbehavior.

Consequences should be thought of in terms of small, logical blocks of time, permitting parents to use punishment in a precise manner as well as insuring that parents will be able to follow through. Therefore, in contrast to grounding a child for a month or a year (a situation in which children can anticipate that their parents will give in), play time can be taken away in 15-minute blocks, whereas TV can be taken away in 30-minute blocks of time.

To enhance children's motivation to comply despite being punished, parents can give their children the opportunity to earn back part of what they have lost because of punishment. However, this should be done judiciously and generally only for nonserious misbehavior. For example, parents may not want to offer their children a chance to earn back privileges lost for hitting a sibling (because of the potential danger of such behavior), but may consider such action for a neglected chore. It is important to stress that only a portion of the lost privilege, activity, or reward can be earned back. For example, a child might earn back part of TV time lost by completing some extra chores.

Natural consequences. Natural consequences refers to the fact that the events that follow children's misbehavior may be sufficiently unpleasant to reduce the frequency of the behavior if the parent does not intervene to prevent the unpleasant consequence. For example, a natural consequence of a child spending money foolishly, may be that he or she will not have it for something wanted later. A natural consequence of breaking a toy, is that it cannot be used again. A natural consequence of picking on another child may be getting punched in the face. The parent should intervene if the child's safety is in danger, but many natural consequences can be permitted to occur without undue danger.

Correction/overcorrection. Because the purpose of punishment is to teach, it seems fitting that many misbehaviors can be dealt with by having the child correct the inappropriate situation that he or she has created. A child who has spilled milk or has created a mess by playing with food can be required to clean up the mess before leaving the dinner table. A child who has drawn on a wall or a table can be required to clean or paint the wall or table to correct the situation. Correction can also be used when children have difficulty with homework, destroy property, leave toys on the floor, dirty the kitchen and so forth.

In some instances, parents may choose to use overcorrection. This form of punishment involves having the child do even more than is necessary to minimally correct a situation. For instance, a child who slams the door upon entering the house can be asked to go back and reenter the house five times, being careful to close the door quietly. The child in the earlier example may be asked to clean the entire dining room table in addition to cleaning up the spilled milk. In many situations, overcorrection has a positive side effect, in that it allows the child to practice a skill (e.g., closing the door quietly). The therapist can encourage parents to identify and list misbehavior that might be dealt with by using either correction or overcorrection.

Time-Out. When a stronger form of punishment is required, removing all reinforcement in a systematic fashion, for a specified period of time is effective. This approach is called time-out from positive reinforcement or simply time-out. Below is a general protocol to guide a parent's use of time-out.

A. *Preparation:*
   1. Select a place for time-out. It is best to use a chair placed in an out-of-the-way corner that can still be monitored by the parent. Keep in mind that this should not be a frightening place for the child, but a place where there is not much going on.
   2. Develop a list of behaviors that will result in time-out and post them in a central location.
   3. Have the parents explain to the child that they will not be yelling or spankings. Rather, the child will have to sit in the chair for several minutes (1 minute for each year of age, i.e., a 6-year-old for 6 minutes, a 7-year-old for 7 minutes, etc.). The parent will set the timer (a kitchen timer will do). The child will remain in the chair until the bell sounds and the parent says it is all right to get up. If the child argues or refuses to go, the parents can add a minute each time the instructions are not followed or take the

child to the chair and physically restrain him or her there with an additional 3 minutes added to the time.

4. Have the parents then explain that they want to show the child what will happen if he or she is noncompliant and walk him or her through the process.

5. Finally, have the parents ask the child to tell them what will happen if he or she misbehaves to be sure that the child understands.

B. *Procedure:*

1. Parents should be instructed to use the format described previously for giving commands. When the child is noncompliant, the parent should say, "I've asked you twice not to hit your brother and you haven't stopped. Now you'll have to go to time-out for 9 minutes (age 9)."

2. If the child argues or refuses to go, parents should add 1 minute each time they have to repeat the request for the child to go to time-out. If a predetermined maximum time (e.g. 15 minutes) is reached, a privilege or activity (e.g., a half hour of TV time or 15 minutes of play time outside) should be taken away. Parents should be instructed to say, "If you don't go right now, I'm going to take away another 15 minutes of play time." Have parents continue until the child complies and be sure that they follow through.

3. The parent sets the timer when the child is quietly sitting in the chair.

4. When the timer bell rings, the parent should review with the child why his or her behavior was unacceptable and what the appropriate behavior is. The child is then told that she or he may leave the chair.

5. The parent should immediately restate the original request. If the child is again noncompliant, the process should be repeated.

6. Parents should be reminded that the slate is wiped clean after the child spends time in time-out.

Parents should be encouraged to use time-out even when they are visiting other people's homes or when they are in stores. As with other punishment techniques, the power of time-out is enhanced by a parent's use of reinforcement for appropriate, incompatible behaviors.

Developing a Punishment Hierarchy. Parents often report that punishment is ineffective with their children. However, this may not be due to their choice of target behaviors or punishment techniques, but rather it may result from the sequence in which parents use punishment techniques. When a parent depletes his or her options for future punishment (e.g.,

"You cannot watch TV for a month) a situation is created in which the child both feels that he or she has little else to lose and at the same time questions whether the parent will actually follow through. Such a circumstance undermines the parents' effectiveness. Parents should have a predetermined plan of action for punishment. Certain behaviors should always be dealt with by time-out. Other types of misbehavior should result in the loss of a privilege, an activity, or a favorite toy. As stated previously, punishment should match the severity of the misbehavior. Minor infringements, for example, might be handled with ignoring or correction. More serious problems may require the use of response cost, time-out, or some other procedure. If punishment fails to work with a problem, it may be necessary to proceed to another level of punishment. For example, if correction does not eliminate the problem, overcorrection or response cost may be needed.

The therapist can help parents prepare a plan of action by first listing target misbehaviors including as many common behavior problems as they can identify. Next, the misbehaviors should be matched to the most appropriate forms of punishment. The therapist can suggest hypothetical situations in which the child's misbehavior may escalate and ask the parents to indicate which form of punishment they would use in dealing with each situation. Following this the therapist will give the parents feedback and repeat the exercise until it is clear that they will be able to generate an appropriate sequence of punishers in a real-life situation with their children. Finally, the therapist will instruct the parents to monitor their behavior at home and report on a situation with one of their children in which this type of approach was used. At this time the therapist can give additional training, if needed.

Anger and Impulse Control

Clinical research indicates that abusive parents frequently display greater levels of anger, anxiety, and aggression (Kaufman & Sandler, 1985; Berkowitz, 1983; Vasta, 1982) as well as poorer impulse control (Rohrbeck & Twentyman, 1983) than do their nonabusive counterparts. Vasta (1982) and others (Wolfe, Fairbanks, Kelly, & Bradlyn, 1983; Disbrow et al., 1977) have suggested that higher levels of arousal underlie these emotional states and may facilitate their maintenance. Furthermore, arousal may mediate aggression when it takes the form of anger (Rule & Nesdale, 1976). This assertion is strongly supported by numerous reports of abusive parents' aggression directed toward their children (Lorber, Felton, & Reid, 1984; Bousha & Twentyman, 1984; Bauer & Twentyman, 1985).

Because abusive parents' difficulties with anger seem to be linked with unusually high levels of arousal, impulsivity, and anxiety, treatment approaches have typically included a combination of relaxation training, self-control, and cognitive coping components (Kelly, 1983; Wolfe, Kaufman, Aragona, and Sandler, 1981). A systematic treatment package, incorporating these elements and adding a detailed self-monitoring component is presented below.

Defining Anger. Parents' perceptions of what anger is can greatly influence their attempts to deal with it. All too often, anger is seen as biologically and culturally determined (e.g., "Latins tend to be hot tempered" or "The men in the Jones family have always had bad tempers"), strictly negative in nature, and a discrete event (i.e., you are either angry or not angry). These myths not only perpetuate an angry response but also make attempts at change a futile waste of time. For treatment to be successful, parents first must be educated in what constitutes anger and when it becomes a problem.

The therapist can begin by suggesting that responding to certain situations with anger is mostly a learned response. That is, we learn to respond with anger by observing and imitating family members and other significant individuals while growing up. This pattern is maintained either indirectly through approval given for using this approach or more directly by otaining payoffs from others as a result of expressing anger.

Parents should also learn that anger has both positive and negative functions. On the positive side, anger can serve as a cue that something is unjust or frustrating, it can energize us to take action, it is a legitimate means of expressing important feelings, and it can give us a sense of control over our environment. Conversely, anger can disrupt our thoughts and actions, it can interfere with recognizing our real feelings (e.g., being hurt or disappointed), it can instigate aggression, and it can promote a negative impression. In actuality, moderate levels of anger can serve a variety of positive functions. Anger becomes problematic when it occurs too frequently, is too intense, lasts too long or interferes with relationships.

When parents are made more aware of the associated complexity of anger, it is easier for them to see anger as a continuum rather than an all or nothing phenomenon. This perception can be enhanced by discussing with them the early signs of arousal.

Identifying Personal Anger Patterns. Once parents have a general perspective on what anger is and is not, their attention should be directed to applying this information to themselves, which is best accomplished by helping parents recognize their own anger pattern. This pattern can be gleaned from a list of cognitive, physical, and behavioral cues that they exhibit during their course of becoming angry. Cognitive cues are the things we say to ourselves about a particular situation. Physical cues reflect noticeable changes in our body, and behavioral cues are the things we do. Once articulated, these cues can be arranged to approximate the progression from calm to angry. Parents should be encouraged tô complete lists for each area, arrange them from calm to angry and then enter them onto a continuum similar to the example presented below.

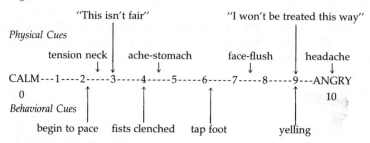

Cognitive Cues

"This isn't fair"   "I won't be treated this way"

Physical Cues

tension neck | ache-stomach   face-flush   headache

CALM---1----2-----3-----4-----5-----6-----7-----8-----9---ANGRY
0   10

Behavioral Cues

begin to pace fists clenched tap foot   yelling

Parents often will need help in completing their personal anger pattern. Although this exercise can be given as a homework assignment, best results are obtained when the exercise is started under the supervision of the therapist.

Self-Monitoring. Rather than treatment simply reflecting implementation of a packaged program applied to all parents in the same way, it should be customized for each parent. For this to be a reality, additional data including what situations make a parent angry, how the anger manifests itself, and in whose presence it occurs must be gathered. This can be accomplished by having parents keep a simple anger diary. The diary should include space for a parent to record the anger-provoking situation, behavioral anger cues, cognitive cues, physical cues and attempts to deal with the anger. This diary should be reviewed weekly by the therapist so that treatment strategies can be fitted to the parents' particular difficulties. Strengths should be built upon to balance out weaknesses.

Helping Parents Recognize When to Leave the Scene. Parents' difficulties typically arise when they ignore cues that their anger has reached excessive levels. At these times, their responses to minimally aversive misbehavior can be considerably exaggerated (e.g., punitive physical discipline). Prevention or early intervention strategies (see following sections) can be effective with parents experiencing low to moderate levels of anger. However, they are of little value when parents' anger and arousal reach higher levels, because judgment and decision-making are often impaired. It is at these times when anger and arousal are high that parents need a preplanned strategy to guide their actions if violence is to be averted.

The first step in this process is to review parents' personal anger pattern with the goal of identifying cues that anger-arousal has begun to impair their judgment. The therapist might ask parents, "When do you get so angry that you begin to feel that your actions are happening automatically?"

Once such a point is selected, the therapist should highlight the associated cues as reference points, telling the parent that he or she can no longer act rationally in this situation. Parents can be instructed to use these cues as a signal to literally leave the scene until their anger has subsided. They may then use a relaxation strategy or a cognitive coping technique to calm down. Finally, the parent can reexamine personal cues before reentering the situation to insure that he or she has calmed down.

This procedure should be role played in the therapist's office because it must be well rehearsed for parents to draw upon it in a stressful situation. The therapist can ask the parents to close their eyes and imagine their child repeatedly misbehaving. Have them notice the cues that let them know that their anger is building and suggest that, despite their best efforts, they notice cues that they have reached the bailout point. Tell them to see themselves leaving the situation, calming down, returning to their child, and successfully intervening. Give parents permission to actually walk outside for a few moments, go to their room or to the bathroom, and lock the door. Parents may share with the therapist their concern that they are afraid to leave their children alone. The therapist can point out that it is better to leave than to stay with the potential of impulsively hurting them. If this concern persists, the therapist can have them call a friend, neighbor, or relative to watch the children for a while.

Generalizing to the Home Environment. It is one thing for a parent to be able to demonstrate mastery of skill in a therapist's office and quite another thing for that same parent to display equal competence when alone at home and dealing with repeated child misbehavior. Generalization from clinic to home is a particular concern with anger management techniques and should not be avoided. If a therapist can afford the luxury of making home visits (or if assistants can play this role), the process of generalization will flow more smoothly. Parents can be prompted during the home visit to practice appropriate anger management techniques, with success insured by the therapist's guidance. When home visits are not a viable option, weekly homework assignments involving planned practice of relaxation skills and/or recording situations in which cognitive coping strategies are used will facilitate generalization. It may also be possible to have families sample their at-home behavior by leaving a tape recorder on at some time during the day. Review of such tapes can be helpful to the therapist in both assessing the extent of treatment generalization and in providing useful feedback to the family. A therapist can also enhance generalization by using imagery techniques during the sessions. For instance, a therapist might suggest that the parent imagine a difficult situation that results in angry feelings (e.g., your child breaks your favorite glass vase after you have asked him or her numerous times not to play with it). The parent is then given a suggestion to notice the mounting anger cues, followed by the use of appropriate coping techniques, a reduction in anger, successful resolution of the situation, and self-reinforcement. If this sequence is practiced often enough, it should increase the probability that parents will use it on their own.

Chapter 5

Treatment of the Victim and Family in Physical Abuse

VICTIM

Despite dramatic increases in attention directed toward the identification and treatment of abusive parents, abused children have rarely been the focus of research investigations. The studies that have been done have restricted their emphasis to either case illustrations of the most seriously pathological consequences of abuse (Barahal, Waterman, & Martin, 1981) or the identification of particular deficits noted in abused children such as low self-esteem (Oates, Forrest, & Peacock, 1985). The existing literature therefore reflects the effects of only a small segment of abusive behavior. As a result, there is a paucity of literature describing treatment interventions intended to remediate the effects of abuse. The purpose of this section is to briefly review treatment strategies currently available in the literature and to expand upon this knowledge base by suggesting additional approaches that would enhance the treatment of abused children.

Treatment of the child should follow logically from a comprehensive assessment. Emphasis should be placed on identification of discrete problem areas and the severity of the deficit. With this information in mind, the therapist should custom design an intervention protocol to meet the needs of each abused child. The conceptual model presented in Figure 2.1 will greatly facilitate this process. A small subgroup of the children who are victims of physical abuse may be characterized by severe pathology arising from their experiences. These children are represented by the top box in the third column of the model presented in Figure 2.1. Such pathology may manifest in a multitude of forms. Yet, in most cases, these children will require specialized services. Inpatient hospitalization may be most appropriate for children exhibiting signs of psychotic behavior, severe depression, or severe anxiety reactions. When the physical consequences of abuse have been severe (e.g., neurological impairment), referral for specialized placement is indicated. Many such children will benefit from involvement in a highly structured school or workshop. Typically, practitioners will not involve themselves in the outpatient treatment of severely disturbed victims of abuse. However, many cases of abuse that reflect a moderate to minimum degree of severity (Figure 2.1, column 3, rows 2 and 3) are a routine part of the clinician's practice. Despite reductions in the severity of abuse and its consequences, some children may exhibit a cluster of difficulties that are similar to those seen in cases of posttraumatic stress disorders (e.g., withdrawal, depression, guilt, and sleep disturbance). Although this constellation of symptoms has not been adequately investigated in the literature, it may be a precursor to later difficulties, as has been found with sexual abuse (Lindberg & Distad, 1985) in which women who experienced childhood incest exhibit frank symptoms of posttraumatic stress disorders later in life. Although such patients may require more intensive individual psychotherapy, most children will benefit from some combination of skills remediation and supportive care. This chapter is directed towards these children with emphasis on both remediating deficits and enhancing children's skills as prophylactic strategy.

Relaxation Skills for Children

Reports in the literature suggest that abused children typically display significantly greater levels of anxiety, aggression and behavioral difficulties than do their nonabused counterparts (Reid, Taplin, & Lorber, 1981). Although this may be true in general, a thorough assessment should be conducted in each area to gauge the child's need for such services. Specific areas of emphasis should include physical tension, general anxiety, and fears. Such an approach will ensure the functional utility of treatment efforts.

Treatment Approaches. The type of relaxation techniques used with children will vary considerably based on their age and associated cognitive capabilities. Younger children will require concrete instructions, simpler techniques, and much more guidance than will older children. Younger children also seem to do better with approaches that allow them to be active in the process of relaxing. Given variations in normal development, the therapist should explore the usefulness of different techniques independent of the child's age. Relaxation skills can be categorized into four distinct theoretical approaches: reducing muscle tension; breathing techniques; use of imagery; and cognitive strategies. Although components can be taught individually, maximal benefit will be achieved when approaches are fitted to the child's difficulties.

Reducing Muscle Tension. The most common technique for reducing muscle tension in adults has been the progressive muscle relaxation (PMR) program described by Bernstein and Borkovec (1973) and Walker, Hedberg, Clement, and Wright (1981). The PMR program involves tensing and then relaxing various muscle groups in an effort to develop both a greater awareness of muscle tension in different parts of the body and an enhanced ability to reduce this tension. The following muscle groups might be isolated for this purpose: scalp and forehead; eyes, nose, and mouth; jaw; neck; back; arms; chest; stomach, thighs and buttocks; calves; and feet. Specifically, the therapist asks the child to tense a particular muscle group (e.g., "Tense your forehead and scalp by raising your eyebrows as high as you can."). Then he requests that the child maintain the tension for 15 to 30 seconds and notice the sensations associated with tension in that area (e.g., "As you hold that, notice the way it feels when the muscles are tense and tight."). Finally, the child is asked to allow the muscles to relax and again notice the accompanying sensations (e.g., "As you let your eyebrows fall back into place, notice how the muscles feel. Notice all the feelings that are associated with a muscle relaxing.")

For most children above the age of 8 or 9 years, such an approach will be applicable with only minor modifications. To adapt PMR to children in this age range, consideration should be given to the child's attention span and motivational factors. The length of sessions should reflect the child's ability to comfortably attend without becoming fidgety. Fifteen minutes is typically a good starting point. Because children rarely see their inability to relax as a problem, they often lack motivation to learn PMR. Such a situation can be remedied by incorporating a reward program into PMR training. For this can be as simple as offering the child a positive consequence completion of the 15-minute training period or as complicated as a token system that includes reinforcers for practicing associated skills.

Although PMR may be successful with younger children, its application involves much effort. In addition to reductions in attention span and motivational levels with decreases in children's age, the therapist must also contend with cognitive limitations that can greatly restrict generalization. Incorporating a self-instructional approach (see section on Problem-Solving Strategies, which follows in this chapter) as well as concrete cues for the use of PMR (e.g., "Relaxation should be practiced prior to dinner to reduce acting out behavior during the meal") will facilitate its use with younger children.

Independent of the age of the child being taught, PMR should be modeled by the therapist at the onset of the session. The child can then practice PMR with the therapist. Children should be reminded to notice the sensations associated with both tensing and relaxing each muscle. The therapist should provide technique-oriented feedback when necessary, and regular practice should be assigned as homework, with parents supervising and providing reinforcement. Finally, PMR should be linked to cognitive strategies (see subsequent section on Cognitive Strategies) to enhance its appropriate application.

Breathing Techniques. Most children can quickly learn diaphragmatic breathing as a relaxation technique. The therapist can instruct the child to first place the hands on the shoulders and take a deep breath. The child can then be asked if he or she felt the shoulders go up. Most will say yes. The therapist can explain that most people breathe that way and suggest that the child can learn to be an expert in breathing a better way. With the full attention of the child, the therapist can explain that a deeper, fuller breath can be had by breathing from the stomach (diaphragm). To do this the child should place his or her hands on the stomach, inhale, and try to exaggerate the motion of the stomach being pushed out. The child can try this a number of times to feel the difference. If the child puts his or her hands on the shoulders during diaphragmatic breathing, a significant reduction in upward motion of the shoulders should be noticed. (The shoulders may still be felt moving downward.)

A simpler alternative is available for use with children as young as 3 years of age. The child is asked to, "Make believe that you are a tire or a balloon," and next, "Fill up the tire or balloon with air until it is as full as it can be." Finally, the child is asked to, "Make believe that there is a small hole in the tire or balloon and let the air out slowly" (making a "ssssss" sound by allowing the air to escape between the lips or teeth). This process is repeated a number of times and can be used in a variety of instances to help a child relax and calm down.

Guided Imagery. Children's seemingly inherent ability to creatively visualize can be drawn upon to enhance relaxation. Although any relaxing scene can be suggested, an attempt should be made to choose one in which the child can play an active role. For example, the child can describe the things that he or she is doing in the scene. It is helpful, but not imperative, for the child to close the eyes while imagining the scene.

A useful framework for teaching relaxation to children is called "The Magic Carpet." This can be introduced by telling children that "We are going to play a game to see how well you can make pictures in your head." The first step in the game is to have the child close his or her eyes and picture a magic carpet. The therapist should spend some time explaining what a magic carpet is and having the child describe the carpet. The properties of a magic carpet are: (a) It can go anywhere, real or make believe; (b) It belongs to the child: and (c) It is safe because the child controls it. Have the child choose a place to visit and then guide him or her through the trip, from calling the carpet to bringing it home.

With younger children or to enhance the affect, some preparatory work can be done. Either at home or in the office, the therapist can have the child flip through magazines or travel brochures, and so forth to find pictures of places that it would be fun to visit. These pictures can then be cut out and discussed. (Be sure this is a supervised activity to reduce the probability of children destroying magazines that their parents value.) Also, the child can draw pictures of a place he or she might like to visit.

The Magic Carpet approach can be used as a reward for doing PMR or in conjunction with breathing techniques. The therapist can suggest that the child practice taking trips while at home and report on progress during the following session. To enhance the experience, the child can be told to notice different sensory modalities,(sight, smell, hearing, and touch) during the visualization. The therapist can then solicit information on which modalities were particularly salient to the child. This information should be recorded and incorporated into future practice.

An excellent set of prerecorded tapes has been prepared by Lupin (1981). These tapes guide children through a variety of relaxing outings, which include a trip to the beach, a trip to the Colorado Rockies, and a walk in the woods. After the child has relaxed and become engrossed in the excursion, suggestions are made by the narrator regarding positive behavior change. The tapes can be used either as part of a therapy session or for home practice.

It should be noted that imagery constitutes a significant part of many other types of therapy that may be used with abused children. These include, but are not limited to, play therapy, psychodrama, and hypnosis. The interested reader is referred to an excellent chapter by Elliott and Ozolins (1983) which discusses these techniques as well as many others.

Systematic Desensitization. When children present with fears or phobias, a treatment of choice is often systematic desensitization. Briefly, the technique involves the creation of an anxiety hierarchy, teaching of anxiety-inhibiting skills (i.e., relaxation and cognitive coping), and counterconditioning (e.g., imagining feared stimuli from the constructed hierarchy after achieving a state of relaxation). Patients repeatedly imagine hierarchy items (from least to most anxiety producing) until they no longer elicit anxiety. Systematic desensitization can also be carried out using real stimuli and real-life situations; this is called in vivo desensitization. If imagined scenes are used initially, in vivo practice is required to make sure that the treatment transfers to real-life situations. A detailed discussion of this procedure and case examples can be found in Walker et al.'s (1981) book. Abused children often have strong fears and phobias for which systematic desensitization can be used. For example, fear of the dark might be treated with imagined scenes, whereas fear of adults might be treated through in vivo desensitization with a warm, accepting caretaker.

Problem-Solving Strategies

Assessment efforts may delineate patterns of behavior that reflect underlying deficits in children's problem-solving ability. Although studies examining abused children are lacking in the literature, a number of investigations support the use of cognitive-behavioral problem-solving strategies with hyperactive (Goodwin & Mahoney, 1975; Varni & Henker, 1979), aggressive (Pitkanen, 1974), and impulsive (Nelson & Birkimer, 1978) children. (See Kendall & Braswell's, 1985, book for a review of the literature.) Because abused children frequently display these behaviors, such strategies can serve a remedial function and may have a long-term prophylactic effect. The three most commonly used approaches with children are Interpersonal Cognitive Problem-Solving (Shure & Spivack, 1978; Spivack, Platt, & Shure, 1976; Spivack & Shure, 1974), Self-Instructional Training (Kaufer, 1980; Kendall & Finch, 1979; Meichenbaum, 1977; Meichenbaum & Goodman, 1971), and the Turtle Technique (Schneider & Robin, 1976; Robin, Schneider, & Dolnick, 1976; Robin & Schneider, 1974).

Interpersonal Cognitive Problem-Solving. Cognitive problem-solving strategies typically contain similar elements. These can be enumerated for the patient as follows:

1. Determine that a problem exists.
2. Specifically and accurately define the problem.
3. Examine the situation:
   a. from your perspective.
   b. from the perspective of others.
4. Decide if change is:
   a. within your control.
   b. outside your control.
5. If change is *outside* your control (few situations really fall in this category), consider methods of emotional and attitudinal adjustment.
6. If change is *within* your control, continue the problem-solving process by generating alternative solutions.

7. Evaluate the merits and consequences of alternatives.
8. Select the "best" alternative and follow through with its implementation.
9. Evaluate the effectiveness of the chosen solution.
10. If the problem is not resolved, select the next best alternative and so on until a satisfactory solution is obtained.

Although this process may seem complex, even young children can be taught the use of this model by first demonstrating its use and then role-playing interpersonal situations that children frequently encounter (e.g., getting along with peers or asking the teacher for something).

Self-Instructional Training. Self-instructional training capitalizes on the combined effects of modeling, role-playing, self-statements, and self-reinforcement to aid children in completing tasks. It is particularly useful for children who have a short attention span and are impulsive. The therapist begins by explaining that he or she is going to teach the child a way of getting work done more consistently. The therapist then demonstrates (models) the successful completion of a task while talking aloud to himself or herself. The content of the therapist's self-statements reflect instructions on how to complete the task, maintaining a satisfactory pace, remaining focused on the task, selecting a response, coping with failures, and self-rewarding for successful completion of the task. After observing the therapist, the child performs the task while making appropriate self-statements aloud. The therapist prompts as necessary to develop the child's skill and gradually fades his or her verbalizations to a whisper and then no sound at all. Later, the child decreases his or her voice volume to a whisper and then finally only thinks the words to himself or herself. Over time, the child's self-instruction becomes an effective covert means of problem-solving. Kendall and Braswell (1985) present a more detailed description of this approach as well as a verbatim clinical example.

The Turtle Technique. The Turtle Technique was designed to facilitate the interruption of impulsive and aggressive behaviors, so that children could carry on the appropriate steps involved in effective problem-solving. The child is taught to display a turtle-like response when faced with a provocative situation. He or she is to pull the limbs in, lower the head, and draw away from the provoking situation. The child then practices relaxation skills to remain calm, and finally follows a problem-solving sequence, with a focus on generation of alternative responses to aggression.

The three techniques just briefly described are discussed in detail by Kendall and Braswell (1985). These authors also provide an excellent intervention manual that can easily be adapted to a variety of settings and situations.

Social Skills and Peer Relations

Investigations of abused children's social interactions consistently point to severe problems in peer relations (Reidy, 1977; Kinard, 1980; Kent, 1976) as well as general deficits in social skills (Wolfe & Mosk, 1983; Mash, Johnson, & Kovitz, 1983). For example, Garbarino and Shermen (1980) found that children who live in neighborhoods with a high incidence of child abuse report fewer contacts with persons outside their immediate family as compared with children living in a neighborhood with a low incidence of abuse. Young abused children (1 to 3 years old) were found to be twice as physically aggressive toward peers as were nonabused children (George & Main, 1979), and similar signs of aggression were noted with older children (Reid, Taplin, & Lorber, 1981).

Barahal, Waterman, and Martin (1981) suggested that abused children's difficulties with peer relations may be related to a combination of an external locus of control and skills deficits in areas such as social sensitivity (recognizing emotional states in others), perspective taking (seeing the other point of view), and comprehending social roles (understanding different social roles that an individual plays). It would seem that the external locus of control would make these children more sensitive to their peers' opinions of them, whereas the skills deficits would provide ample opportunity for them to be seen as different or not fitting in. Intervention approaches have typically attempted to either remediate these skills deficits (Silvern, Waterman, Sobesky, & Ryan, 1979) or change children's behavior through operant approaches (e.g., Weinrott, Carson, & Wilchesky, 1979).

Treatment Strategies. Skills remediation. Teaching children social skills can assume a variety of different forms. For example, Howes and Espinosa (1985) in one study involving abused children demonstrated the efficacy of using day care groups that include socially appropriate children as models. The best results were achieved when groups were well established as opposed to newly formed groups. Other strategies have involved the use of role-playing, demonstration, and filmed modeling to teach children social sensitivity, perspective taking, and comprehension of social roles (Silvern et al., 1979; Spivack et al., 1976).

Operant approaches. Operant approaches to children's social skills deficits have been in use since the early 1960s. Operant interventions have been based on strategies that include: contingent adult reinforcement of prosocial behavior (Allen, Hart, Buell, Harris, & Wolf, 1964); reinforcement for learning to play with toys as a means of engaging other children (Romanczyk, Diament, Goren, Trunell, & Harris, 1975); the use of socially competent peers as co-therapists (Strain, Shores, & Timm, 1977); having college undergraduates serve as social skills coaches (Gottman, Gonso, & Shuler, 1976); and teaching social skills within the context of elementary school teacher-child pairings (Weinrott, Carson, & Wilchesky, 1979).

A variety of different approaches seem to show promise. Yet, the most efficacious intervention combined a number of popular strategies (Weinrott et al., 1979). Contingent teacher reinforcement for prosocial behavior was provided by the child's teacher. In addition, other children were reinforced for approaching and playing with the target children, and group contingencies for socialization were provided.

Although a detailed description of these techniques is outside the scope of this book, an excellent review of such approaches is provided by Ross (1981) in his chapter on social skills training. Suggestions for treatment are outlined by Combs & Slaby (1977) in their chapter on social skills training.

Dealing with Children's Developmental Delays

The presence of developmental delays in abused children, especially in language skills, is well documented in the literature (Klien, 1981; Martin, 1976; Gregg & Elmer, 1969; Elmer & Gregg, 1967; Johnson & Morse, 1968). In a recent study Allen and Wasserman (1985) concluded that abused infants' language delays were due to a recursive pattern of neglect in parent-child interaction patterns. Maternal ignoring and lack of stimulation may contribute to children's delays. In turn, the child's failure to develop age-appropriate language skills results in disturbances in the parent-child relationship, school performance, peer interactions, and self-esteem. It is likely that a similar cycle may exist with regard to other developmental skills.

Treatment Strategies. Remediation of developmental delays can be an arduous process. In many cases, children's lack of environmental stimulation has placed them many months behind their chronological peers. In such instances, involving the child in a formal Infant Stimulation program may be the most appropriate tact. Parish, Myers, Brandner, and Templin (1985) demonstrated that the use of a Family Development Center, which combines a developmental preschool with services to parents (e.g., parent support group and parenting skills classes), can produce substantial gains in developmentally delayed, abused children.

When deficits are moderate, the therapist may choose to attempt interventions on an individual basis. These attempts should include both the child and his or her parents, as home practice will play a crucial role in the remediation process. The Denver Developmental Screening Test (DDST; Frankenburg & Dodds, 1967) can serve as a helpful guide for parent-child stimulation tasks. Parents can be assigned practice tasks to carry out with their child that either appear on the DDST or are similar in content. Tasks should be assigned in areas reflecting deficits that were identified during the initial assessment period. Assignments can be chosen from more than one DDST area (Personal-Social, Fine Motor-Adaptive, Language, and Gross Motor) if necessary. Practice should begin with tasks that the child is already capable of performing to ensure initial success experiences. The therapist should encourage parents to reinforce their child generously for his or her efforts (rather than outcomes) during practice sessions and help parents plan times during each week for developmental practice. Practice sessions should be kept relatively brief, with at least one per day. The therapist should solicit information on practice sessions at each meeting with the family. If there is some question as to the parents' compliance, a diary may be needed to track the child's response to practice sessions. Retesting the child with the DDST on a regular basis will also monitor progress.

Also helpful in guiding parents work with their children is a commercially available poster called Directions in Development. This poster includes slightly different categories (Relating to Other Children, Daily Activities, and Body Control Skills) from the DDST, but it can be used in a similar manner.

Simulating a positive home environment. Many studies suggest that the specific characteristics of the child may play a role in eliciting abusive acts (Friedman, Sandler, Hermandez, & Wolfe, 1981; Bell & Harper, 1977; Fredrich & Boriskin, 1976). Hoffman-Plotkin and Twentyman (1984) suggest that children may exhibit a variety of aversive behaviors that decrease their reinforcement quality to their parents. Furthermore, abused children show higher levels of noncompliance than do control subjects (Bousha & Twentyman, 1984), a higher rate of verbal and physical aggression directed toward their parents (Bousha & Twentyman, 1984), and a greater likelihood to reciprocate their parents' negative behaviors (Anderson and Burgess, 1977). Considered together, these findings indicate the need to both increase the reinforcement value of abused children and decrease the aversiveness of their day-to-day behaviors. Although these goals may be approached in a number of ways, simulating a positive home environment during therapy sessions can be a vehicle for their accomplishment.

Treatment approach. This approach, modeled after one used by Wolfe et al. (1981) involves the creation of a simulated environment conducive to demonstrating to children the advantages of becoming involved with the approaches that their parents are introducing into their homes. Practically, this type of strategy makes the most sense for the therapist treating abusive families in a group format. However, these concepts can be adapted to individual treatment. When parents are being treated in group sessions, their children can simultaneously be involved in the simulated environment, using a co-therapist to supervise the children involved. The first step in the process is to develop a set of environmental guidelines. The intent of the guidelines is to create an environment that includes the same rules that the children's parents are learning to implement in their parent training classes. The simplest form might be rules of conduct for the playroom that the children are in while their parents are attending the group sessions. The rules should cover both appropriate and inappropriate behaviors and their respective consequences. For example, playing cooperatively may result in 10 minutes of special play time, whereas the consequence for destroying toys may be 10 minutes in time-out.

During the early sessions, children are taught the basics through the use of modeling and role-playing. Lessons include: How to earn rewards by obeying commands promptly; what you are supposed to do when sent to time-out; and how to avoid getting into trouble. Once basic rules are learned, a token economy may be added to increase motivation. As each component is added, it is explained, demonstrated, role-played and reexplained to ensure that its purpose is clear to the child.

After the basic parameters are set out, attention can be directed to other skill areas that can be taught within the simulated context. Skills may include those already discussed (e.g., problem-solving) as well as those specific to increasing the reinforcing value of the child (e.g., recognizing when parents are in a bad mood and knowing what to do). In this way children can not only learn new skills directly, but also become accustomed to functioning in an environment with clear rules and contingencies.

Other Treatment Approaches

Improving Self-Esteem. Investigations of abused children suggest that they have lower self-esteem than do their nonabused peers (Martin & Beezley, 1977; Lynch & Roberts, 1982). The presence of anxiety, extreme shyness and a fear of failure may underly these difficulties (Lynch & Roberts, 1982). Treatment approaches might involve arranging mastery experiences for the child to bolster his or her self-concept or identifying areas of strength (e.g., math, spelling, or art) to be fostered. Another approach is to target fears and/or anxiety reduction as preliminary steps in improving the child's self-esteem. (See Ross', 1981, chapter on "Excessive Avoidance Behavior: Fears and Phobias" for more details on this approach.) Self-reenforcement approaches that involve teaching a child to monitor his or her behavior and to internally reinforce appropriate responses can also be effective. (See Walker et al., 1981, for a more detailed discussion of these approaches.)

Anger Management Techniques. Abused children have been found to emit high levels of aversive behavior directed toward both peers (George & Main, 1979) and parents (Reid, Taplin, & Lorber, 1981). This in combination with substantial evidence that abusive adults have significant difficulty controlling their anger (Bousha & Twentyman, 1984; Vasta, 1982) seem to suggest the need for teaching abused children anger management skills.

Treatment approaches generally will be similar to those used with abusive parents. (See section on Anger Management Techniques for abusive parents.) Relaxation training, stress inoculation, and cognitive coping skills are likely components of this treatment. A particularly good approach for use with children and adolescents, which has not previously been discussed, is called the Barb Technique. This approach involves first discussing the anger management problem with the child on an individual basis. Next, the child is taught some basic cognitive coping techniques. The child is then told that he or she will be given opportunities to practice these techniques without warning. This involves the parent (or any other designated person) presenting barbs to the child as an opportunity to practice appropriate anger management. A barb may be any statement intended to arouse the child's anger. Each time the child responds appropriately, he or she should be rewarded. When the child responds inappropriately, the situation should be reviewed and alternative (appropriate) responses should be solicited from the child. Over time, additional persons should be asked to present barbs to the child to enhance generalization. The therapist should closely monitor the approach to avoid its use as a punitive, rather than teaching, technique.

The Handicapped Child. A number of investigators report that handicapped children are more likely to be abused than are nonhandicapped children (Gray, 1979; Davidson, 1977; Soeffing, 1975; Gil, 1970). This may occur as a result of parents' inability to deal with their loss of the expected normal child (Solnit & Stark, 1961). Despite the apparent prevalence of abuse, the diverse ways in which families attempt to care for a handicapped child are only beginning to be a focus of attention (Stein & Jessop, 1984). Keinberger and Diamond (1985) presented an excellent review in this area, which may be of additional assistance to the clinician.

The special needs of the handicapped child should be a priority concern of the therapist working with this population. Necessary interventions may include helping the child accept limitations, helping the parents overcome their grief over the loss of the expected normal child, fostering independence by the child, and changing family attitudes. Often, specialized referrals (e.g., occupational or recreational therapy program) can significantly improve the situation.

Working with the Schools. Abusive children are more likely to display intellectual deficits (Barahal, Waterman, & Martin, 1981) that may adversely affect their academic performance (Perry, Doran, & Wells, 1983). It is likely that behavioral difficulties, reported elsewhere, will also extend to the school setting, further disrupting the child's education.

The therapist's role can be diverse in dealing with school difficulties. He or she can provide assessment services, consultation, or intensive individual and family therapy. In many cases the therapist will need to initiate contact with the child's teacher, principal, and school psychologist. Maintaining contact with appropriate sources is often crucial to successful school interventions.

FAMILY

The family as a unit has been a much neglected topic in the child abuse literature, possibly due, in part, to a dependence on crisis intervention and individually based models of treatment. Many early treatment agents, particularly those characterized as understaffed public agencies, found it necessary to use approaches that were cost effective (e.g., parenting groups) as well as consistent with agency guidelines (e.g., individual treatment) to meet client contact requirements. As such, few agencies were in a position to provide intensive family-oriented services (Boszormenyi-Nagy & Spark, 1973). It is only recently that greater financial resources (i.e., national/local grant programs) and an emphasis on improved intervention strategies have made the family a more popular focus of treatment.

Despite the continued prevalence of individual/group treatment practices, an increasing body of literature supports the need for greater use of family-oriented techniques. Research indicates that abusive families display higher rates of negative interaction and lower rates of positive interaction than do either nonabusive families with behavior problems or normal controls (Burgess & Conger, 1978; Reid et al., 1981). Furthermore, they show less cohesion, expressiveness, encouragement of independence, and intellectual/cultural interest than do behavior problem families (Lamphear, Stets, Whitaker, & Ross, 1985). Wolfe (1985) concluded that child abuse is significantly associated with observable levels of conflict and problem behavior in the home. Additional attention has been given to marital discord as an influential factor in the occurrence of physical abuse. Higher rates of interspouse aversive behavior and marital discord have been noticed in abusive couples compared with nonabusive couples (Reid, et al., 1981; Lamphear et al., 1985). In fact, Lamphear et al. (1985) found that marital difficulties were related to measures of negative family environment that were, in turn, related to children's behavior problems. Based on these findings, Lamphear et al. (1985) concluded that marital discord and family factors were necessary treatment targets for impacting physical abuse.

The purpose of this chapter is to briefly examine family therapy techniques and family-focused interventions that may serve as useful approaches in the treatment of physically abusive families. Although a detailed discussion of the various schools of family therapy is beyond the scope of this book, the interested reader is referred to works by Gurman and Kniskern (1981), Wolman & Stricker (1983), and L'Abate (1985).

Assessment-Guided Treatment

As with other areas of intervention, treatment should follow directly from assessment. The model presented in Figure 2.1 is a useful adjunct to facilitating this process. The initial decisions that the clinician should make include whether the abusive acts are related to family or marital difficulties, and if these difficulties exist, how severe they are and whether the clinician has sufficient training to deal with them. Some families will present with family/marital difficulties of such immense proportions that referral to a family therapist (if the clinician is not well trained in this area) is necessary before dealing with other deficits (e.g., child management skills). These families are considered to be at high risk for future abuse because of severe family pathology (Figure 2.1, column two, row one). In contrast, families exhibiting moderate (Figure 2.1, column two, row two) and minimal (Figure 2.1, column two, row one) levels of risk due to family factors can often be treated while receiving other services (e.g., child management skills training). Families displaying a moderate level of risk often require interventions designed to remediate a variety of marital difficulties (e.g., inequitable division of household chores, lack of intimacy, communication difficulties). In contrast, families at minimal risk may simply require support to deal with a difficult situation or intervention focused on one particular problem.

Whereas other areas of assessment and treatment (e.g., assessing and treating the abusive parent) can easily be dealt with as discrete components, family therapy does not lend itself to such a simple dichotomy. In most forms of family therapy a recursive pattern of assessment-intervention-assessment-intervention and so forth predominates. Although this is true to some extent in all forms of therapy, this pattern seems more prominent in family therapy. That is, the therapist gathers information to understand the family system and its dysfunctional properties. Based on this understanding, the therapist designs and implements an intervention. During the following session, the impact of the intervention is assessed and another (or the same) intervention is offered. Through this process of repeated assessments and interventions, treatment can remain sensitive to an evolving family system.

Although the focus of the assessment may vary from model to model, the most common assessment targets across orientations include: (a) the balance of power in the marital hierarchy, (b) the specifics surrounding the presenting symptom/problem, (c) attempted solutions, (d) family coalitions/alliances, (e) behavioral definition of the problem, (f) reinforcers and contingencies, (g) cross-generational alliances, and (h) the symptom as a metaphor for other family problems. In addition to understanding the family's interactions, it is also important to examine how the family fits into the larger system of the family's relationship with state agencies, the community, other professional helpers, and the like.

The Family as a System

Most family therapy models view families as systems that strive to maintain a certain balance or homeostasis. In this way an individual family member may be sacrificed or may sacrifice himself or herself to maintain the system's balance. Such a perspective might suggest, for example, that a child may engage in behaviors that he or she knows will elicit abuse to keep the father from abusing the mother, which may lead to dissolution of the family. The therapist's goal is typically to facilitate a change in the way in which homeostasis is maintained, so that abuse will not be necessary to maintain the system's balance.

Treatment Approaches

Strategic Approach. Proponents of the strategic school of family therapy (Haley, 1984; Madanes, 1984) believe that families present with symptoms that metaphorically represent some other problem. For example, a mother's abuse of her son may, in part, be representative of the emotional and psychological neglect that she experiences when her husband is drinking. Most problems would be seen as stemming from incongruent or unbalanced hierarchies, usually the marital hierarchy, that is, a situation in which either the husband or the wife has more power with regard to intimacy, affection, or decision-making. In this situation the person with more power is referred to as one-up and the person with less power is one-down. Two common extensions of imbalances in power include: (a) a child's behavior protecting the weaker parent by distracting the stronger parent from direct attacks; and (b) the child's problem representing an arena for parental fighting that is less threatening than the parents' real dispute (e.g., fighting about a child's misbehavior rather than a parental lack of sexual intimacy).

Strategic interventions frequently involve rebalancing the marital hierarchy. For instance, a therapist might put the one-down parent in charge of implementing behavioral parenting directives, with the one-up parent serving as expert consultant. The one-up parent is likely to agree to be an expert consultant but can only discuss the one-down parent's parental shortcomings at nightly meetings. The one-up parent is not allowed to directly intervene with any of the children and must keep a list of things to be discussed at the nightly consultation meeting. Although the one-up parent has the facade of being the one in charge, he or she is not allowed to actually carry out any discipline, thus restricting the scope of their real power. In this way, the one-down parent gains status and power in the marital hierarchy by actually being in charge of carrying out parental responsibilities. At the same time the one-up parent will be reluctant to sabotage the spouse's efforts for fear that failure may reflect on his or her own competency as a consultant.

Another strategic intervention keys in on situations in which children seem to exhibit symptoms in an effort to protect a parent. In the case of a parent who must seek a job after many years of not working, a child's recurrent stomachaches allow the parent to avoid facing the issue of employment. A strategic solution to this problem might involve the therapist suggesting both that the child pretend to have stomachache and that the parent pretend to care for the child. In this way the child no longer needs to actually have the stomachaches to protect the parent. Furthermore, the parent-child interaction assumes a game-like quality of caring for each other. A final approach relies heavily on the use of paradoxical intentions. For example, parents who abdicate decision-making to a child to avoid control issues surrounding cooperative decision-making might be asked to allow the child to make all the family decisions for a week. The possibility of losing all control is often enough to motivate the couple to cooperatively assume more responsibility. These and other strategic techniques are discussed in greater detail in *"Behind the One-Way Mirror; Advances in the Practice of Strategic Therapy"* (Madanes, 1981 & 1984) and *"Ordeal Therapy"* (Haley, 1984).

Structural Approach. Rather than focusing on power as a strategic practitioner would, adherents to this model emphasize the structual aspects of the family (Minuchin & Fishman, 1981). They interest themselves with both intergenerational boundaries (i.e., the need for members of different generations to maintain their place in the family structure) and the formation of alliances/coalitions. They believe that difficulties are most likely to occur during critical life cycle points (e.g., marriage, birth of a child, a child beginning school, and the beginning of adolescence). From their perspective, dysfunctional patterns arise most often when generational boundaries are unclear or absent. This is illustrated by a family in which decision-making is not typically relegated to the parental level or in which grandparents are overly involved in the parenting of their grandchildren. The classic dysfunctional family structures include enmeshed (over-involved) and disengaged (uninvolved) families. This model further suggests that unclear boundaries may lead to triangulation, the process that occurs when decision-making is going on at more than one level in the family structure (e.g., when two parents involve their daughter in the parental decision-making process). In the case of physical abuse, a structural explanation for its occurrence in a particular family might highlight the disengagement of the father and the enmeshment of the mother and son. Furthermore, it might be suggested that the mother covertly precipitates the child's acting out, which necessitates dad's presence at home to discipline him, thereby increasing dad's involvement in the family, but also angering dad and increasing the probability of abuse.

The structural family therapist should attempt to elicit a behavior as close as possible to the problem behavior during a session. In this way he or she will have a first-hand opportunity to observe the process of family interaction around this issue. An attempt should then be made to facilitate change in the family's structure. The therapist may either reframe a crucial element of the process or direct family members to respond in a different way. For example, reframing the son's behavior (in the abuse just cited) as helpful in keeping dad involved in the family may pave the way to asking the dad to suggest more appropriate ways that the son can continue to involve him (e.g., having the son plan a Saturday family activity). A directive to change the process underlying this problem might involve having the parents meet briefly to develop an agreed-upon punishment for the child and then alternating responsibility for implementation of the punishment. In this way, a pattern would be established in which parents make discipline decisions as a team, without triangulating the child, and then share responsibility for the discipline, while increasing their interactions. Other structural interventions, which include a focus on conflict resolution and the use of paradox, are discussed by Minuchin and Fishman (1981).

Behavioral/Cognitive Behavioral Approach. Rather than being based on a purely systems conceptualization, behavioral family therapy has its roots in social learning theory which suggests that reciprocal determinism exists among personal, behavioral, and situational forces that shape every human behavior (Stuart, 1980). In other words, family dysfunction can be related to some combination of an individual's behaviors, thoughts, and feelings (although focus is typically on behaviors and thoughts) and the environment's response. A behavioral conceptualization of physical abuse might include the identification of skills deficits (e.g., child management skills or communication skills between the couple), unrealistic developmental expectations, feelings (e.g., anxiety), and difficulties in the response to environmental stressors (e.g., child care demands and financial stress).

Practitioners of this model believe that change involves a three-step process: (a) modifying behavior and/or cognition to facilitate change, (b) prompting further behavioral change to increase enhanced social interaction, and (c) facilitating the cognitive integration of the true meaning of these changes to potentiate maintenance of changes.

Relabeling and changing expectations are techniques commonly utilized. In work with couples an individual might be asked to assume the other person's viewpoint and continue the discussion or an attempt might be made to explore the accuracy of certain expectations. Behavior change with couples might involve the use of caring days, a technique in which couples identify behaviors that their spouse could engage in to demonstrate their caring. Each partner then commits to displaying one to five of these behaviors each day and maintaining a written record. Other techniques, which include communication skills training, contracting, problem-solving, activity structuring, and negotiation skills, are described by Stuart (1980) and Jacobson and Margolin (1979).

Illustrative Family Therapy Approach for Abusive Families

Dale and his associates (Dale, Morrison, Davies, Noyes & Roberts, 1983; Dale & Davies, 1985) described a family systems approach as the basis for the work of a borough-wide child protection team in the United Kingdom. The team is composed of five social workers (one of whom serves as team leader) who have been working together since the team was founded in 1980. Referrals come directly from child abuse case conferences, requests from other agencies, and the public. The team limits their work load and typically selects the more difficult cases. Initial assessment contacts with the family are intended to facilitate an understanding of the family's history (across generations) and recurrent family processes as well as to establish a firm contract, outlining expectations, responsibilities, consequences, and legal involvement. Emphasis is placed on establishing rapport, which can be difficult with families who have long histories of defeating agencies.

Office-based co-therapy is seen as essential despite initial time demands placed on the staff. In fact, the authors suggest that such an approach is more effective because it reduces the overall length of involvement with families. This, in addition to less frequent appointments during treatment (by traditional child abuse treatment standards), may result in long-term time savings. Much early treatment focus is on family resistance which typically takes two forms: (a) intrapsychic, which reflects the personal resistance an individual directs towards other family members as much as towards the therapist, and (b) systemic, which is a response to the threat to the system's equilibrium. The six major categories of resistance that have been identified are: (a) hostility; (b) passive-hopeless; (c) passive-aggressive; (d) challenging; (e) chaotic; and (f) psychotic. Initially, direct approaches are attempted to have impact on resistance. However, more strategic, systemic, and structural techniques are used if they fail. (See Dale et al., 1983, for an excellent discussion of such approaches with various types of resistance.) For some families, treatment goals are modified after resistance is dealt with; for others, dealing with resistance is an ongoing part of facilitating more concrete changes in the family conducive to preventing further abuse. Treatment itself is individualized to meet a family's particular needs. Systemic, strategic, and structural approaches are used at different times.

Dale's approach seems both theoretically sound and clinically plausible. Moreover, his articles offer anecdotal reports of success over the past 5 years. Given the potential of such an approach, we hope that additional work will be attempted in this area.

Other Services to the Family

In addition to providing or referring for family therapy, there are a number of ways in which the clinician can have a positive impact on family members. All too often families enter into treatment without a clear understanding of what they need to do to satisfy the referral source or the treatment. The clinician can be helpful by facilitating the development of a contract that stipulates what is expected of the family, what is expected of the treatment and referral agencies, what will occur if the family meets its obligations, and what will occur if the obligations are not met. The contract should be reviewed before the beginning of treatment and signed by all concerned.

When families have been known to the system repeatedly or over a long period, it is not uncommon for many service agencies and providers to have contact with the family. To ensure that services do not overlap and that efforts are coordinated, it is useful to arrange a meeting of all providers involved with the particular family. Again, this is best arranged at the onset of treatment and can provide additional assessment information.

Although we have previously discussed parents' potential for social isolation (see section on Social and Situational Factors), family patterns of this sort bear mention. In some cases, attempting to modify a parent's social network alone will have only minor impact in light of the family's propensity to isolate itself. In these instances, a more global approach to networking is in order and might involve exploring the availability of family activities as well as individual contacts.

Somewhat related to issues of networking is how the family spends its time. For some families a review of time management and the division of responsibilities should be part of the treatment process. This is especially true for chaotic families and those families in which conflict is centered around who is responsible for completing household chores, who is missing at dinner, and the like. In a more proactive manner, the clinician can also become involved in the family's planning of leisure time. Many families would benefit from an increase in the time they spend positively interacting with each other.

Finally, when parent-child interactions are particularly poor, the clinician may want to initiate Parent-Child Interaction Training (PCIT, Eyberg, in press), a highly structured systematic technique for teaching parents to interact more positively with their children. Although it can be time consuming, in families in which parent-child interactions are poor, the resulting gains may be well worth the time invested.

Chapter 6

Intervention with Social and Situational Factors in Physical Abuse

As the model in Figure 2.1 indicates, social and situational factors have been identified as contributing significantly to the incidence of physical abuse (Wahler, 1980; Conger, Burgess & Barrett, 1979; Garbarino, 1977; Justice & Duncan, 1976). Factors mentioned include financial stress (Barbarino, 1976), life changes (Justice & Duncan, 1976), unemployment and excessive child care demands (Pelton, 1978; Gelles, 1973), social isolation (Wahler, 1980; Spinetta, 1978), inadequate social skills (Kelly, 1983), and deficits in problem-solving (Kaufman & Sandler, 1985). To effectively intervene with problems of this nature, the professional may be called upon to assume roles that have not traditionally been considered part of the therapist's repertoire. At times, the professional may be asked to serve as case manager, resource developer, social director, activities planner, and network developer as well as therapist and skills trainer to meet these diverse needs. Although such a generalist approach may seem unusual in a world of specialization, an integrated continuum of services is a necessity to guarantee a successful outcome. That is not necessarily to say that the therapist will assume all roles; rather, he or she will insure that these needs are met either through her or his own efforts or those of other professionals in the community.

ASSESSMENT-GUIDED TREATMENT

A therapist's decision to focus on social and/or situational factors should be guided by data collected as part of the assessment process. Following the suggestions in Chapter 3, the therapist should evaluate social/situational factors that have impact on the family. Of particular interest are the family's social network, parental and familial attitudes/ expectations, and the adequacy of parents' social skills. Situational factors reflecting heightened levels of stress should also be investigated. Based on findings from such an assessment, the therapist should make determinations as to which areas warrant intervention and their relative priority.

In some cases, social and situational difficulties will be of such magnitude that they threaten the immediate welfare of the family. These situations are reflected in Figure 2.1 by the top boxes in rows 4 and 5. Examples may include families that are so socially withdrawn that they do not seek needed medical services and homeless families without food or without minimal financial resources. When families present with problems of this severity, the therapist can be most helpful by assuming the role of the family advocate. He or she can identify community resources and facilitate the family's linkage with the proper agencies. Often these referrals constitute a necessary prerequisite to other forms of treatment.

In most families, however, social and situational factors do not constitute the most immediate treatment concern. Although they may still contribute to a moderate level of risk for future abuse (Figure 2.1, row 2, columns 4 and 5), they need not be dealt with before other treatment interventions. Rather, they may be considered for prioritization purposes at the same time that determinations are made about treatment for the abusive parent, the victim, and so forth. Moderate risk factors might include a parent's recent unemployment, social isolation, social skills deficits, excessive child care demands, and problem-solving deficits. Situations in which social and situational factors contribute only minimally to the risk of abuse are represented in Figure 2.1 by the boxes in the third row of columns 4 and 5. These families will differ from those in the moderate category in both the number of difficulties they are experiencing and the relative severity of the problems. Such families will typically lack a history of social or situations difficulties, yet may be currently experiencing some situationally related difficulties.

The purpose of this chapter is to suggest intervention strategies for some of the most common social and situational problems that abusive families encounter. This chapter will be oriented towards the treatment of families that may be characterized as exhibiting minimal to moderate levels of risk due to social and situational factors.

Social Factors

Social Isolation. Although abusive parents have previously been identified as socially isolated (Garbarino, 1977; Parke & Collmer, 1975), the work of

Wahler and his associates (Wahler, 1980; Wahler, Leske, & Rogers, 1979) has been particularly enlightening. Rather than simply rearticulating this relationship, they have suggested an underlying mechanism that may perpetuate the maintenance of isolation. Wahler (1980) suggests that when the isolated (or insular) parent responds to others' demands to start or stop particular childrearing practices, the parent is negatively reinforced (i.e., demands are terminated) and the other party is positively reinforced (i.e., parent has complied), thus setting up a "coercion trap." (See Patterson & Reid, 1970, for further discussion.) However, shifts in parenting behavior (i.e., in compliance with professional helpers or family members' demands) occur only in the presence of these change agents and their demands. At other times, these parents tend to revert to former childrearing approaches, a fact that may explain good treatment outcomes and poor follow-up findings for some parents.

Wahler (1980) suggests that it is not simply mothers' isolation that predisposes parents to this coercion trap, but rather it is the aversive nature of the social contacts that they do have. For many of these parents it becomes easier to avoid social contacts than to deal with their aversive nature. Wahler's findings also suggest that insular mothers are more likely to have "mother-child coercive problems" (p. 218) on days when their extra-family contacts are few and/or adversive in nature, thus supporting friendship as an inverse predictor of these difficulties. These findings support an earlier conclusion (Wahler, Leske, & Rogers, 1979) that implied that the most troubled mothers had only contacts with helpers and extended family.

These findings are significant in that they offer a number of treatment suggestions. First, social factors should be addressed for reasons other than their own significance as they may indirectly influence a parents' ability to maintain treatment gains. Second, assisting parents in developing a social network composed primarily of extended family may actually facilitate continued punitive behavior by the parents. Instead, networks should be heavily weighted toward the inclusion of friends and community contacts other than family. Finally, many abusive parents have a history of avoiding social contacts as they have proved aversive in the past. Therefore, it is unlikely that these parents will be easily motivated to develop a broader social sphere.

Networking. Many parents live in communities in which resources are available, yet remain untapped. For these parents the first step is to identify groups that represent the best fit for their particular family. Professionals attempting to develop resource lists will benefit from contacting local telephone hotlines and referral services, as their information is typically the most current. The local mental health association can also be a helpful resource. Special interest groups and classes should not be overlooked as viable resources for some parents (e.g., hospital volunteer organizations, pottery/ceramics classes). Groups have been organized nationally for the expressed purpose of bringing parents together who have similar life situations (e.g., Parents Without Partners and Widow to Widow). Such groups can meet a multitude of parents' needs and should be used as appropriate. Many professionals will find it helpful to discuss their clientele with someone from each of these groups. Preparation of this nature can insure appropriate referrals as well as an accurate knowledge of group function and criteria for membership. In addition to groups, parents' personal contacts should be assessed and evaluated with the intent of identifying individuals who show potential for friendship and support. Parents will often need to be prompted to identify persons with whom they have had only minimal contact but who have shown some interest in their welfare.

Once potential supports are identified, an attempt should be made to heighten parents' motivation to use these resources. As noted, many parents are reluctant to seek out social contacts as a result of previous aversive interactions. This is particularly true with groups that may be connected with or may be perceived as connected with state agencies. In the early phases of the resocialization process it is important to anticipate and dispel myths on the purpose of the group (e.g., "The group is to help you make new friends and no one from the group will be checking-up on you.") Furthermore, an attempt should be made to insure attendance at the first few meetings. This may involve arranging transportation, baby sitting, or even contracting with the parents for attendance. Parents often will become intrinsically motivated after attending a few meetings or making a number of contacts with a friend or neighbor. At this point, external motivation is less of an issue.

Visitation Programs. In recognition of abusive parents' social plight, some communities have developed home visitation programs that pair successful parents with abusive parents. These programs are modeled after the work of Kempe (1973) and Kempe and Helfer (1972) who used primarily senior citizen volunteers. The Parent to Parent (Tampa, Florida) program is representative of such programs. The program screens community volunteers to select individuals with appropriate parenting experience. Volunteers then go through a rigorous training program to familiarize them with a variety of intervention approaches, ethical dilemmas, and potential crisis situations. Volunteers are assigned to follow one or two abusive families. There commitment involves one visit per week as well as attendance at volunteer meetings. Similar programs are also available which assign visiting nurses to "at risk" families. The goal of the program is to provide support as well as a positive role model. With adequate screening and supervision, visitation programs can offer much to abusive parents.

Expectations and Attitudes. As Wahler (1980) has suggested, the parents' extended family may have a negative influence on discipline practices. For parents who have few other social contacts, family members may represent the only input they receive. This is particularly problematic when family members are advocating punitive discipline practices. In addition to broadening parents' social sphere it may be useful to have some impact on familial attitudes and expectations. This approach will both introduce positive role models and at the same time increase the appropriateness of those family members that have frequent contact with the parents.

Inappropriate developmental expectations (Azar, Robinson, Hekimian, & Twentyman, 1984), negative behavioral expectations (Larrance & Twentyman, 1983), and misattributions of children's behavior (Azar, Fantuzzo, & Twentyman, 1984; Mash, Johnson, & Kovitz, 1983) have previously been cited as correlates of abusive behavior. Although these studies queried only parents themselves, we would expect similar attitudes and expectations to also exist in many extended family members. Informational approaches are typically most effective in reversing these trends.

An approach that has proved successful was described by Wolfe et al. in 1981. A commercially available developmental poster (Directions in Development) is displayed to the group and associated handouts (reflecting poster items) outlining expected development in a variety of areas (e.g., language and motor development) are reviewed. After reviewing these outlines on a number of occasions a developmental game is played. Particular developmental milestones from handouts are written on index cards. Parents are asked to sort these cards into piles reflecting age ranges from 1 month to approximately 12 years. In a group treatment situation this game can be played for prizes based on the number of correct card placements.

Parents' attitudes can be assessed as well as modified using a group discussion format. Correcting myths and misinformation should be the first order of business. The next priority should be facilitating changes in attitudes that perpetuate punitive discipline practices and create additional tensions in the family. Attitude change is typically slow in coming; however, when such efforts are attempted in conjunction with other techniques (e.g., child management skills and anger management), the probability of success increases.

Skills Training. Although social skills training has not been extensively used to deal with abusive parents, there is little doubt that they would benefit from such an approach. Deficits are likely to manifest themselves primarily in general social interaction, marital/dating situations, and situations calling for appropriate assertion. Social skills interventions, which include modeling, role playing, feedback, and systematic desensitization, have been used successfully in increasing the frequency of socially anxious persons' interactions (Trower, Yardley, Bryant, & Shaw, 1978; Marzillier, Lambert, & Kellet, 1976). Deficits in dating behavior have been positively affected through practice dating (Kramer, 1975), social skills training (Twentyman & McFall, 1975), and a combination of systematic desensitization and social skills training (Curran, 1975; Curran & Gilbert, 1975; Curran, Gilbert, & Little, 1976). Furthermore, Stuart (1980) has demonstrated the effectiveness of behavioral approaches for marital skills training. Finally, assertion training programs have relied upon modeling (Kazdin, 1976), covert modeling (Hersen, Kazdin, & Bellack, & Turner, 1979), and a combination of behavioral rehearsal, video modeling, video feedback, group feedback, bibliotherapy, and homework assignments (Galassi, Kosta, & Galassi, 1975). A more extensive discussion of these techniques is beyond the scope of this book; however, the interested reader should consult reviews of the literature completed by Arkowitz (1977) and Curran (1977).

Situational Factors

Wolfe (1985) suggested that, "child abuse can be considered as an attempt by a parent to gain control over multiple aversive events present in their environment." Many of these events reflect situational factors (e.g., financial difficulties, unemployment, excessive child care demands, and dangerous living conditions) that which can adversely affect treatment outcome (Dumas, 1984; Dumas & Wahler, 1983; Wahler, 1980). Many of these factors have traditionally fallen outside of the therapist's purview. However, for treatment programs to have consistently successful outcomes these situational elements must be dealt with.

Economic Factors. For many families referred for treatment, immediate situational concerns predominate their thoughts. In such cases the therapist must assume the role of advocate, facilitating the stabilization of the family before any attempt can be made to tackle long-term goals (e.g., skills acquisition). When economic needs represent a pressing concern the therapist can help the family pursue emergency loans, food, and emergency shelter arrangements. Local church groups, the Salvation Army, and similar groups can frequently help families who are in immediate need of food, shelter, or clothing. For families in slightly better circumstances, assistance in obtaining food stamps, Aid to Families with Dependent Children (AFDC), child support, or transportation to appointments and the doctor's office may suffice. Often this entails little more than help in filling out a state form, putting them in contact with the proper state office, or helping them arrange an appointment with a state eligibility worker.

If the family's immediate stability is not at issue, attention may be turned towards improving job-seeking or interviewing skills, facilitating completion of a high school equivalency diploma, or enrolling in a vocational/technical school or a state job program. In some instances the therapist may become directly involved in these activities. At other times he or she may simply act as a conduit between the family and the appropriate resources.

Child Care Demands. Abusive parents have been identified as having fewer child-care options (Gelles, 1973) while at the same time feeling overwhelmed with their parental responsibilities (Pelton, 1978). These stressors may be exacerbated by parents' sense of isolation (Wahler, 1980) and helplessness. When parents report being overwhelmed by their child care demands, practical action by the therapist is indicated. Recent emphasis on respite care services for overly burdened parents has made resources available in greater numbers. Children often can be enrolled in preschool programs or head start centers. When such resources are not available, the therapist may consider organizing cooperative community day-care programs with parents serving as part-time child care workers. Community centers and/or smaller day-care operations are potential sites for these informal day-care enterprises. If a day-care program cannot be arranged, another acceptable option may be "mothers day out" programs, which provide child care for parents a morning or two each week. Other informal options may include neighbors, family members, and friends. With some families, parents need a gentle push to take advantage of resources that already exist. The therapist should assign parents time away from their children the same way that other homework might be assigned. At times, coupons and gift certificates solicited from local merchants will make parents' outings a practical reality.

Parents who continue to struggle with their abusive impulses require the availability of emergency child care services. Many communities now have crisis nurseries designed specifically for this purpose. These nurseries are intended as short-term, 24-hour residential care facilities for children suspected or in danger of abuse or neglect (Beezley & McQuiston, 1977). Although nurseries vary in purpose, many strive to provide: (a) the child with a safe environment; (b) parents with a nonthreatening resource; (c) developmental and medical screening; and (d) referral to appropriate programs. Therapists should seek out local crisis nursery services and make volatile parents aware of procedures for use in the nursery.

PROBLEM-SOLVING

A recent study has suggested that abusive parents may frequently exhibit problem-solving deficits, particularly in narrowing alternatives and implementing a chosen solution (Kaufman & Sandler, 1985). With this in mind therapists should ensure that parents receive adequate practice in these areas. The therapist should ask parents to identify problems that they are currently struggling to solve and then guide them through the steps as outlined. Whenever possible, parents should be asked to implement the chosen solutions during the week between sessions. Reviewing the results of these attempts and reinforcing parents' efforts are included in the following session. When solutions are implemented, but not successful, discuss other alternatives and reassign them as homework for the week to come. Proceeding in this manner will increase the probability of parents' compliance and eventually ensure success experiences for the parent.

With regard to generalized problem-solving, parents should be taught to implement a solution-oriented framework each time they are faced with a problematic situation. Much has been written on teaching problem-solving to adults. (The interested reader is referred to Spivack, Platt, & Shure, 1976.) In treating abusive parents, the following framework will provide a basic foundation: (a) specifically define the problem situation; (b) generate alternative solutions; (c) evaluate the pros and cons of each alternative solution; (d) select the best alternative; (e) implement the alternative; (f) evaluate the outcome of the alternative selection; and (g) if the problem is not resolved, select another alternative and start over.

In an interesting article, Wolfe et al. (1981) described the use of a filmed modeling procedure for parents whose problem-solving deficits center around their childrearing practices. In this approach parents view a videotaped illustration of a common childrearing difficulty (e.g., child will not go to bed). The tape is then stopped and the parents are asked to critique the problem and offer intervention strategies. These are discussed in terms of the appropriateness of their application to the particular problem. Finally, the tape is again started and an illustration of one potential solution is presented. The 12 problem illustrations are shown two to three per session and are complemented by discussions of parents' real-life childrearing problems. (See Wolfe et al., 1981, pp. 138 to 140 for additional details.)

Part III
Sexual Abuse

Chapter 7
Understanding Sexual Abuse

As we turn from a discussion of physical abuse of children to sexual abuse of children, it may be useful to compare the two phenomena. Although both represent a misuse of power over children by adults, there are a number of significant differences between the two. For example, as indicated earlier in this volume, girls are predominantly the victims of sexual abuse; however, in physical abuse, there is a more nearly equal distribution, with a slight tendency for boys to be more abused. Physical abuse is frequent at very young ages (2 years and under) and tends to decrease with age. Sexual abuse is less frequent at very young ages but increases considerably from about age 6 (National Center on Child Abuse & Neglect, 1981). Physical abuse is almost always a result of actions by the parents. In sexual abuse, parents are involved to a large degree, but a substantial amount of abuse also occurs from relatives, friends, and strangers. In physical abuse, both mothers and fathers are frequently involved, with a slight tendency for mothers to be more involved. In sexual abuse, between 85 and 95% of the incidents are by males, frequently fathers or step-fathers. Females and mothers are seldom involved in sexual abuse. Statistically, physical abuse appears to be more prevalent than sexual abuse, although the rates for both are high. With physical abuse, generally obvious signs of injury or other trauma are present to substantiate the abuse. In sexual abuse, seldom can physical signs or trauma be used to substantiate the abuse. Physical and sexual abuse tend to occur largely in lower socioeconomic classes, although they can occur at any level. However, families in which sexual abuse occurs have incomes two to three thousand dollars higher than those of families in which physical abuse occurs (Finkelhor, 1985c). In sexual abuse, one of the motivators is sexual drive which results in appetitive behavior of a physical nature. Although there may be some organic basis to anger and hostility, there is certainly no clearly developed drive or appetite to physically abuse children. Sexual abusers enjoy what they are doing; physical abusers seldom do. Sexual abuse more often involves the police and legal justice systems because they perceive that a serious crime has been committed. Only extreme forms of physical abuse are percieved in this manner (Finkelhor, 1985c). Finally, in terms of learning theory, sexual abuse follows a positive reinforcement model in that the behavior itself is highly pleasurable and reinforcing. Conversely, physical abuse follows a negative reinforcement model, in that the behavior is intended to remove or eliminate an aversive stimulus

As pointed out in earlier chapters of this volume, physical abuse is not a unitary phenomenon. There are numerous interacting factors that may result in abuse. A conceptual model was presented in Chapter 3 to help organize the factors that contribute to physical abuse. When we approach the topic of sexual abuse, the fact that it is not a unitary phenomenon is even more impressive than is the case with physical abuse. If we trace the various pathways that may lead to sexual abuse, we discover that a wide range of possibilities exists. We must, in some sensible framework, account for a range of behaviors that at one end of the continuum may involve simply exposure of the person's own genitals or observing children nude (exhibitionism and voyeurism) and that then ranges through fondling, mutual fondling, masturbation, mutual masturbation, various forms of oral stimulation, vaginal intercourse, anal intercourse, group sex, a variety of sadomasochistic involvements, and sometimes the taking of photographs or videotapes of the behaviors. We must account for a pedophile who has a long-established preference for and habit of interacting sexually with children and who is not involved in any meaningful or significant way with an adult sexual partner. We must account for adults who are involved in significant relationships with age-appropriate partners but who, in times of stress or under certain circumstances, become involved with children. We must account for parents who become involved with their own children and for siblings who become involved with each other as well as teenage and/or adult friends or relatives who become involved with individuals younger than themselves. We must account for individuals who use enticement and relationship-oriented inducements to involve children in sexual behavior as well as those who use force, threats, and other forms of coercion (which constitutes rape) to involve children. Finally, we must account for heterosexual, homosexual, or bisexual preferences in the perpetrator. Therefore, when we consider sexual abuse of children, we are addressing a wide range of behaviors that involve individuals who are different from each other. Some of these individuals are just barely over the line of what would be considered normal. For example, it is not uncommon for a divorced mother to marry a man younger than herself. When he begins living in the home, he may discover that a teenage girl is present who may be as close, if not closer, to his age than her mother whom he has married. They are not biologically related, and if he had met her under other circumstances, they may have had some romantic attraction and married. Furthermore, she may feel competitive with her mother for his attention. Given these circumstances, they may become sexually involved, making him an abusive stepfather. However, the individual involved in such behavior would not be deviant from the norm in the same sense that a 40- or 50-year-old individual who has no adult sexual interests or contacts and who chooses 3- or 4-year-old children as sexual partners would be.

Numerous typologies and models have been proposed to organize the possibilities into some comprehensible pattern. None of these are completely satisfactory or account adequately for all of the possibilities. To a large extent this is true because little empirical data are available on many important points that would be necessary to provide clear definitions and a universally accepted typology. One of the more useful typologies has been proposed by Groth & Birnbaum (1979). They first divide sexual offenders against children into two major categories, molesters and rapists. Molesters are individuals who use enticement, negotiation, entrapment, and mild pressure to involve a child in sexual behavior. Rapists are individuals who use force and assault. Molesters may be further broken down, in this system, into those who are fixated and those who are regressed (Groth & Birnbaum, 1979). Fixated abusers are individuals who have never matured sexually to the point where they relate effectively to adult age-appropriate sexual partners. These individuals have a strong or exclusive preference for children and find their major form of sexual satisfaction in interacting with children. They find adult contacts as either less satisfying or abhorrent. This group would include pedophiles as well as a variety of other offenders. These individuals are generally described as immature and interacting with the child in a manner that is appropriate to the age of the child rather than to their own age. A common speculation about these individuals is that they find adult contacts threatening in that such contacts raise anxieties about who controls the relationship, the adequacy of their performance, possible negative comparisons with other lovers, rejection, and so forth. It is thought that individuals who engage in this behavior find children more easily controlled and less critical because of their more limited experience. This places the adult in the position of being the one who is powerful and all knowing, in control of the situation, and who introduces the child to many things that the child does not know rather than being in the position of a rather inept adult partner. The regressed offender within this classification system is an individual who has a normal sexual orientation and relates in general to age-appropriate adult partners. However, under certain circumstances such as (a) times of stress during which the individual finds his self-esteem threatened; (b) cases in which marital conflict or difficulties eliminate normal sexual outlet; or (c) following excessive use of alcohol or other drugs, the individual may impulsively choose a sexual partner of a younger age. In contrast to the fixated offender, these offenders generally treat the child as an older person and attribute a high degree of maturity and experience to the child, which then classifies the child as an acceptable substitute adult partner. Whereas fixated molesters generally have come to terms with their attraction for children and regard this as a basic part of their personality, the regressed offender tends to deny that this is a basic facet of his sexual orientation. Such individuals rationalize their behavior on the basis that the child was more mature than others realized and that special circumstances resulted in sexual involvement. They consider themselves to be normal in their sexual orientation—certainly not a child molester. The second major category of sexual offenders against children, rapists, can also be divided into subcategories. Groth & Birnbaum (1979) suggest three major categories: anger, power, and sadism. Thus, some rapists who attack children may do so because of displaced anger in which the child victim becomes the object of rage that has developed out of other sources. The power rapist uses force because of a desire to control and dominate another individual. Choice of a young child makes successful exertion of power more likely; therefore, a young person becomes an extremely attractive target. Sadistic rapists are the most dangerous of all in that they experience a high degree of sexual satisfaction and arousal (in some cases it is only under such circumstances that they experience sexual excitement), through inflicting pain on another individual during sexual interaction. Fortunately, there are fewer rapists than molesters of children, and sadistic rapists represent only a small percentage of all rapists. Although this typology may not be perfect or totally comprehensive, it is certainly one of the more useful typologies and accounts for the vast majority of cases.

Figure 7.1 presents a model that parallels the model earlier presented for physical abuse of children. Within this model, the typology presented by Groth accounts for most of the major factors that would be involved under characteristics of the abuser.

In the second component of the model, the siblings and other family members have not been carefully studied or evaluated. A general clinical impression supported by some research is that siblings do show considerable confusion, upset, and fearfulness as has been demonstrated when any type of family crisis occurs or when any child in the family becomes victim of a serious illness or trauma (Lourie, 1984). It is important to remember such siblings in the evaluation and treatment of families in which sexual abuse has occurred, because these individuals can be affected by the family circumstances and may also later become victims of sexual abuse themselves if preventive measures are not taken.

The mothers of sexually abused children are frequently characterized as being passive, dependent, immature, sexually inhibited, unable to protect their children, subtly promoting abuse of the daughter to divert sexual demands from themselves, lacking in emotional bonding toward their children, involved in role reversal with a daughter (the daughter cooks, cares for the house, and eventually becomes the sexual partner of the father in lieu of the mother), and having been sexually abused themselves as children (Mrazek, 1981; Sgroi, 1982b; Holder & Schene, 1981; Rosenzweig, 1985). Because any of these may be present in a given case, they should be explored during the evaluation. Additional characteristics involving the mother are discussed in connection with the social context component of the model.

The next factor in the model concerns the characteristics of the child. The age and sex of the child interact with the preferences of the perpetrator in determining whether or not the child will be an attractive target. Commonly, the oldest female child will be at greatest initial risk for sexual abuse in the home. The male abuser in the family may then involve other children as they become older. Boys are more at risk for abuse by strangers outside of the home (Finkelhor, 1984).

Children who are precocious in their interests and sensitivity to sex may thereby make themselves more at risk. Such precociousness in some cases may be biological. In others, it may result from observing sexual behavior of adults who are not discreet, (e.g., divorced mothers who entertain boyfriends in the home). This should not be misunderstood as meaning that such children are responsible for the sexual behavior or have seduced unwitting adults. The latter is an extremely rare occurrence, if it occurs at all and the adult must ultimately assume responsibility for his or her own behavior.

Individuals who are the object of rape are often described as passive people who present with a demeanor that suggests they would be an easy victim (Amir, 1971). Similarly, children who are low in self-esteem, highly seeking of nurturance, and do not have a good bond with their mother may well be easy victims (Sgroi, 1975; Summit & Kryso, 1978). Finally, retarded children often make relatively easy targets for abuse.

As we move to the next factor in the model, which deals with the social context, numerous possibilities have been proposed in the literature. Many writers and researchers have commented on the social isolation of families in which sexual abuse occurs (Finkelhor, 1984). An interesting clinical observation by the present authors is the high degree of religiosity that appears to pervade many families in which sexual abuse of children occurs. Strong religious belief does not prevent sexual abuse of children. Low intelligence and/or low educational level have been implicated

(Groth, Hobson, & Gary, 1982) although most individuals involved in sexual abuse are probably normal in these respects.

Finkelhor has reviewed the data in a recent article and developed the Sexual Abuse Risk Factor Checklist, which he found to be highly related to the occurrence of sexual abuse of female children. The factors that he includes in his list are: (a) a step-father is present; (b) the child has lived for a time away from the mother; (c) the child is not emotionally close to the mother; (d) the mother never finished high school; (e) the mother is sexually punitive in her attitudes toward the sex education of the child; (f) there is no physical affection from the father; (g) income is under $10,000; and, (h) the child had two or fewer friends in childhood (Finkelhor, 1984).

The final factor in the model concerns the situational context. Numerous circumstances appear to produce a situation in which abuse is more likely to occur. As suggested under some of the other factors, if the mother is unavailable or unwilling to engage in normal sexual relations with the father, there is a higher risk that he will turn to one of the children. Inadequate supervision of children (e.g., single-parent families and latchkey children) may place them at higher risk to be involved in sexual activity. Circumstances in which the perpetrator is given major responsibility over the child, such as caring for the child in the evening while the mother works, assisting the child in taking baths, and putting the child to bed, make the child particularly vulnerable. Sleeping arrangements in which adults sleep in the same room or in the same bed with children because of either space limitations of the house or an occasional visitor increase risks.

As noted earlier when discussing physical abuse, all of the components interact in complex combinations. The result may be abuse or no abuse depending on the force of the factors that might produce sexual abuse as opposed to the strength of the factors that would tend to prevent it. A couple of examples may help to clarify the use of this model in the area of sexual abuse. It would be possible to have an individual in the family who has a relatively high sexual drive and interest but who is well functioning in all areas of life. If such a person (a) is coupled with a well-functioning partner who is in very good control of his or her behavior, (b) has a child who does not have many of the risk factors associated with abuse, and (c) is in a stable family in which there are few times when the children are in the care of the possible abuser, it would be unlikely that any abuse would occur. However, assume that this same individual loses his or her job with the result that the other parent must find a job outside the home (the job turns out to be a night shift). Therefore, the parent with the potential to abuse is home alone with the children and must see that they get a bath and are put to bed with the full knowledge that the other partner is at work and will not be home for several hours. If this occurs, the possibility of abuse greatly increases.

Let us examine another possibility, an individual who (a) has some personality characteristics similar to those of abusers, (b) has a partner who is significantly depressed and shows no interest in sex, and (c) has a partner who does not endeavor to provide much support or care for the children. If the child in this family is either significantly disturbed or has some of the risk factors, such as being overly solicitous of adult attention, there would be a significant possibility that sexual abuse may occur.

Likewise, consider the highly pathological individual such as a severe drug abuser or a schizophrenic who has characteristics of a possible abuser. If this person is paired with a partner who is disorganized or incapacitated by pathology and a child who is, say, retarded and they live in one room with very minimal income and a variety of other factors of this sort, it is highly likely that abuse will occur. However, this same individual paired with a well-functioning partner might be prevented from abusing the children by the skillful management of the situation and protection of the children by the well-functioning partner.

One final example might be a stranger who would be in the middle or the high end of the continuum and who might sexually molest a child in a family that is well functioning, socioeconomically advantaged, and in a very favorable general living environment. Generally speaking, this child will rebound from the experience with relatively little difficulty and the parents will take precautions to see that no further abuse occurs. As a result, there may be little consequence to the episode. Therefore, it can be seen that a wide variety of situations may be accounted for by reference to the model in Figure 7.1 The worksheet presented in Figure 7.2 may be used to systematically evaluate all of the factors in order to develop a treatment plan.

Another interesting model that has been proposed to account for sexual abuse was developed by Finkelhor (1984). In his model, he includes four major components that must be present before sexual abuse will occur. The first he terms motivation to sexually abuse. This component includes emotional congruence (relating sexually to a child satisfies some important emotional need), sexual arousal (the child comes to be a potential source of sexual gratification for the individual), and blockage (alternative sources of sexual gratification are not available or not completely satisfying). The second factor in his model he calls overcoming internal inhibitors. A variety of personal and social factors may serve to overcome inhibitions that the individual might have towards becoming sexually involved with a child, such as alcohol abuse, emotional disturbance, senility, social toleration of sexual interest in children, and weak criminal

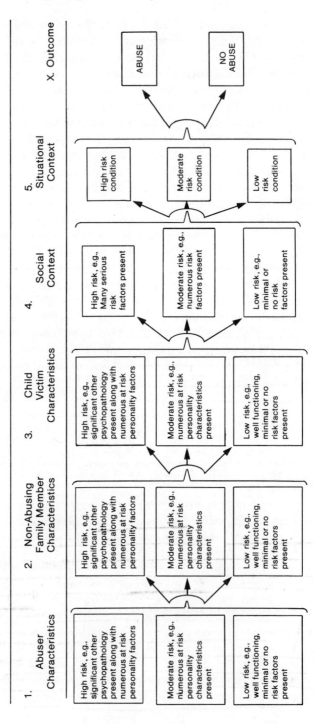

Figure 7.1

SEXUAL ABUSE ASSESSMENT:

MODEL

sanctions against offenders. The third component of the model is overcoming external inhibitors. A variety of individual or social circumstances may have the effect of reducing the normal external inhibitors of sexual activity with children, such as a mother who is absent or ill, a mother who is not close to or protective of the child, a mother who is dominated by an abusive father, social isolation of the family, erosion of social networks, and unusual sleeping or rooming conditions. The final component of the model refers to overcoming the child's resistance. Again, individual or social considerations may be involved such as coercion, social powerlessness of children, an emotionally insecure or deprived child, or a child who lacks knowledge about sexual abuse. In this model, all of the foregoing factors play a role in determining whether or not sexual abuse occurs. If there is no motivation to sexually abuse, sexual abuse will not occur. However, if there is motivation to sexually abuse children, the individual may be inhibited by internal inhibitors and therefore will not abuse. If the internal inhibitors are overcome, there may be external inhibitors that will prevent the abuse. If both internal and external inhibitors are overcome, the resistance of the child may still prevent abuse. However, if the motivation is present and the various inhibiting factors and the resistance of the child are overcome, abuse will occur. This is a very interesting and useful model. As with the model proposed in this chapter, it can account for all of the variations of behavior that are involved when abuse occurs. Finkelhor's model employs the same types of information as does our model but simply organizes them in a different way. The model presented in the present chapter is believed to be more clinically useful in planning treatment strategies although both models employ similar concepts and combine them in such a way that the wide variety of types of sexual abuse can be understood in a systematic and organized fashion.

CONSEQUENCES OF SEXUAL
ABUSE OF CHILDREN

There are several reports dealing with the effects of sexual abuse on children both during their developing years and in terms of their later adjustment as adults. Although some writers have attempted to argue that the trauma from such experiences is greatly overstated or that sexual interaction with adults may even be beneficial (Constantine, 1977; Henderson, 1983; Ramey, 1979; Yorukoglu & Kemph, 1966), the evidence, although somewhat meager at this point, appears to be clearly in the other direction. Studies are currently underway and there should be more information based on rigorous research in the future. However, at the

Figure 7.2. Sexual abuse process therapy worksheet.

1. Abuser				2. Nonabusing Family Members				3. Child Victim				4. Social Context				5. Situational Context			
a. Identified Problems	b. Planned Intervention	c. Identified Assets	d. Planned Use	a. Identified Problems	b. Planned Intervention	c. Identified Assets	d. Planned Use	a. Identified Problems	b. Planned Intervention	c. Identified Assets	d. Planned Use	a. Identified Problems	b. Planned Intervention	c. Identified Assets	d. Planned Use	a. Identified Problems	b. Planned Intervention	c. Identified Assets	d. Planned Use
1.	1.	1.	1.	1.	1.	1.	1.	1.	1.	1.	1.	1.	1.	1.	1.	1.	1.	1.	1.
2.	2.	2.	2.	2.	2.	2.	2.	2.	2.	2.	2.	2.	2.	2.	2.	2.	2.	2.	2.
3.	3.	3.	3.	3.	3.	3.	3.	3.	3.	3.	3.	3.	3.	3.	3.	3.	3.	3.	3.
4.	4.	4.	4.	4.	4.	4.	4.	4.	4.	4.	4.	4.	4.	4.	4.	4.	4.	4.	4.
5.	5.	5.	5.	5.	5.	5.	5.	5.	5.	5.	5.	5.	5.	5.	5.	5.	5.	5.	5.
6.	6.	6.	6.	6.	6.	6.	6.	6.	6.	6.	6.	6.	6.	6.	6.	6.	6.	6.	6.

present time a wide variety of detrimental effects have been noted. Studies indicate that women who have been sexually abused as children suffer specific sexual dysfunctions as adults including higher levels of frigidity, vaginismus, terrifying flashbacks, emotional problems related to intimacy, sex guilt, and sex anxiety (Finkelhor, 1984; Browne & Finkelhor, 1986a). Individuals sexually abused as children also appear to show higher vulnerability to revictimization later in life. Studies report a higher incidence of adult rape among former child sexual abuse victims (de Young, 1982; Fromuth, 1983; Herman, 1981, Miller, Moeller, Kaufman, Divasto, Pather, & Christy, 1978; Russell, 1984), and some studies show that they are even more subject to physical abuse by spouses (Briere, 1984; Russell, 1983). A history of childhood sexual abuse was found in studies of prostitutes (Fields, 1981; James & Megerding, 1977; Silbert & Pines, 1981), child molesters (Groth & Burgess, 1979; Langevin, Handy, Hook, Day, & Rosson, 1983, Pelto, 1981; Bard et al., 1983), rapists, and physically abusing parents (Finkelhor & Browne et al., 1986). Finkelhor reported a connection between homosexuality in male adults and child sexual abuse (Finkelhor, 1984). There is evidence that children of adults who were sexually abused when they were children are more likely to suffer sexual abuse in their lifetime (Finkelhor & Brown et al., 1986). Sexually abused individuals generally show impaired personal and emotional functioning as adults (Steele & Alexander, 1981). For example, in adult life they show more signs of depression (Bagley & Ramsay, 1985; Briere, 1984; Briere & Runtz, 1985; Peters, 1985; Sedney & Brooks 1984), a high incidence of substance abuse (Briere, 1984; Herman, 1981; Peters, 1985), high levels of anxiety (Bagley & Ramsay, 1985; Briere, 1984; Sedney & Brooks, 1984), poor self-esteem (Bagley & Ramsay, 1985; Courtois, 1979; Herman, 1981), poor sexual self-esteem (Finkelhor, 1984), feelings of isolation and stigma (Briere, 1984; Courtois, 1979; Herman, 1981), fear of others (particularly men) (Briere, 1984; Courtois, 1979; Meiselman, 1978), hostility towards parents (especially their mothers) (Herman, 1981; Meiselman, 1978; Wickes & Madigan, 1985), and a higher incidence of eating disorders (Oppenheimer, Palmer, & Braden, 1984). They are reported to have a higher incidence of self-destructive behavior, suicide (Bagley & Ramsay, 1985), multiple personality disorder (Kluft, Braun, & Sachs, 1984), and borderline disorder (Meiselman, 1978). As noted, in most cases these effects are not conclusively demonstrated by carefully conducted research, but the data are accumulating and are impressive. As data accumulate, it should be possible to make more definitive statements in this area. It should also be possible to relate specific characteristics of the sexual abuse, such as frequency, relation to the abuser, and whether or not force was used, to the degree of harm incurred. Although the details must remain sketchy because of the limited data, there is little doubt that many individuals who suffered sexual abuse as children have significant emotional and adjustment problems as adults because of the abuse (Browne & Finkelhor, 1986).

Recently, Finkelhor and Browne (1986) reviewed the existing literature on the effects of sexual abuse on children and identified four general components that they referred to as 'traumagenic dynamics, which appear to summarize the data. The first traumagenic factor is traumatic sexualization, by which they mean that a child who is sexually abused is introduced to sexual experiences that are developmentally inappropriate. Such experiences interfere with the normal and healthy development of sexuality as well as predisposing the individual to future episodes of inappropriate sexual involvement. For example, children who have been sexually abused often aggressively and inappropriately make sexual approaches to other adults and children. They also are more likely to be sexually victimized in other contexts later in life.

The second factor is betrayal, which refers to the loss of a sense of security and trust that results when someone that the child has depended on and trusted starts to take advantage of the child and use him or her in an abusive and callous manner. Third is powerlessness or disempowerment. This component reflects the anxiety, fear, and helplessness that develops in the child because he or she is unable to prevent or terminate the abusive situation. This traumagenic effect is heightened if satisfactory action is not taken when the child reports the abuse. Finally is stigmatization, which refers to the negative connotations applied to individuals who have been sexually abused. The child realizes that this is a socially unacceptable thing to happen and feels "bad," guilty, and ashamed. Therefore, the child often feels ruined for life and has very low self-esteem. Finkelhor and Browne (1986) point out that these factors can serve as a model in evaluation and treatment as well as guide future research on the effects of sexual abuse in children.

Chapter 8

Assessment of Sexual Abuse

As with physical abuse, there are two major phases to the assessment of sexual abuse in children. The first phase involves determination of whether abuse has occurred. There have been numerous articles on medical examination of sexual abuse victims which outline clearly developed procedures, protocols, and prescriptions regarding laboratory tests and gathering of evidence (e.g., Kerns, 1981; Orr, 1978; Sgroi, 1982; Tilelli, Turek, & Gaffe, 1980; Hunter, Kilstrom, Kraybill & Loda, 1985). In addition, procedures have been carefully developed for interviewing children following an episode in which sexual abuse is suspected in order to validate the occurrence (Sgori, Porter, & Blick, 1982; Goodwin, 1982). Of particular concern is the problem of validating abuse among children who are too young to be interviewed or to communicate the events that have occurred to them because of their limited vocabulary and abstract reasoning abilities. Data are being accumulated on the use of psychological tests in this area. Particularly popular are projective test instruments, especially drawings (Goodwin, 1982) and structured doll interviews. Various protocols have been developed to evaluate sexual abuse in children using dolls (Boat & Everson, 1986; Rambasek, White, Strom, & Santilli, 1985). Data are currently being collected on the reactions of abused and non-abused children, which are crucial in determining the validity of reports of sexual abuse (White, et al., 1986). A useful audiotape for professionals using dolls to interview child victims is available through Migima Designs (Friedmann, Morgan, & Bosche, 1986).

Because clinicians will become involved in cases after the validation process has been completed, the details of the validation process will not be covered in the present chapter. Such a discussion would take us too far afield from the focus of this volume. The reader who is interested in the validation and examination process is directed to the references previously noted. Also, reviews of the literature and discussions of the legal aspects of such evaluations are available (e.g., Fraser, 1981; Doek, 1981).

Once the sexual abuse has been validated, however, it is necessary to develop a treatment strategy. Many of the points with respect to rapport and techniques of interviewing that were made in Chapter 3 on physical abuse of children would apply equally well to evaluation of the family in which sexual abuse is suspected. To avoid redundancy, those comments will not be repeated here. However, the reader may want to reexamine that chapter before reading the present chapter. This represents the second phase of assessment of sexual abuse. As in physical abuse, we can follow the model presented in the preceding chapter in developing the assessment strategy and determining appropriate interventions. The worksheet provided in Figure 7.2 can be very useful in facilitating this process.

Starting with the first factor in the model, the perpetrator of sexual abuse, the clinician can use any of the wide range of standard clinical assessment instruments to evaluate the intellectual level of the individual and the personality factors that may be pertinent. In particular, the MMPI, the Rorschach, and other similar instruments can be very useful in this process. The presence or absence of serious psychopathology can be determined through these instruments. Some judgment also can be made regarding impulse control and deviant sexual tendencies. These instruments can also be used to examine the strengths of the individual and resources that can be employed in treatment.

Beyond the standard clinical assessment instruments, there are several other devices that the clinician will frequently find useful. For example, the Locke-Wallace Marital Adjustment Inventory can be very helpful in evaluating the marital relationship and marriage happiness (Locke & Wallace, 1959; Locke & Williamson, 1958). A standardized sexual history inventory such as that used by Masters and Johnson (1970) can be very useful in uncovering a variety of types of sexual dysfunction that may be present. The present author has been developing an instrument called The Sex Form, which consists of 324 true and false items that are presented to the subject. Built into the item pool in terms of content are such factors as tendency toward aggressive sexual deviancy, tendency toward nonaggressive sexual deviancy, sex guilt, receptivity to therapy, conservative values, romanticism, fantasy versus action potential, gender identity confusion, sex drive, impulse control, marital happiness, sex knowledge, and overall adjustment. The long-range research goal for this instrument is to develop empirically and logically keyed scales for each of the aforementioned content areas. Research is currently in progress. The end result would then be a profile of scores that would depict the various dimensions of a person's sexual attitudes, behaviors, and functioning in relation to each other. Individuals interested in the use of this instrument may contact the senior author of this volume. The Thorne Sex Inventories (Thorne, 1965) for males and females have some limited use in evaluating sexual behaviour, although much more research is needed with these instruments. In addition, although it would be out of the scope of competence and practicality for most clinicians, there has been a considerable amount of research on measurements of penile tumescence and vaginal temperature with respect to auditorally or visually presented stimuli as a diagnostic assessment for sexual arousal and orientation (Geer, 1980).

Moving to the second component of the model involves evaluating the parent(s) and siblings who have not been actively involved in the abuse. Again, most standard clinical assessment instruments can be used to determine the level of intellectual functioning and emotional status as well as to evaluate other characteristics that might be relevant. In most cases, however, careful interview will be all that is necessary for evaluation of these individuals. The interview would ideally cover their understanding of what occurred, whether or not they were aware of it; their reaction to the situation; their feelings of adequacy in dealing with any future problems or occurrences; and similar issues. Behavioral observations are also useful with these individuals. Noting their relationship and interactions with other members of the family can often provide very useful information. Two intriguing instruments that have been used in research are the Ward Attribution of Rape Blame scale (1980) and the Jackson Incest Blame scale (Jackson & Ferguson, 1983). These scales can be used with the offender and the family to evaluate their perception of the situation and help plan treatment. Table 8.1 presents a checklist developed by Orten & Rich to assess family characteristics in cases of sex abuse. The variables in this system were developed out of existing literature, and the present authors have found it to be clinically useful; however, empirical support for the scale is not yet available, and therefore it should be used with caution.

Table 8.1. Family Assessment: Father–Daughter Incest

I FATHER OR FATHER-FIGURE

							Score
1.	Admits incestuous behavior		Cautious or vague in acknowledging incestuous behavior			Categorically denies abuse	
		1	2	3	4	5	____
2.	Accepts responsibility for incest		Projects blame to wife, alcohol, etc.			Blames victim for incest	
		1	2	3	4	5	____

3. Seems to understand impact on child and shows remorse | Minimizes seriousness of incident and impact on child | Main concern over consequences for self | _____

1	2	3	4	5

4. Abuse limited to touching, fondling, exposure, no use of force | Abuse included manual or oral genital contact or intercourse, use of threats | Rape through threat or force; injured, terrorized, or involved child in pornography | _____

1	2	3	4	5

5. Past relationship with child showed general empathy | Role reversal, lack of empathy for child | History of physical abuse or extreme discipline | _____

1	2	3	4	5

6. No history of drug or alcohol abuse | Sporadic alcohol or drug abuse | Alcoholism or drug addiction | _____

1	2	3	4	5

7. No history of anti-social behavior or criminal acts | Few and less serious law infractions | Extensive anti-social behavior, criminal record | _____

1	2	3	4	5

8. No previous history of sexual abuse | History of sexual abuse of current victim and/or other children in family | Past or current sexual abuse of children outside of family | _____

1	2	3	4	5

FATHER'S SCORE _____

II MOTHER

1. Believes child | Vague about incident, doubts child's report | Does not believe child, denies abuse | _____

1	2	3	4	5

2. Historically adequate relationship with child | Ambivalent bond to child, role reversal | History of abuse, neglect, inadequate parenting | _____

1	2	3	4	5

3. Quickly forms bond with therapist | Forms bond with therapist after resistance | Distrustful, resistent to help | _____

1	2	3	4	5

4. Takes action to protect child, i.e. reports incident | Minimizes need to protect or takes ineffectual action | Primary concern is protection partner and self | _____

1	2	3	4	5

5.	Demonstrates ability to be independent	Dependent on partner but can act independently with support	Strong dependency on partner	_____
	1	2 3 4	5	

6.	Active social support system	Limited social support system	Socially isolated	_____
	1	2 3 4	5	

7.	Holds adults responsible for limits of sexuality and for protection of children	Partially blames daughter or blames alcohol, etc.	Blames daughter for incestuous behavior	_____
	1	2 3 4	5	

8.	No history of alcohol or drug abuse	Sporadic alcohol or drug abuse	Alcoholism, drug abuse or addiction	_____
	1	2 3 4	5	

9.	No physical or mental handicap that limits ability to protect	Intellectual, physical or psychiatric condition that compromises ability to protect child	Serious physical, intellectual or psychiatric handicapping condition	_____
	1	2 3 4	5	

MOTHER'S SCORE _____

III CHILD

1.	Adolescent, age 13 or above	Latency age, age 6 through 12	Preschool age, age five or less	_____
	1	2 3 4	5	

2.	Normal intellectual, emotional, and physical functioning	Borderline intelligence, mild physical or emotional handicap	Vulnerable child: serious mental, physical or emotional handicap	_____
	1	2 3 4	5	

3.	Expresses confidence in mother's ability to protect	Protective of mother or sees mother as unable to protect	Fearful of mother or sees her as potential abuser	_____
	1	2 3 4	5	

4.	Can identify viable adult resource person outside family	Can identify possible adult resource persons	Socially isolated, distrustful of adults	_____
	1	2 3 4	5	

5.	Easily develops rapport with therapist	Ability to develop bond with therapist after initial caution		Distrustful, resistant to therapist and other helpers	
	1	2	3	4	5

CHILD'S SCORE _____

From Orten & Rich (unpublished manuscript).

The third component of the model is the abused child. Evaluation of the child may include any of the standard child assessment instruments; however, there are a few instruments that may be especially helpful. For example, the Cassell Behavior Checklist (1962) or a variety of similar instruments can be used to evaluate the parents' perception of the child's functioning in various areas and to identify possible problems.

Such instruments as the State-Trait Anxiety Scale (Spielberger, Gorsuch, & Lushene, 1970) and the Children's Depression Inventory (Kovacs, 1981) have been helpful. Fear surveys have been developed by several authors (e.g., Scherer & Nakamura, 1968; Miller, Barrett, Hampe, & Noble, 1972) and often provide useful information on sources of anxiety or stress. Self-concept can be evaluated by using the Piers-Harris Self-Concept Scale (Piers 1969) or the Tennessee Self-Concept Scale (Fitts, 1964). Finally, studies have identified common reactions of children to sexual abuse. Table 8.2 (Goodwin & Flanagan, 1983) lists the symptoms that have been noted by clinicians. These should be carefully examined and assessed by testing and interview. Many of the symptoms present suggest posttraumatic shock syndrome (American Psychiatric Association, 1980), and this appears to be a useful model for understanding the effects of abuse in some cases. The criteria for posttraumatic stress disorder are clearly outlined in DSM-III. There must first be the existence of a recognizable stressor that would be traumatic for and evoke significant symptoms of stress in almost any individual. Therefore, sexual abuse of children would appear to fit readily into this pattern. Secondly, the individual must have flashbacks or reexperience the trauma through intrusive thoughts about the event, recurrent dreams, or sudden experiences in which he or she act or feel as though the traumatic event were recurring. Finally, other symptoms associated with posttraumatic stress disorder are markedly diminished interest in activities that were enjoyed before the event, feelings of detachment or estrangement from others, flattened or constricted affect, hyperalertness, sleep disturbances, feelings of guilt, trouble concentrating, and a high degree of sensitivity to any activities that arouse recollection of the traumatic event or are similar to it. Posttraumatic stress disorders may be acute, in that they occur immediately or shortly after the trauma and dissipate in 6 months or less, chronic or delayed. It is delayed if the onset of symptoms is at least 6 months after the traumatic event and chronic if they persist 6 months or more following onset.

Table 8.2. Evaluation and Treatment Based on Developmental Age

State	Presentation	Issues	Therapy
Infancy to age 4	Loss of toilet training Sleep disturbances Fear of men Excessive clinging Vulvar reddening Sex talk ("Joe poke bum-bum")	Safe placement of primary import Abusive father often flees (often quite disturbed) Mothers are cooperative	Play therapy (2–8 sessions) Goals: (1) Help child express anger toward perpetrator (2) Help child say goodbye to departing father perpetrator (3) Resolve anxiety, e.g. sleeping in own bed
4–6 (Oedipal)	Physical complaint e.g., vaginal discharge, pharyngeal gonorrhea Depression Family conflict	Conflict between parents Child guilty with alienation from mother Angry mother Divorce frequent	Marital therapy (often becomes divorce therapy) Play therapy allows child to express anger at both parents; compulsive cleaning may express feelings of guilt Child often must be removed from home until resolution of marital situation
7–12 (Latency)	Majority of victims are age 9–12 Report with desire for justice Recent decline in grades Stomach pain Depression	Child wants to stay at home (fear of loss) Child's need for confidentiality Physical fear more prominent than sexual aspects of abuse	Family therapy often indicated: same sex therapist or male female team helpful in individual and group therapy Earliest stage when groups are useful Child uses metaphor, play, drawing, fairy tales: may avoid discussing problems directly
Adolescence	Runaway Promiscuity Suicide attempts	Increased focus on individuation in family Teenager shows mood swings, pregnancy fears, guilt about increased independence and a critical view of parents	Group therapy Earliest stage when victims explore details of incidents and of emotional relationships of family members

State	Presentation	Issues	Therapy
Adult victim	Suicidal depression Sexual problems Multiple rape or victimization Parenting problems	Victim's relationship with husband or partner Concern about protection of children, especially from perpetrator Feeling blocked or paralyzed	Group and individual therapy Improve self-esteem, competence Vent pent-up angers and frustrations Apply adult strengths to incest situation Explore needs to confront the perpetrator

From Goodwin & Flanagan, 1983.

One very common occurrence is assessment and treatment of sexual abuse victims should be noted before closing this section. That is, after the abuse has been reported and validated, many children begin to recant and deny earlier statements that they made. This occurs in a variety of forms. Some children simply deny what they said and indicate that they made it up to get even with their parents or to punish them for something they did to them. Others say that they are confused and wonder if maybe they misunderstood or if it really was their fault. At this point, they generally want the family to be reunited and everything to go back to the way it was before the report of abuse. Such statements must be evaluated carefully and certainly cannot be taken at face value. In many cases, there is overwhelming evidence that the abuse has occurred, sometimes including a confession from the perpetrator. Further evaluation of the situation may reveal that the child is simply upset and feels that the remedy for the abuse is worse than the disease. For example, they note that their parents' relationship has been disrupted; they have been removed from the home; the other children are upset by the disruption of the family; and they are told their father may go to prison. They may also have some feelings of guilt because they think they may have brought on the abuse or that they should have prevented it. They may also feel guilt because they experienced some pleasure out of the experience or used it to gain favors from the adult involved. At the same time they are experiencing these mixed feelings, relatives and friends may be telling them that they have trouble believing their story and asking if they are sure it really happened. Such factors may lead the child to the point where he or she wants to forget the whole thing and return to the way it was before. Generally, they feel that the abuser will no longer approach them or that they will be able to defend themselves. Unfortunately, such is not the case and it is important to see that the child is protected.

Therefore, the clinician should not be shocked to learn during or following an evaluation that the child has suddenly changed his or her mind and is now telling a different story. This development must be evaluated on its own merits. Children seldom make up convincing stories of sexual abuse that has not occurred. However, they may sometimes, and in these cases the rights of the accused must be protected. In most cases, however, the safety of the child is the main concern.

The social and situational context for the abuse (components 4 and 5 of the model) is evaluated primarily by examining the home situation and living arrangements of the family. For example, is the family isolated or is there an extended family/social network; are the parents employed or unemployed; what is the educational level of the parents; and is it an intact family or a divorced single-parent family or a reconstituted family with stepparents and step-siblings? With respect to the situation, does the mother work an evening or night shift, leaving the father home alone with the children to see to their baths and get them to bed? Are there sufficient bedrooms to accommodate all of the family without having people in the same room in such a manner that abuse is likely to occur? What is the health of the mother and her relationship to the child in terms of her willingness and ability to be protective? The safety of the other children in the household should also be evaluated. It is not uncommon for an offender to proceed from one child to the next in the family and continue down the line through all the siblings irrespective of sex and age.

As with the earlier model of physical abuse, it should be stressed that the present model is strictly a conceptual model. It will assist the clinician in understanding the process by which abuse occurs and in organizing all of the information necessary to evaluate and treat a family in which sexual abuse has occurred. Although the model is presented as a linear one, it should be understood that any of the factors involved can interact with any of the other factors in a variety of complex ways that will influence whether or not abuse will occur. The possible interactions and combinations are of such magnitude that it is not possible to represent them in a model. However, the astute clinician will need to be aware that reality, in fact, embodies that very complexity. Completion of the worksheet in Figure 7.2 will set the stage for effective intervention. We shall now turn to a discussion of treatment modalities.

Chapter 9
Treatment of the Sexual Abuser of Children

The sexual abuse of children by adults must be viewed as a multidimensional phenomenon. As increasing professional attention is focused on individuals who sexually abuse children, it is becoming clear that offenders are a diverse group who present with a wide range of pathology (Araji & Finkelhor, 1986; Quinsey, in press; Wolf, 1985). Although most of the literature on the treatment of offenders correctly focuses on adult males, sexual abuse is perpetrated by both males and females, although abuse by females is relatively rare (Araji & Finkelhor, 1986). Offenders vary in age from juveniles to the elderly, are found in all socioeconomic classes, and present with mild to significant psychological and behavioral dysfunctions.

The assessment model (Figure 7.1) is designed to systematically evaluate the broad continuum of behavioral dysfunctions and psychopathology found among sexual abuse offenders. As the model indicates, offenders can range from individuals with significant pathology that calls for immediate, aggressive intervention; to individuals whose sexual behavior is deviant but who function adequately in other areas of their lives; to well-functioning individuals who may have impulsively become involved in inappropriate sexual behavior that is uncharacteristic of their typical behavior and unlikely to be repeated. The model will assist clinicians in conducting a thorough assessment across significant areas of the abuser's life to determine the extent and severity of the offender's psychological dysfunctions as well as his or her assets that can be used in the therapeutic setting.

Because of the diversity of presenting problems, treatment plans will differ significantly in terms of recommended location of treatment, expected duration of therapy, and the forms of treatment selected. At this stage in the development of knowledge in the treatment of sexual offenders, no one approach or program is known to be successful for all types of offenders.

As the model presented in Figure 7.1 suggests, at one end of the continuum are those offenders whose significant psychopathology places them at high risk for reabuse. The pathology may be relatively unrelated to the sexual abuse, as in cases of schizophrenia, antisocial personality, alcoholism, drug abuse, and some other forms of pathology. In other offenders, the pathology may be an integral part of the abusive behavior, as in cases of sexual sadism, rape, chronic child molestation, and pedophilia. These offenders are identified as the endpoint on the continuum because the seriousness of their pathology requires that it be addressed specifically and intensively before other treatment interventions are implemented.

This group generally is relatively small in number, but these offenders are seen as extremely dangerous individuals who may require prolonged therapeutic intervention. In cases of intrafamilial abuse, the safety of the child victim as well as any other children present in the family is of utmost importance. The offender and the victim must be separated during the treatment period by removing one or the other from the home. It should be pointed out that in some cases it may never be possible to entrust the care of children to an offender of this type. The initial recommendation for such offenders may include a referral for psychiatric hospitalization or inpatient treatment for drug or alcohol abuse. Other individuals may be treated and their condition stabilized through intensive outpatient treatment while living out of the home in a shelter, halfway house, motel or with relatives. If that cannot be accomplished, the children should be removed from the home and placed in safe custody either with relatives or through placements arranged by social service agencies. This latter course is generally less desirable, but it is sometimes necessary.

Once sufficient improvement in the offender's pathology is realized, it may be possible to proceed with other treatment modalities, such as family or group therapy aimed at reuniting the family. However, as noted, it may never be possible to proceed beyond attempts to deal with the offender's more serious psychopathology.

Treatment for the major forms of psychopathology that do not involve sexual deviation are well known and will not be discussed here as it would take us too far afield from the purpose of this volume. Treatment of the pathologies that do involve sexual deviation is in the embryonic stages. Some comments may be made about the state of the art in this area of treatment.

Although it is increasingly evident that sexual offenders present with a variety of significant dysfunctions, there are certain common problematic areas. Sex offenders are described as being immature and feeling inadequate, isolated, and vulnerable (Groth, Hobson, & Gary, 1982). Other studies have indicated that offenders have poor heterosocial skills (Hayes, Brownell, & Barlow, 1983; Overholser & Beck, 1986), deviant sexual arousal patterns (Abel, Becker, & Skinner, 1985; Brownell, Hayes, & Barlow, 1977; Quinsey, Chaplin, & Carrigan, 1980), and poor impulse control (Watkins, 1983). In addition, some adult male offenders may present with problems such as an irregular work history, acute financial problems, marital difficulties, and chronic interpersonal problems (Sgroi, 1982b). Clinicians also report that many offenders refuse to admit the abuse and do not enter into treatment voluntarily. Likewise, they terminate prematurely unless they are required by court order to remain in treatment.

Some clinicians may hesitate to work with individuals who are ordered into treatment as they may question whether therapeutic gains can be made under these conditions. Other clinicians view this as a challenge and find that court-ordered therapy does not preclude establishing a workable therapeutic relationship. A study by Maletzky (1980) lends support to this view. In working with self-referred and court-referred exhibitionists and pedophiles, Maletzky found no significant differences in treatment outcome measures at termination or at five follow-up assessments.

Early attempts to deal with these offenders relied heavily on group therapy (Quinsey, 1977). Many programs still use this as the primary modality. For example, Groth, Hobson, & Gary (1982) describe the treatment program at the Connecticut Correctional Institution as a psychosocial education approach. This program, designed for incarcerated sex offenders, uses group therapy settings to discuss issues related to the offensive behavior. Offenders can choose to attend groups that discuss sex education, management of anger and aggression, relationships to women, and so forth. Attending Parents Anonymous meetings and utilizing biofeedback to learn relaxation are other program options.

Behavioral approaches have been employed extensively in the treatment of child sexual abusers. These techniques have been used to modify the offender's deviant sexual orientation, and particularly to decrease inappropriate sexual arousal. Kelly (1982) systematically reviewed 32 studies that used behavior therapy with pedophiliacs and reported that some form of aversive procedure was typically utilized. Aversion therapy is used to treat disorders in which a person's behavior is dangerous or unacceptable both to society and to the person, but which has become self-reinforcing.

Aversive therapy is designed to directly reduce inappropriate sexual arousal by presenting an aversive stimulus following the occurrence of a maladaptive or inappropriate behavior, in this case a deviant sexual arousal. The goal of aversive therapy is to form a strong association between the maladaptive behavior and the aversive consequences.

Several forms of aversive therapy, such as the use of noxious odors or images, electrical shock, or shame aversion, have been used in the treatment of deviant sexual arousal. However, the most frequently used method is aversive imagery or covert sensitization, either alone or in conjunction with other techniques. The use of behavioral techniques, and particularly covert sensitization, has been shown to have a relatively high success rate (Abel et al., 1984; Kelly, 1982; Lanyon, 1986; Maletzky, 1980). Clinicians who are interested in the use of aversive treatment, in addition to behavioral procedures that can be employed to increase appropriate sexual behavior, can read the excellent chapter by Adams, Tollison & Carson (1981).

Other clinicians have taken a more cognitive-behavioral approach to treatment and have used strategies that focus on the offender's poor impulse control (Watkins, 1973, 1977). Watkins (1983) contends that individuals with impulse control disorders are not acting on the spur of the moment and are not responding to uncontrollable, irresistible urges. He describes a treatment approach that incorporates stress innoculation, cognitive restructuring, and the development of coping skills.

Based on Watkins' model, Boyer & Beckham (in press) hypothesize that impulsive behavior is in fact a planned sequence that has identifiable cognitive antecedents. To test this hypothesis, they developed and implemented a cognitive-behavioral treatment program with a group of outpatient sex offenders and other impulse disorder clients. The program uses seven major techniques: (a) cognitive restructuring; (b) self-instructional training; (c) cognitive rehearsal; (d) generation of alternatives; (e) homework assignments; (f) decisions on maladaptive assumptions; and (g) masturbation satiation.

One exercise that is assigned as homework is the keeping of an "urge book." Used to focus the offender's attention on the cognitive precursors to deviant behavior, the client is to record thoughts and urges three times a day, 7 days a week. The books are read weekly by the therapist. Data from an initial pilot study using these techniques indicate that cognitive behavioral techniques can be used effectively with sex offenders (Boyer & Beckham, in press).

In addition to group therapy, behavioral therapy, and cognitive techniques, several medical procedures have been developed in an effort to manage the behavior of offenders with significant sexual deviancies. Selected drug therapies and surgical techniques have been employed in an attempt to bring sexual offenders' behavior under better control. The use of these procedures is recommended in only a small number of cases, and the procedures should be implemented in conjunction with a physician trained in this area.

In some cases, physicians have recommended the use of sedative or tranquilizer drugs, female sex hormones, and antiandrogenic drugs (Cordoba & Chapel, 1983). The medications have been used in an attempt to decrease the offenders' sexual drive. They are not intended to induce impotence and may be most useful in assisting a cooperative offender to gain better self-control (Berlin, 1983). Unfortunately, these medications do not specifically decrease deviant sexual desires, but rather they suppress sexual drive in general.

Although there is little substantive evidence that tranquilizers are effective in the treatment of sexual offenders, other drug treatments may be more helpful. Two antiandrogenic preparations, cyproterone acetate and medroxyprogesterone acetate (Depo-Provera), have been used in recent empirical studies. Depo-Provera was useful in reducing sexual drive and modifying the offender's deviant sexual behavior to various degrees (Berlin & Meinecke, 1981; Cordoba & Chapel, 1983; Gagne, 1981; Money & Bennett, 1981). The use of medications is still being tested and additional research is needed to confirm its efficacy. However, it appears to be a promising avenue of treatment, and clinicians should be aware of the possibility of using chemotherapy with certain offenders. (See Berlin & Meinecke, 1981, and Berlin, 1983, for comprehensive reviews.)

Two surgical procedures have been used in the treatment of sex offenders: orchidectomy (castration) and stereotactic neurosurgery. The effects of these techniques in both male sexual offenders and animals have been studied. Castration is not seen as an acceptable form of treatment in this country, but modest success has been reported in other countries (Heim, 1981; Ortmann, 1980). Researchers generally agree that the findings do not justify the recommendation of surgical castration as a reliable form of treatment for sex offenders (Heim, 1981).

The second surgical procedure sometimes used with sex offenders is stereotactic neurosurgery. This operation is performed with microscopic-sized instruments that produce minimal-sized brain lesions in the ventromedial nucleus of the hypothalamus. Berlin (1983) reports that although this technique appears promising, a governmental task force has recommended that it be used only in designated research centers to provide adequate safeguards. For a summary on the use of surgery with paraphiliacs, see Berlin (1983) and Freund (1980).

In considering these medical approaches to the treatment of sexual offenders, clinicians may recoil because of the severity of the consequences to the offender, and rightfully so. However, it should be emphasized that these procedures are recommended in only a small number of cases. Some of the milder forms of drug intervention, such as Depo-

Provera, act to temporarily reduce the sex drive of the individual, but the effects are reversible when the medication is stopped. Furthermore, many offenders welcome medical treatment because they sometimes feel as much a victim of their uncontrollable sex drives as is the person they offend. The use of drugs can be seen as a humane approach to treatment, as the offender stays out of trouble, is in better self-control, and is not hurting others. If drugs can be employed to safely free an offender from compulsive sex drives that result in the abuse of children or adults or both, their use may greatly enhance the possibility that offenders with significant pathology can lead more productive lives.

More recently, clinicians have combined various therapeutic approaches in working with offenders who evidence long-standing abusive behavior. Based on an assessment of the individual's strengths and areas of dysfunction, clinicians initially may recommend a combination of approaches such as group therapy, education, behavioral techniques, cognitive restructuring, social skills training, and, in selected cases, biomedical treatment. Later in the course of therapy, it may be recommended that the offender be seen in marital or family therapy.

An example of a multicomponent behavioral treatment program is one developed and evaluated by Abel and his associates (1984). In a study using 194 outpatients, voluntary offenders from ages 18 to 76 years, follow-up evaluations indicated a high rate of success in decreasing the incidence of child molestation. Rates ranged from 98.9% success rate at 1 week, to 88.6% success at 6 months, to 79.2% 6 to 12 months after treatment. It should be noted that these figures are based on offenders' self-reports of their behavior. Abel et al. (1984) report that arrest records are poor criteria for evaluating treatment outcome as approximately only 1 in 60 sexual crimes leads to arrest. These researchers have established an effective system of confidentiality for the offenders and believe that self-reports are an appropriate criterion for treatment evaluation.

The treatment program is for 30 weeks and incorporates six specific treatment elements. The six components of the program are: (1) satiation, (2) covert sensitization, (3) social skills training, (4) assertive skills training, (5) cognitive restructuring, and (6) sex education. Each element is focused on for five group treatment sessions of 1.5 hours each. The treatment elements are seen as applicable for any type of sexual deviation, not just child molestation.

The first two elements, satiation and covert sensitization, are designed to assist the offender in decreasing his sexual arousal to young children. The next two elements, social skills training and assertive skills training, teach offenders more effective ways to communicate with adults in both social and sexual situations. Cognitive restructuring and sex education are used to attack offenders' faulty cognitions regarding their involvement with children and to provide information and skills in interacting with adult partners. A description of the six program elements follows. Clinicians interested in a more detailed description can order the treatment manual (Abel et al., 1984).

Element 1: Satiation

Masturbatory satiation is a therapeutic technique that has been effective in eliminating deviant sexual arousal. It works by having the offender pair his deviant sexual fantasies with an aversive, boring task—masturbating for approximately 55 minutes after an orgasm. The offenders are first given a theoretical framework to understand their arousal to children and how satiation therapy can effectively reduce this arousal.

It is explained that early childhood memories of either a very positive or aversive sexual or emotional experience became associated with genital arousal. The recalling of the memory during arousal and orgasm has maintained the association between young children and sexual pleasure. Satiation therapy is used to dissociate the offender's thoughts and fantasies of young children from pleasurable sexual activities.

Specifically, the offender masturbates at home while he verbally describes nondeviant sexual fantasies until he ejaculates or until a predetermined maximum time, the switch point, is reached. From orgasm or the switch point to the end of 1 hour, the patient describes deviant fantasy material, such as sexual activities with children, while he continues to masturbate. The activity of masturbating to deviant themes when orgasm is difficult or impossible to achieve decreases the erotic stimulation of the previously arousing fantasies. The exercises at home are tape recorded and the therapist spot checks the tapes at therapy sessions to make any necessary corrections to the procedures. Charts are used to record various aspects of the satiation process over the 5-week period. The treatment manual has examples of charts for accurate record keeping and a helpful section that deals with problems arising during satiation therapy, such as inability to masturbate, the recurrence of a second or multiple orgasm during deviant fantasies, or fear that impotence will result from the satiation therapy.

Element 2: Covert Sensitization

Covert sensitization is a technique using the offender's imagination to reduce deviant sexual urges. The reduction is accomplished by the offender using his imagination to associate the deviant urges with thoughts of highly aversive consequences. Offenders grasp the explanation of this concept rather easily as they most likely have found it useful at times in reducing their urges to molest children. In this approach, covert sensitization is used systematically to maximize the effects of these aversive thoughts. By repeatedly associating the sexually deviant fantasies with aversive consequences, the deviant thoughts become aversive and produce less pleasure and stimulation.

Offenders are taught that their molestation of children is the end behavior in a long chain of events and that a clear delineation of each behavior in that chain is critical to interrupting and ultimately stopping the abusive behavior. The patients learn to insert the aversive scenes early in the chain of events before their behavior gets out of control.

There are four steps in the covert sensitization cycle: (a) a neutral scene that lasts about 30 seconds; (b) a deviant sexual scene of 1 to 2 minutes; (c) an aversive scene of 2 to 5 minutes; and (d) for half the trials, the addition of an escape scene.

Careful instruction is given to patients regarding the development of appropriate material for each step in the cycle. For example, the patient might begin with a neutral scene such as describing himself watching a baseball game or reading a newspaper in his home. The deviant scene could be a fantasy of molesting a child, followed by imagining a highly aversive social consequence, such as being arrested at his place of employment or being beaten up in prison. The patient is taught to repeatedly switch back and forth between the deviant fantasy and the aversive consequence scenes to strengthen their association. In half the trials, the patient is taught to escape the aversive scene by describing appropriate sexual interactions with consenting adults. The escape scene is used to increase the offender's ability to have nondeviant sexual fantasies.

The practice sessions are conducted at home and tape recorded. Each patient completes at least ten 15-minute recorded sessions over 5 weeks, which are checked by the therapist during the weekly group meetings. The manual again addresses problematic issues for clinicians in implementing this therapeutic technique.

Element 3: Social Skills Training

As clinical experience has indicated that child molesters often have deficits in their basic social skills, the third component in the program focuses on improving communication skills and increasing appropriate social interactions with other adults. Five sessions are spent teaching social behaviors, such as initiating conversations, keeping a conversation going, the importance of self-disclosure, and how to approach a dating or sexual relationship with an adult. Role playing is used extensively during the group sessions and patients are given practice assignments to complete between sessions.

Element 4: Assertiveness Training

Assertiveness training is a component of the program designed to improve the molester's ability to communicate and interact with adults. Five sessions of the treatment programs are spent in improving group members' skills in requesting changes in others' behavior, expressing positive and negative feelings, refusing others' requests, and altering aggressive behavior. Abel et al. (1984) recommend the use of *"Your Perfect Right"* (Alberti & Emmons, 1982) for this phase of the program and strongly emphasize the importance of role playing within the group setting.

Element 5: Cognitive Restructuring

This component of the behavioral program is used to examine, indirectly confront, and restructure the cognitive distortions used by child sexual molesters to justify their behavior. Child molesters develop distorted belief systems that lend support to their continued sexual involvement with children. For example, an offender might say to himself, "If a young child stares at my genitals, it means the child likes what she/he sees and enjoys watching my genitals." Abel et al. (1984) state that a direct, frontal attack on these distorted beliefs is often unsuccessful because of the duration of the distortions and the critical role they play in justifying the molester's behavior.

The treatment approach used by Abel and his associates has been to collect cognitive distortions from group members and to spend five sessions indirectly examining these beliefs. Using the process of role reversal as an indirect approach, the therapist role plays a molester who uses these distorted beliefs to justify his behavior. The offenders act the role of a policeman, child protection worker, or family member and attempt to confront the distorted beliefs portrayed by the therapist. The treatment manual lists commonly held cognitive distortions, along with comments and instructions to clinicians for conducting the role-playing exercises.

Element 6: Sex Education

The last five sessions of the treatment program are structured to increase the group members' knowledge of sexuality and sexual dysfunction. These sessions focus on the fallacies molesters may have about their sexual behavior, detailed explanations of male and female anatomy, normal sexual attitudes and behaviors, specific sexual dysfunctions, and sexual communication. The authors recommend using *"Human Sexuality:*

Essentials" (Strong, Wilson, Robbins, & Johns, 1981) as a text for this component of the program.

In addition to programs developed for outpatient offenders, treatment programs for incarcerated offenders have been developed and implemented over the last 15 years (Abel, Blanchard, & Becker, 1978; Freeman-Longo & Wall, 1986; Marshall & McKnight, 1975). Although there is insufficient empirical data on the efficacy of these treatment approaches, the programs are typically based on a multicomponent approach to intervention. Annis (1982) describes a treatment program for mentally disordered, incarcerated sex offenders that includes psychological treatment, vocational, occupational, and recreational therapies, as well as other interventions such as attending school, being in a substance abuse program, or participating in ward government. In Oregon, incarcerated offenders can volunteer to participate in a treatment program at Oregon State Hospital that incorporates many of the approaches just described, such as group therapy, education, behavior therapy, and possibly chemotherapy (Freeman-Longo & Wall, 1986). An added feature of this largely client-run program is its focus on relapse prevention. For offenders who complete all three phases of the program, recidivism is reported to be 10%. However, 50% of the offenders who volunteer for the treatment program drop out and return to prison.

Relapse prevention is a cognitive-behavioral approach to assessment and treatment (Pithers, Marques, Gibat, & Marlatt, 1983). This approach is designed to assist offenders in maintaining changes brought about by other therapeutic interventions during their treatment for sexually aggressive behavior. A recent publication by George and Marlatt (1986) may be useful for clinicians working with sex offenders. These authors have developed a manual that can be used as a guide for posttreatment maintenance. It has guidelines for individual sessions and an outline for six group training sessions.

Other descriptions of treatment programs for adult sex offenders can be found in Knopp's (1984) comprehensive book, *"Retraining Adult Sex Offenders: Methods and Models."* For a review of treatment outcome with sexual offenders, clinicians can see the article by Kilmann, Sabalis, Gearing, Bukstel, & Scovern, 1982.

The middle box in Figure 7.1 refers to a large number of offenders who, were they examined without the knowledge of their sex offenses, more often than not would be viewed as relatively normal individuals. In many areas of their lives, such as their work or involvement in community and civic activities, offenders of this type may function adequately. Sex offenders have been found in positions of community responsibility, such as holding political office, teaching a Sunday school class, or leading a Scout troop. Virtually every occupation including police officers, ministers, and bank presidents has been involved. A psychological assessment might indicate a personality or character disorder, but one of a relatively limited nature. These individuals are significantly more functional than the offenders discussed thus far and their treatment is likely to be less difficult. Although the model indicates three categories of offenders, clinicians are again reminded that the model assumes a continuum of offenders, with each category merging into the next.

When assessing or treating offenders denoted by the middle box of Figure 7.1, clinicians should not be misled by their presentation of normalcy. These individuals may appear to be normal while they are in fact abusing children. In developing treatment goals for these offenders, the therapy worksheet presented in Figure 7.2 will be useful in delineating problematic areas as well as areas of strength. Based on this assessment, clinicians can plan a program of intervention that may include various forms of psychotherapy.

Depending on the availability of services and the needs of the offender, clinicians may recommend individual, group, marital, or family therapy, or a combination thereof. The progression often follows this order, with family therapy usually being the last modality used. Although these offenders are sexually attracted to children or adolescents, they usually have had or are currently involved in an adult sexual relationship. Therefore, although the focus of therapy may be more on marital or family issues, in selected cases the behavioral methods described previously may be employed to decrease the offender's attraction to children. However, aversive techniques should be used selectively with offenders in this category. Other behavioral techniques, such as thought stopping, assertiveness training, or systematic desensitization, can be used to address issues of stress management, impulse control, or cognitive distortions (Walker, Hedberg, Clement, & Wright, 1981; Watkins, 1983). Mayer (1983) presents an approach to incorporating stress management techniques in the treatment of sex offenders. For a complete review of relaxation and stress management techniques, the reader might want to see an excellent article by Denney (1983).   If the offender is married or in a long-term relationship, marital or couples therapy may be recommended. In this modality, focus may be directed to improving communication skills, redefining marital or parental roles within the family, or improving the couple's sexual relationship (Jacobson & Gurman, 1986). Techniques used to improve the couple's sexual relationship could include relaxation training (Walker et al., 1981; Denney, 1983), bibliotherapy (Mayer, 1983), sensate focusing, or other exercises suggested by Masters and Johnson (1970).

Offenders also may be found to suffer from a variety of sexual dysfunctions, such as impotence, inhibited orgasm, or premature ejaculation.

These dysfunctions may serve to further inhibit an appropriate adult relationship, as the offender may experience embarrassment or reluctance when interacting sexually with an adult. At these times, offenders may turn to a child or adolescent in an experimental way, to see if he or she can perform more adequately in a less stressful or demanding situation. If these dysfunctions are present, they should be addressed as part of a treatment program. (For specific treatment suggestions, see Goldberg, 1983, and Leiblum & Pervin, 1980.) It is also likely that offenders in this category need basic sex education information incorporated into their treatment plan.

If the abuse occurred within the offender's family setting and an attempt is to be made to maintain or reunite the family unit, clinicians frequently employ family therapy as part of an overall treatment plan. One approach to treating families in which father-daughter incest has occurred is the Child Sexual Abuse Treatment Program (CSATP) developed in 1972 by Giarretto (1982a; 1982b). The program consists of three interdependent components: professional staff, volunteers, and self-help groups, such as Parents United. The treatment program is used as an alternative to incarceration for the offender and is designed to facilitate the reunification of families. The average length of treatment is 9 months and typically proceeds in the following order: (a) Individual counseling for the child, mother, and father; (b) mother-daughter counseling; (c) marital counseling, which is seen as a key component for families who plan to be reunified; (d) father-daughter counseling; (e) family counseling; and (f) group counseling.

A report by Giarretto (1982a) indicates that of the 4,000 children and family members seen in the Santa Clara, California program since 1972, approximately 85% of the offenders and 90% of the children have been reunited with their families. For the 600 families who received a minimum of 10 hours of treatment and whose cases have been formally terminated, less than 1% recidivism has been reported.

Although these figures are seen as a promising indicator for the effectiveness of this form of treatment, the inadequacies in the research design employed in the evaluation makes these findings suspect (Conte, 1984). Additionally, other programs based on this model have reported substantially different outcome findings. In a study of 55 families, Server and Janzen (1982) found that 38 parents (69%) separated following the disclosure of sexual abuse, with the children remaining with the mother. In the remaining 17 families (30%), the parents chose to remain together and the children were placed in foster care. One year after disclosure, only 11 of these 17 families were reunited or working toward reunification with the children. The children in the remaining six families refused to return home if the offender remained with the family. Although these differences may be due to sample bias, the significant discrepancy highlights the need for well-designed studies to further assess the effectiveness of this form of intervention with offenders and families.

Other clinicians have focused on more specific treatment considerations when discussing therapeutic interventions with families. Hoorwitz (1983) describes issues to be addressed in four stages of treatment with father/daughter incest families. During the first stage of therapy, the therapist meets individually with the father, mother, and child victim, addressing issues of protection, denial, commitment to therapy, and individual emotional reactions. Additionally, the therapist may need to provide referrals to community and social service agencies to assist the family in meeting basic necessities, such as different housing arrangements or food subsidies. During this stage, the therapist prepares the family members for the subsequent therapy stages, which may include group therapy or marital sessions.

In the second stage of treatment, issues such as role confusion, self-esteem, trust, social skills, depression, or stress reduction are addressed in individual or group therapy, or both.

The third stage of treatment utilizes mother-daughter sessions and marital therapy. These modalities are used to strengthen the relationship between the mother and daughter to promote nurturing and protection. Hoorwitz (1983) sees this relationship as pivotal to the success of family therapy in the fourth stage of treatment. Marital sessions are used at this point to prepare the parents for the issues to be addressed in family therapy, that is, parental responsibility for the incest situation, and new household roles or safeguards for protecting the child. Treatment can also focus on aspects of the couples' marital and sexual relationship, such as modifying and redistributing the power and responsibilities between the partners, improving communication, or the sexual relationship.

The fourth stage of therapy, as described by Hoorwitz (1983), involves the use of father-daughter sessions and family sessions. It is recommended that at least one session be scheduled in which the father apologizes to the daughter and describes how their relationship will be different. Family therapy sessions are used to assist the family in establishing and enforcing new limits, clarifying role boundaries, improving communication, and increasing the family's involvement in activities and relationships outside the family.

Clinicians may be asked by child protection workers, clients, or the courts to make recommendations regarding reunification of families in which abuse has occurred. The recommendation will be based primarily on the clinician's assessment of the child's safety from the recurrence of abuse. Factors for the clinician to evaluate are the likelihood of the offender to reabuse, the nonoffending parent's ability to provide adequate protection for the child, and the child's ability to protect himself or herself. Although there are no empirically based criteria for clinicians to follow, some general guidelines have developed in clinical practice. This list should not be seen as exhaustive or as a successful predictive tool. However, clinical experience indicates that the following conditions may be seen as minimal requirements for considering family reunification: (a) The abuser acknowledges the behavior, takes responsibility for the abuse, and does not project blame on the victim; (b) The nonabusing parent does not hold the victim responsible for the abuse; (c) The nonabusing parent demonstrates the ability to protect the child from abuse; (d) The victim demonstrates the ability to obtain professional help if approached by the abuser; (e) The therapist and all family members express reasonable assurance that the victim is safe from future abuse; (f) The family has been restructured with more appropriate role boundaries and an improved marital relationship; (g) The therapist and family members are certain that sufficient progress has been made on short- and long-term treatment goals (adapted from Server & Janzen, 1982). Additionally, O'Connell (1986) provides step-by-step guidelines for clinicians to consider in the reunification process.

In considering a recommendation that a family be reunited, the protection of the child from further abuse is of primary concern. Although the parents are responsible for protecting the child from reabuse, there are some techniques that can be used to assist the child in self-protection. Depending on the age of the victim and other children in the family, the children can be taught to call the therapist's office, the child abuse hotline, or a case worker. A list of emergency numbers can be attached to each phone in the house so that everyone has access to them. Role-playing situations that should be reported can be enacted during family sessions. It is important that the child act out placing the call in front of the parents so that the therapist can offer suggestions and encouragement. When the offender continues to be seen as possessing significant at-risk characteristics, such as a significant alcohol problem, despite therapeutic interventions, the family should not be reunified. If the parents choose to remain together, the child or children may have to be removed from the home on a permanent basis. Additional readings on family therapy with incestuous families can be found in Furniss (1983), Mayer (1983), Ryan (1986), and Sgroi (1982b).

Treatment for offenders represented by the bottom box in Figure 7.1 will be markedly different from that for offenders in the other two categories. These are offenders who impulsively commit a relatively minor sexual offense such as exposing themselves or inappropriately touching a child, often only once or twice. Psychologically, they are generally normal individuals who function adequately in all areas of their lives.

Their inappropriate sexual behavior is seen as out of character for them, and their response is likely to be embarrassment and genuine remorse.

Although their behavior could be the beginning of a more serious dysfunction, these offenders can frequently benefit from short-term supportive intervention. Therapy may focus on delineating factors that contributed to the breakdown in behavior control and assisting the offender to build in safeguards to prevent the recurrence of the abuse. Self-monitoring techniques (e.g., Watkins, 1983), along with relaxation training and stress management as described earlier, might be useful to offenders in this category. If the offense occurred within the family, behavioral contracting among family members (that no future abuse will occur) and instructions to the child to make use of phone calls to the therapist or hot lines may also be useful.

In addition to adult male sex offenders, two other groups of offenders need to be discussed: female perpetrators and juvenile sex offenders. It has long been assumed that very few women sexually abuse children. Although this assumption has begun to be questioned (Groth & Birnbaum, 1979; Justice & Justice, 1979), Finkelhor and Russell (1984) have presented a review of the available data on the incidence of female perpetrators and concluded that the amount of sexual abuse perpetrated by females is indeed small. Estimates suggest that females are perpetrators in approximately 5% of the cases in which girls are abused and 20% of cases in which boys are victims.

As clinicians report referrals of increasing numbers of female offenders for treatment, however, new data appear to be challenging some of the previous assumptions. Contrary to earlier writings on female perpetrators, a recent study of 12 adult female offenders indicate that the women did not suffer from significant psychiatric disturbance and that they were not all coerced into the abusive role by a male (Wolfe, 1985). However, half of the women committed the abuse in conjunction with an adult male. Wolfe's findings further suggest some similarities and differences between male and female child molesters. As with male offenders, these women more frequently victimized children within their own families, did not use physical force to gain compliance, and reported the use of deviant fantasies for sexual arousal. The women were seen as socially isolated and tended to deny and minimize the seriousness of their acts. Conversely, the women were not found to pair the deviant sexual behavior with orgasm as frequently as do male offenders and reported the onset of their abusive behavior at a later age than do male offenders.

Unfortunately, very little data are available on treating women sexual offenders. For those clinicians who are asked to see a female offender, it is suggested that the evaluation follow the model presented in Figure

7.1. Although little is known about the psychological makeup of female perpetrators, clinicians might pay particular attention to those deficit areas reported by Wolfe (1985), such as denial, use of deviant fantasies, lack of social skills, and social isolation.

Another group of sex offenders that have received increasing attention are adolescent offenders. As clinical intervention in treating adult sexual offenders has expanded, it has become evident that the abusive behavior frequently began during the offender's adolescent years (Abel, Mittelman, & Becker, 1985; Deisher, Wenet, Paperny, Clark, & Fehrenbach, 1982; Longo & Groth, 1983). Typically, the behavior was not discovered or was treated as normal adolescent acting out and treatment interventions were not made. In conjunction with the current focus on prevention of sexual abuse, more attention has been placed on intervention with juvenile offenders. However, few clinicians are trained to work with this population and there is little empirical data upon which to base treatment interventions. Although some research projects are currently in progress on treatment strategies with juvenile offenders, this continues to be an area in which clinicians have minimal guidelines. It is certainly recommended that clinicians be experienced in working with adolescents or work under the supervision of a more experienced colleague.

Juvenile offenders are described as being socially isolated, lacking in self-esteem, and having poor peer relationships (Deisher et al., 1982). Although the exact incidence is unknown, it is estimated that many juvenile offenders were themselves victims of sexual assault in their earlier years (Wolf, 1985; Seghorn, Boucher, & Prentky, 1987). Based on the authors' experience in treating young sex offenders, it is recommended that treatment be court mandated because of the offender's, and often the family's, denial or minimization of the behavior and the tendency for offenders to drop out of voluntary treatment.

Treatment programs for adolescent sex offenders are similar to those developed for adult offenders. These programs are currently being implemented in both residential and outpatient settings. Following an assessment of the offender's strengths and degree of psychopathology, one or more of the following treatment modalities are usually employed: individual, group, and family therapy; education in human sexuality; behavioral techniques; values clarification; and social skills and assertiveness training. Most programs place a strong emphasis on involving the adolescent's family in the treatment program, and there are some programs that will not accept the offender unless the family is involved. Knopp (1982) has published descriptions of nine treatment programs, but to date, little data are available on the efficacy of the treatment interventions.

Groth, Hobson, Lucey, & St. Pierre (1981) offer some general guidelines for treatment interventions. These authors view treatment as a process of education, skills training, and counseling, using both individual and group therapy. It is recommended that the therapist take a supportive, but authoritative stance. If possible, the program should involve the offender's family and use a team approach. In addition to focusing on taking responsibility for the abusive behavior and learning more appropriate ways to handle stress, the treatment program should include social skills training and sex education. Specific treatment strategies suggested by Groth et al. (1981) include: (a) having the adolescent write a detailed autobiography, (b) the use of audio and videotapes of adult sex offenders relating their experiences and the consequences, and (c) the involvement of the adolescent in projects designed to prevent sexual abuse, such as meeting with police or crisis center staff to educate her or him about the problems of juvenile offenders or critiquing materials on how to prevent child sexual abuse.

A highly structured, research-based approach to treatment with juvenile sex offenders has been developed by Becker and her associates. Based on the Abel et al. (1984) program in which she worked with adult sex offenders, Becker (1985) developed a cognitive behavioral treatment program for adolescent offenders. Designed as a research project, it is an outpatient program for adolescents aged 13 through 18 who have engaged in deviant sexual behavior and who volunteer to participate in treatment.

The five program components include:

1. Educating the parents or parent surrogates about the nature and extent of the adolescent's problems as a means of motivating them to become more involved in assisting the adolescent to deal with the problems;
2. Using two self-control techniques, satiation and covert sensitization, to decrease the adolescent's deviant sexual fantasies and to alert the adolescent to the precursors of deviant sexual behavior;
3. Treating assertiveness and social skills deficits and assisting the adolescent to relate more effectively with peers;
4. Focusing on sex education and sexual values;
5. Using cognitive restructuring techniques to confront and replace the offenders' faulty beliefs about their behavior.

Initial findings from Becker and her associates' treatment program with adolescent sex offenders indicate that the adolescents have committed more sexual crimes than they have been arrested for, were involved in sexual behavior at an early age, and tend to deny or minimize the extent of their deviant sexual behavior (Becker, Cunningham-Rathner, & Kaplan, 1986; Becker, Kaplan, Cunningham-Rathner, & Kavousi, 1986).

Although Becker qualifies the generalization of the findings due to sample bias (outpatient population of mostly innercity minority adolescents), the study represents an excellent model for further investigation.

Programs such as Becker's, which combine a theoretically based treatment approach and empirical research with a large population of adolescents, can make a significant contribution to the treatment of juvenile offenders. (For additional information on adolescent sex offenders, see Ageton, 1983; Awad, Saunders, & Levene, 1984; Becker & Abel, 1984; Groth & Loredo, 1981; Knopp, 1985; Longo, 1982; Otey & Ryan, 1985; Tarter, Hegedus, Alterman, & Katz-Garris, 1983; Thomas & Rogers, 1983. An annotated bibliography of articles on adolescent perpetrators of child sexual abuse was compiled by Ryan, 1986.)

Chapter 10

Treatment of the Victim and Family in Sexual Abuse

VICTIM

In working with child victims of sexual abuse, clinicians are asked to make decisions on such issues as does the child need treatment and if so, what type and for how long; should the child remain in the home; and does the child need psychiatric hospitalization. Unfortunately, at this point, clinicians have little empirical data on which to base these decisions.

The literature on treating child and adolescent victims of sexual abuse suffers from several of the same deficits as does that on offenders. First, there is no widely accepted conceptual framework on the effects of sexual abuse on either male or female children and adolescents. Although numerous articles describing the psychological impact of child sexual abuse have been published over the past 10 years (Browne & Finkelhor, 1986a, 1986b; Gomes-Schwartz, Horowitz, & Sauzier, 1985; Goodwin & Flanagan, 1983; Knittle & Tuana, 1980; Sgroi, 1982b), only recently has an attempt been made to organize these observations into a coherent framework that describes both the initial and long-term consequences of abuse (Finkelhor & Browne, 1986). Another problem for clinicians is the lack of literature on the treatment of children who have been abused by nonfamily members. Although there has been a great deal of literature on the impact and treatment of father-daughter incest (e.g. Herman, 1981; Mayer, 1983), other forms of sexual abuse have received far less attention. One byproduct of the clinical focus on father-daughter incest is the lack of information available on boy victims.

A third problem for clinicians attempting to provide treatment is the lack of outcome studies that assess treatment effectiveness. For example, some articles strongly recommend group treatment as the most effective method of therapy with child or adolescent victims, but there are few supportive data other than subjective clinical impressions at this time. Clinicians are left with few guidelines as to the severity of the impact on the child and the most appropriate interventions to make across a continuum of victim and family responses.

With these limitations in mind, this chapter will present recommendations for treating child and adolescent victims based on the authors' experience and the current data available. Additionally, a section on treating special populations is presented. This section briefly describes suggestions for treating children who have been involved in pornography and adult women who were molested as children. The chapter is designed to assist clinicians in developing and implementing treatment plans for victims who evidence symptoms ranging from significant psychological dysfunctions to relatively mild reactions.

The assessment model (Figure 7.1) recommends a comprehensive evaluation of the child's psychological, educational, and social functioning. Using this assessment of the child's strengths and areas of dysfunction, clinicians can develop a treatment plan designed to (a) reduce or prevent the negative effects of the abuse, (b) assist the child or adolescent to master appropriate developmental tasks, and (c) prevent further abuse or molestation.

In planning treatment for a child or adolescent, the first task is to evaluate the seriousness of the child's psychopathology. Some children and adolescents will present with serious psychopathology. They may be diagnosed as schizophrenic, mentally retarded, or severely depressed. In some cases, this pathology may have been present before the sexual abuse and may have acted as a contributory factor to the child's victimization. For example, a retarded child may be more at risk to be sexually exploited because of his or her cognitive limitations. For other children, the preexisting pathology may have been significantly worsened by the sexual abuse. In children who were functioning adequately before the abuse, the presenting problem may be seen as a direct result of the abuse. Regardless of the origin of this psychopathology, a specific, aggressive treatment plan needs to be implemented when serious pathology is found.

A variety of approaches are available to treat significant psychopathology in children and adolescents. These are well known and will not be discussed at length in this chapter. For some children, the clinician may find it necessary to recommend a period of inpatient treatment in a facility designed to care for children and adolescents. Depending on the extent of the child's pathology and the length of hospitalization, it is possible that some of the treatment suggestions discussed in the next section on the impact and consequences of the sexual abuse could be implemented as part of the inpatient treatment plan.

Other children and adolescents may present with severe psychological handicaps, such as mental retardation, that may make traditional forms of therapy difficult or impossible to implement. In these cases, clinicians may need to make recommendations on residential placement, educational resources, and other appropriate forms of treatment. Based on the family and community resources available, clinicians should recommend settings in which the child will receive maximum protection, the probability of reabuse is minimal, and personnel to provide specialized treatment are available, whether it be a physical therapist, an educational specialist, or a mental health professional. Special attention should be placed on assertiveness and prevention skills with handicapped children, as it is possible these children are at higher risk of reabuse (Finkelhor & Baron, 1986b; Varley, 1984).

Although the group of sexual abuse victims with significant psychopathology will be relatively small, it is important for clinicians to recognize a continuum of severity and to develop treatment plans accordingly. When these patients' psychopathology becomes more stabilized, their treatment plans can be expanded to include a focus on the psychological issues related to the sexual abuse discussed in the next section.

Children and adolescents in the mid-range of the continuum are seen as having significant psychological problems related to the sexual abuse. The response of a child or adolescent to sexual abuse can vary greatly, depending on such factors as the child's age and cognitive ability, duration and frequency of the abuse, form of inducement or coercion used, relationship to the perpetrator, type of sexual abuse, and the response of family members when the abuse is disclosed (Friedrich, Urquiza, & Beilke, 1986; Gomes-Schwartz et al., 1985). The impact of victimization is different for each child and clinicians must remember to assess the child's perception of the abuse.

Clinical experience with child and adolescent victims of sexual abuse indicates that the abusive experience can significantly affect a child's cognitive and emotional response to the environment and distort the child's self-perception, relationships with others, and adaptive capabilities. A useful way to understand the possible repercussions of sexual abuse and to discuss appropriate treatment interventions is to use the four-component model suggested by Finkelhor and Browne (1986). It appears that the impact on the child of traumatic sexualization, stigmatization, betrayal, and powerlessness makes the treatment of these children and adolescents somewhat different than that of children who have other presenting problems. Therefore, each of these factors will be discussed along with the behavioral manifestations associated with each factor and treatment possibilities for the behaviors.

Traumatic sexualization is the process by which a child's sexuality becomes distorted over the course of the abuse. This process can occur to a child when the offender: (a) repeatedly rewards a child for inappropriate sexual behavior, (b) exchanges gifts, affection, privileges, or attention for sexual activity with the child, (c) overly attends to or distorts the meaning and importance of certain parts of the child's body, (d) conveys misconceptions and confusion about sexual behavior and accepted morality to the child, and (e) abuses the child to a degree that the child associates fearful memories and events with sexual behavior.

Children tend to evidence greater degrees of sexual traumatization when the offender attempts to arouse the child's sexual responses rather than merely interacting with the child as a passive object. Additionally, children appear to experience more severe levels of traumatization when they are enticed to participate, when high levels of fear become associated with sexual experiences, and when they have a better understanding of the implications of the sexual behavior.

Children who have experienced significant traumatic sexualization are likely to evidence behavioral and cognitive dysfunctions that must be addressed in treatment. These children may have distorted views of sexual norms, become confused as to their sexual identity, or become sexually aggressive. They may have a heightened sensitivity to sexual issues and respond by being highly attracted to sexual behavior or, at the other extreme, associate highly negative feelings with any sexual activity or arousal. Young children may indiscriminately act out sexual behaviors that are developmentally inappropriate, develop sexual preoccupations, or engage in compulsive sexual behavior. Older children and adolescents may become involved in numerous sexual relationships or in some cases work as a prostitute. Conversely, children may avoid any sexual contact as they have a strong aversion to sexual activities, arousal, or intimacy. These extreme reactions may lead to a variety of adult sexual dysfunctions, such as difficulty in arousal or orgasm.

Many children will need assistance in relearning acceptable sexual behavior. Depending on their age and cognitive ability, they will need education about normal sexual activity for different ages. Therapists might use books such as, "Where Did I Come From?" (Mayle, 1973), "What's Happening To Me?" (Mayle, 1975), or "Let's Talk about S-E-X" (Gitchel & Foster, 1982), as a means of discussing this issue with children.

For those children who show inappropriate or compulsive sexual behaviors or who appear preoccupied with sexual activities, therapists might employ behavioral techniques, such as shaping and modeling acceptable behavior and reinforcing more age-appropriate behavior (e.g.,

Bornstein & Kazdin, 1985). Other techniques that might be used are role playing appropriate child-child and child-adult interactions related to friendship, affection, and care-giving. With older children, a cognitive behavioral approach may be useful in helping the child gain more control over compulsive, unacceptable behavior. Shaw and Walker (1979) describe the usefulness of relaxation training in the treatment of inappropriate sexual behavior in an 8-year-old boy.

A planned behavioral program that consistently reinforces appropriate behavior can be a useful therapeutic tool. To insure that the program is properly implemented, the parents, teachers, or day-care personnel may need to be involved in designing a program that can be carried out in different settings. For examples of behavioral programs designed for children, clinicians can refer to Forehand and McMahon (1981), Keat (1979), Patterson (1976), and Shapiro (1984).

Boys may be particularly vulnerable to react to sexual traumatization by becoming more aggressive. Although few articles have been written about the impact of sexual abuse on boys, Rogers and Terry (1984) indicate that boys typically attempt to reassert their masculinity through aggressive behavior. In treating boy victims, therapists may want to implement a program that assists boys in channeling these aggressive feelings through involvement in team sports or improving a particular skill such as swimming or karate. They might also be encouraged to redirect their aggressive impulses in prosocial directions such as asserting their masculinity by helping and protecting others. (See following section on treating male victims.)

A second traumagenic factor in child sexual abuse is stigmatization. This develops when the offender blames and denegrates the victim and the child comes to feel a sense of shame and responsibility for the abuse or when other people in the child's environment have shocked, horrified reactions to the disclosure, blame the child for the abuse, or fail to believe that the abuse occurred. The psychological consequences to the child are feelings of guilt and shame, lowered self-esteem, and a sense of being different from other children. Behaviorally, the child or adolescent may become isolated from peers, involved in criminal activity, abuse drugs or alcohol, engage in self-mutilation, or attempt suicide.

Several therapeutic strategies can be employed to decrease the negative effects of stigmatization. Although these effects may be initially addressed in individual therapy, several clinicians have reported that group therapy is particularly effective in dealing with issues of blame, responsibility for the abuse, and isolation from peers (e.g., Berliner & MacQuivey, 1983). The therapist needs to clearly convey that responsibility for the abuse lies with the offender and that the child is not to blame. Books such as "Alice Doesn't Babysit Anymore" (McGovern, 1985) or

"No More Secrets For Me" (Wachter, 1983), can be used to help younger children correctly identify where blame should be placed in an abusive situation. Older victims may benefit from viewing and discussing films or videotapes that show victims and offenders discussing blame and responsibility for sexual abuse.

Children and adolescents who have been involved in abusive situations sometimes have poor social skills and have had only limited interactions with their peers outside of school. If a child is extremely shy or has little experience in age-appropriate peer relationships, the therapist may need to help the child learn basic skills in making friends, that is, how to approach another child, what to talk about, or how to invite a friend to a movie. The therapist can also encourage the child or adolescent to join age-appropriate activities, such as a church choir or youth group, a sports team, or a school club.

Betrayal is another traumagenic factor frequently observed in victims of sexual abuse. The child's sense of trust and vulnerability are manipulated by the offender. As a result, the child's normal expectation that others will provide care and protection is significantly damaged. This sense of betrayal is particularly relevant in cases of intrafamilial abuse when children realize that someone they trusted or depended on has harmed them. Children may feel betrayed not only by the perpetrator of the abuse but also by other family members. If other members of the family knew about the abuse and were unwilling to believe or protect the child, or if their attitude toward the child changed dramatically when the abuse was disclosed, the child may feel an overwhelming sense of betrayal.

In response to these feelings, the child may experience a grief reaction, significant depression, and an impaired ability to judge the trustworthiness of others. Children may become hostile or angry and show a pervasive mistrust of adults. This sense of betrayal may be evidenced by high levels of aggressive behavior, delinquency, and discomfort in close relationships. Conversely, some children may go to the opposite extreme. They may become indiscriminately overly attached to adults, which may act to increase their risk to be reabused.

With children who experience a strong sense of betrayal, individual therapy may be recommended (Jones, 1986). In this relationship, the child can gradually learn to trust adults again. Another consideration that may be important is therapist gender. As most known offenders are male, it may be helpful for children, particularly girls, to work initially with a female therapist. If the child later moves to a group setting, the use of a male and female as co-therapists can be productive in helping the child resolve any conflicts in dealing with adult males. A technique that might be useful in dealing with the issue of trust is for the child to keep a chart or booklet at the therapist's office with one page entitled, "Who Can I Trust?" Over the course of therapy, the child can add names to the list, such as a friend, parent or caretaker, relative, teacher, or therapist.

Cognitive behavior therapy can be implemented for children and adolescents suffering from depression and to increase a child's problem-solving and decision-making abilities. Children whose trust in others is significantly damaged are likely to mistrust their own reactions and behaviors. A therapist is in an ideal position to help children review decisions that they make and reinforce those that are appropriate. Anticipatory guidance can be used to help a child think through possible future problems, such as an impending court appearance or what to say to schoolmates about living in foster care.

The fourth traumagenic factor observed in sexual abuse victims is that of powerlessness. An unwanted invasion of a child's body territory may have occurred repeatedly over time, resulting in feelings of vulnerability and an inability to protect himself or herself. Additionally, a child's sense of self-efficacy may be damaged if he or she was unable to convince others that the abuse occurred. As a result, children may become anxious, highly fearful, and at significant risk for reabuse. Other manifestations of a feeling of powerlessness are nightmares, phobias, eating and sleeping disorders, depression, running away, and truancy. Some children may show an inordinate need to control events or people or recapitulate the abusive experience by abusing other children.

Several behavioral techniques can be used to reduce children's fears, phobic reactions, and eating and sleeping disturbances. Becker, Skinner, & Abel (1982) report on the behavioral treatment of a 4-year-old who was sexually abused by her father in the home of her paternal grandmother. The problem behaviors included a significant weight loss, phobic behaviors, self-injurious behaviors, and verbal comments about her father and grandmother. Following a brief training session, the child's mother acted as both data collector and therapist. A modified token program was used to increase the child's weight and reverse what could have developed into a life-threatening condition. The family was instructed to ignore the phobic and self-injurious behaviors as it appeared that the child was not in significant danger. Additionally, the family was not to initiate a discussion, but they were to listen to the child and reassure her when she talked about the assault. This study indicates that a relatively simple behavioral program implemented by a trained parent can be effectively used in the treatment of young sexual assault victims.

For children experiencing nightmares and other sleeping disorders, relaxation tapes played at bedtime have been found helpful. Systematic desensitization may be used to help children overcome specific phobias or to decrease a child's anxiety. Other clinicians have used techniques such as an unsent letter by the child to the offender, journal keeping, role playing, and bibliotherapy to assist the child in regaining a sense of self-efficacy and confidence (Berliner & Ernst, 1984; Delson & Clark, 1981; Mayer, 1983; Sturkie, 1983).

Because children who have been abused often feel a sense of helplessness, therapists should focus their efforts on the prevention of reabuse. Various techniques may be helpful to therapists in approaching this issue, such as books, films, and role playing. Numerous books and pamphlets designed to educate and inform both children and adults are available and can be read with a child in the therapy setting. Parents can be asked to reinforce prevention techniques by re-reading the books at home with their children. In addition to the McGovern and Wachter books mentioned earlier, therapists could use *Talking About Touching for Parents and Kids* (Beland, 1985), *Spiderman and Powerpak: Secrets* (Salicrup, 1984), or *Top Secret: Sexual Assault Information for Teenagers Only* (Fay & Flerchinger, 1982).

One skill that children often need to learn is assertiveness. Mayer (1983, 1985) describes an approach to teaching assertiveness to children that can be useful to clinicians. She recommends that (a) cognitive material be kept to a minimum, (b) the material be repeated in different forms, and (c) tangible rewards and social reinforcers be used to reward the child's efforts. Clinicians can teach children to recognize potentially dangerous situations and how to be assertive if they are approached in a sexual way again. It is important that children role play or act out scenarios of appropriate behavior rather than just cognitively understand the concepts of prevention. A game entitled, "The Assertion Game" (Berg, 1986), could be used in either individual therapy or with a group of children in helping them learn general assertive skills.

Several techniques to improve children's ability to protect themselves have been developed by Hadden & Gober Zimmerman (1985) in their group treatment program for sexually abused children. The first is a group exercise designed to help the children learn strategies to prevent reabuse. In this exercise, the children discuss and determine whether a particular strategy is safe or risky. The materials needed for the game include a clothesline, clothespins, long strips of paper, and pencils. The children are divided into groups of two to four children, and each group is to write down two safe defenses and two risky defenses on the strips of paper. The children are regrouped and attempt to identify the other groups' strategies as safe or risky. The safe strategies can be pinned at one end of the line, risky strategies at the other, and ones that involve some risk pinned in the middle. It is helpful for the therapists to direct the discussion on how situational factors make certain strategies a better choice.

Another technique designed by Hadden & Gober Zimmerman is a game entitled, "I Can Protect Me." The game is designed to indicate the degree to which children have internalized principles of assertiveness training and their ability to protect themselves. To construct the game, a poster board, blank 3 by 5 cards, colored markers, tokens of children or animals, and a pair of dice are needed. First, draw a road of any type on the poster board. Divide the route into equal spaces and color each one, alternating the colors in any pattern. Vignettes describing self-protective and nonprotective behaviors are written by the leaders on 3 by 5 cards. The cards are shuffled and placed face down beside the board. The following are examples of vignettes that have been found useful for younger children.

> "You are walking home from school and a woman asks you to help her carry her grocery sack home. You say firmly that your mother expects you home by 3:30. You cross the street and begin running home."

> "You are spending the night at your friend's house. His (or her) 14-year-old brother asks you to come into the bathroom with him. You wonder what he wants, but you say 'Okay' and follow him."

> "Your father molested you several months ago. He has just been allowed by the court to return home. He has started going to therapy. When you take a bath, you lock the bathroom door first."

Each child rolls the dice and the one with the highest number begins. First, the child rolls the dice. Without moving the token, the player takes the top card off the pile and reads it aloud (or a leader reads the card). The player decides if the vignette describes a self-protective or nonprotective behavior. The other group members decide if the child is correct, with the group leaders making a final decision if necessary. Group discussion of why the behavior is nonprotective is encouraged. If the child makes the correct decision he or she can move a token the number of spaces indicated on the dice. If they are incorrect, the token remains in place. In a clockwise direction, the other players take their turns. The person who reaches the end space first is the winner and could wear a self-protection badge for the remainder of the session.

Other forms of treatment may also be used in treating victims of sexual abuse. For example, play therapy has been used with young children to assist victims in the recovery process (Burgess, Holmstrom, & McCausland, 1978; Jones, 1986). A recent publication by MacFarlane, Waterman, Conerly, Damon, Durfee, and Long (1986) discusses the use of play therapy and provides in-depth information on the evaluation and treatment of young sexual assault victims.

Several authors have suggested the usefulness of art therapy with young children and adolescent victims (Kelley, 1984; Mayer, 1983; Sgroi, 1982b). Art techniques have been used for both assessing and treating the impact of sexual abuse. Clay and other art media can be used to express emotions, stimulate dialogue with shy or resistant children, and monitor a child's progress during treatment. Carozza & Heirsteiner (1983) describe the use of art techniques in a group setting with school-age female victims. The authors employed clay, life-size body tracings, Group Scribble, collages, finger painting, and theme drawings to enhance individual and group growth.

Many clinicians who have had extensive experience working with school-age and adolescent victims have strongly endorsed the use of group therapy (Berliner & Ernst, 1984; Knittle & Tauna, 1980; Lubell & Soong, 1982; Mayer,1983; Sgroi, 1982b; Sturkie,1983). As part of an overall treatment approach, Delsen and Clark (1981) reported beneficial results from the use of a group approach with 6- to 11-year-old girls. Focusing on improving the children's self-esteem, the therapists employed art, free play, and role-playing techniques in the group sessions.

For clinicians considering the use of group therapy, possibly in conjunction with other forms of treatment for victims, the article by Berliner and Ernst (1984) is particularly useful. The authors clearly establish the rationale for group therapy, set out steps for establishing a group, describe the role of the therapist and structure of the group, and suggest a detailed format for a six-session therapy group.

The group experiences are designed to address issues related to the sexual assault, such as acknowledgment of the abusive incident, understanding of who is responsible for the abuse, and learning means of self-protection, as well as the psychological consequences of the abuse. The authors use positive interactions with other victims, discussion groups, physical exercises, and art therapy to enhance the victims' self-esteem.

The six sessions follow a format that is designed for different age groups. Each session begins with a snack and the children being reminded of why they are in the group. A group leader might say something like, "Everyone is in the group because another person touched/molested/abused them in a way that wasn't right." The children then tell about a positive event that happened to them during the last week. After 10 to 15 minutes, a group activity is introduced. This is usually art or drawing and includes activities such as making a personal name tag, a rogue's gallery of offender pictures, drawing self-portraits, kinetic family drawings, or a group mural.

Following an art activity, each session moves to a more didactic format, using a discussion, demonstration, or mini-lecture. Topics to be covered in this part of the session are defining sexual abuse, feelings and thoughts about the abuse and the perpetrator, age-appropriate sex education, family roles and friends, solving problems related to the abuse, and prevention of reabuse. A group exercise or game is used to close the session and it may include learning relaxation techniques, role playing a court-room scene, practicing prevention techniques, or playing a game like, "The Thinking, Feeling, and Doing Game" (Gardner, 1973).

The sessions end with a closing activity, such as an assignment to bring a family photo or a joke to the next group meeting. The authors list books, films, ideas for teaching problem-solving skills, self-esteem exercises, and prevention activities that clinicians will find helpful in designing a therapy group for children or adolescents.

A commonly overlooked factor in writing about sexually abused children is the frequency with which they are removed from their homes, either on a short- or long-term basis. By the time they are brought for evaluation and treatment, they may have lived for several days or weeks in a children's shelter, followed by placement in new school and family surroundings. The impact of these changes, combined with the crisis precipitated by disclosure of the abuse, may well tax most children's ability to cope adequately. In these cases, it is recommended that the foster parents or relatives with whom the child resides be included as part of the child's treatment plan. The caretakers may need not only basic information about sexual abuse and its impact on children at different ages, but also assistance in dealing with disruptive or highly depressed, anxious children. Finally, because reports indicate that children have been sexually reabused while they are in foster care (Borgman, 1984), the clinician will have to be alert to this possibility as treatment progresses.

As most clinicians are aware, the bulk of the literature on treating child sexual abuse victims has been based on therapy with girls. In the past, fewer boys have presented for treatment and until recently, little attention has been paid to the patterns and characteristics of sexual victimization of boys (Finkelhor, 1984; Showers, Farber, Joseph, Oshins, & Johnson, 1983; Zaphiris, 1986). With more recent studies indicating a cycle of sexual abuse, wherein a boy who is sexually victimized may become an adolescent or adult perpetrator, more professional attention has turned to the impact of abuse on boys (Freeman-Longo, 1986).

Although the data remain limited on how treatment of boy victims may or may not be different from that of girls, several studies have indicated that boys are more often abused by nonfamily members, are less likely to tell about the abuse, and therefore are less often seen in a clinical setting (e.g., Rogers & Terry, 1984). Fortunately, there are two publications that can be useful for clinicians who are asked to treat male victims.

Rogers and Terry (1984) discuss similarities and differences in the patterns of victimization between boys and girls and present guidelines for intervention with boy victims. Based on 101 cases, their data indicate that boys are primarily victimized by nonfamily members or strangers and that boys are more frequently assaulted by juveniles than are girls.

Although this may not be a typical finding, over 50% of the boys in this study were subjected to anal intercourse.

In addition to the symptoms typically seen in female victims, such as shame, depression, guilt, and inappropriate sexual behavior, Rogers & Terry (1984) have described other issues encountered in the treatment of boy victims, which include: (a) confusion over sexual identity and fears of homosexuality; (b) the tendency of boy victims to reenact their victimization by sexually abusing other children; (c) increased aggressive behavior; and (d) strong denial or minimization of the impact by the boys' parents. The authors provide suggestions for clinical interventions that could be used in addition to those described earlier in this chapter. They recommend providing a clear cognitive framework to increase the victims' and family's understanding of the abuse. This approach may help reduce the parents' blaming the child and the child's self-blame. Another recommended technique is to help the boy channel his need for assertiveness into socially acceptable outlets. This might include joining a sports team or taking a course in self-defense techniques. These authors suggest that intervention with boy victims may be a productive long-term approach to preventing sexual crimes.

A recent publication by Porter (1986) summarizes the current information on male victims and discusses various treatment approaches, such as group, family, and individual therapy. Although empirical data on boy victims are limited, this book offers some helpful suggestions on therapeutic interventions. (For additional information on the victimization of boys, see Ellerstein & Canavan, 1980; Finkelhor, 1985b; Fritz, Stoll, & Wagner, 1981; Johnson & Shrier, 1985; Nielsen, 1983; Rush, 1980).

At the other end of the severity continuum are children and adolescents who may need only minimal therapeutic intervention as a result of being sexually abused. This may include children who have experienced more minor forms of abuse on a limited basis and very young children who are less aware of the social implications of the abuse. Children in this category typically have supportive families, are developmentally normal, were considered well adjusted before the abusive incident, and are not seen as high risk for repeated sexual abuse.

Treatment for these children and adolescents may be limited to crisis intervention or brief psychotherapy for the family (e.g., Aguilera & Messick, 1978; Swensen & Hartsough, 1983). The intervention can be from two to six sessions in which the therapist assesses the child's current functioning; provides information to the family about the medical, legal, and possible psychological consequences of sexual abuse; and arranges to see the child for a follow-up evaluation. With children who appear to be functioning well, treatment may focus primarily on assisting the parents to cope appropriately with the situation. (See section on treating the nonabusing parent.)

Clinicians may also be asked to consult with other professionals, such as pediatricians or school nurses, in handling cases involving less severe molestation. Funk (1981) describes a consultant-directed approach that may be useful for clinicians in working with other health-related professionals. Funk suggests that a consultant approach be used when the sexual abuse is a one-time, nonviolent, nonfamilial incident. This method operates on the assumption that a child is not necessarily traumatized by a single incident of abuse. Funk's approach does not include direct assessment of the child by a mental health professional. However, most clinicians would probably prefer to evaluate the child and then act as a consultant on the case. For clinicians who choose to consult with other professionals on case management, this article will be useful as it discusses pertinent issues that must be addressed, such as suggestions for parents to prevent further abuse, dealing with extended family members and neighbors about the incident, and possible involvement with the legal system.

TREATMENT OF SPECIAL POPULATIONS

Although this chapter has dealt primarily with the treatment of children who were abused through direct sexual contact with individual adults, there are other groups of sexual abuse victims who are increasingly being presented to mental health professionals for treatment. Two of these groups are children who have been involved in the production of pornographic materials and/or sex rings and adults who were sexually abused as children. This section will briefly describe suggested treatment approaches for these groups and list references for the professional who wishes to obtain additional information.

Child Pornography Victims

Current data on sexual abuse indicate that most children and adolescents are sexually abused on a one-to-one basis by adults that they know. However, recent publications describe the abuse and exploitation of groups of children and adolescents by involving them in adult organized sex rings and the production of pornographic materials (Burgess, Groth, & McCausland, 1981; Pierce, 1984; Schoettle, 1980a; Tyler & Stone, 1985). Although professional interest in the problems of sexually abused adults and children has continually increased in the past decade, until recently little mention was made about the involvement of children in pornography, as either participants or viewers.

Although data on the effects of involving children or adolescents in sex rings or pornography are limited, it is likely that these children experience many of the same symptoms in differing levels of severity as do other child victims of sexual abuse. A 1984 study of 66 children and adolescents who had been involved in adult organized sex rings and pornographic photography indicated that three fourths of the victims had negative psychological and social adjustments following public exposure of the rings (Burgess, Hartman, McCausland, & Powers, 1984). This study further revealed that boys were the preferred gender of the adult male ring-leaders.

Based on the available data, it appears that the traumagenic factors model described by Finkelhor and Browne (1986) and the treatment methods described in this chapter are applicable in the assessment and treatment of these children and adolescents. Hartman, Burgess, & Powers (1984) discuss some of the difficulties in establishing rapport and treating adolescents who have experienced long-term exploitation by adults. These victims may be aggressive, have drug and alcohol problems, and be highly suspicious of adults. (For additional information in this area, see Burgess, 1984, and Schoettle, 1980b.)

Adults Molested as Children

Many adult women are seeking treatment for sexual abuse that occurred when they were children or adolescents. A recent survey of adult women indicates that up to 38% of the women report being sexually molested before they were 18 (Russell, 1983). Russell's study further reports that approximately 90% of the perpetrators were relatives of the victims (29%) or were known but unrelated to the victims (60%).

Numerous studies have documented the long-term effects of sexual abuse in women who present for treatment (Browne & Finkelhor, 1986a, 1986b; Lindberg & Distad, 1985; Silbert & Pines, 1983). Typical symptoms found in adult victims include sexual dysfunctions (Meiselman, 1978; Briere, 1984), depression, suicidal tendencies, anxiety and tension (Bagley & Ramsay, in press; Sedney & Brooks, 1984), guilt, disturbed interpersonal relationships, and drug and/or alcohol abuse (Browne & Finkelhor, 1986a; Gelinas, 1983). Gelinas describes these symptoms as the continuing negative effects of incest. Other authors have described adult victims as suffering from posttraumatic stress disorder or postsexual abuse syndrome (Briere, 1984; Donaldson & Gardner, 1985).

Although there is inadequate space in this chapter to thoroughly describe the assessment and treatment of adult victims, the literature does suggest that this population shows a range of severity comparable to that of child victims. That is, there will be victims who evidence severe psychopathology requiring intensive treatment, those with more moderate dysfunctions who function adequately in some areas of their lives, and those who suffer relatively mild or no repercussions from the abuse.

Although little empirical work has been done on the effectiveness of treatment with adult victims, several therapeutic modalities have been implemented and reported by clinicians to be useful. These include the use of individual counseling, behavioral techniques, and group therapy (Cole, 1985; Rychtarik, Silverman, Van Landingham, & Prue, 1984; Westerlund, 1983).

Because of the commonality of problems presented by these victims, the reported benefits of discussing issues with other victims, and the frequent lack of professionals trained to work with this population, a group therapy approach is frequently mentioned as particularly beneficial. For professionals who are asked to work with these clients, several studies discuss treatment issues and describe both short- and long-term treatment groups (Gordy, 1983; Herman & Schatzow, 1981; Tsai & Wagner, 1978).

The use of behavioral techniques with adult victims is still in the beginning stages. Although the use of systematic desensitization, cognitive behavioral therapy, and sexual dysfunction therapy have all received empirical support in the treatment of rape victims (Becker & Abel, 1981; Turner & Frank, 1981; Wolff, 1977), the use of these techniques with adults victimized as children is much more limited. It is possible that these techniques could be used to benefit adult victims. The interested clinician can find additional information in the reports of Becker and Abel (1981) and Becker and Skinner (1984).

FAMILY

Current research on the variables that influence the impact of sexual abuse indicates that the response of family members is a significant factor in determining both the short- and long-term consequences to victims (e.g., Fromuth, 1986; Peters, 1985). These studies show that victims who are believed and whose families are supportive tend to experience fewer psychological repercussions from the abuse.

The model in Figure 7.1 suggests three categories of nonabusing parents. The categories are, in reality, anchor points on a continuum. The first category (one end of the continuum) consists of those parents who have significant psychopathology. For example, one or both nonabusing parents may be psychotic, suicidal, or suffer from chronic drug or alcohol abuse. Because of their level of psychological dysfunction, these individuals would be able to participate only minimally, if at all, in treatment related to their child's victimization. Clinicians should recommend that an appropriate treatment plan be implemented that would aggressively address the areas of parental dysfunction. When the parent's condition is stabilized, an additional assessment can be made regarding the parent's increased involvement in the child's treatment.

The second category (middle range of the continuum) includes parents who are not directly involved in sexually abusing their children but whose psychological problems or dysfunctional life style may have reduced their effectiveness in preventing the abuse. Such parents may present with a range of psychological difficulties from affective and behavioral disorders to inadequate parenting skills. However, these parents are not significantly dysfunctional and could be involved productively in their child's treatment program.

In cases of intrafamilial abuse in which the perpetrator is the father, stepfather, or father surrogate, treatment issues often focus on the mother. Early studies of incest families place particular focus on the involvement of the mother (e.g., Gordon, 1955), often depicting the mother as pivotal in promoting the father-daughter sexual relationship (Gutheil & Avery, 1977). Although these descriptions may be accurate in some cases, more recent studies question these theoretical premises and the number of families that fit this description (Borgman, 1984; Dietz & Craft, 1980; Finkelhor, 1985a; McIntyre, 1981).

The idea that nonabusing mothers in incest families are likely to be a diverse group is supported by a recent study of 43 mothers of incest victims (Myer, 1985). This study indicates that the mothers fell into three groups: (a) those who denied the incest and took no action (9%), (b) those who rejected their daughters and protected their mates (35%), and (c) those who proceeded to protect their daughters and reject their mates (56%).

Myer's study indicates that the mothers in the first group (n = 4) participated in treatment reluctantly and with poor results. These women had a history of neglecting their children and were classified as having Borderline Personality Disorders. In all four cases, the children were removed from their homes. The 15 mothers in the second group were classified as having a Narcissistic Personality Disorder and were highly dependent on their partners for emotional and economic support. Few of these women were seen in treatment as they denied the abuse and gave up their children.

This study suggests that clinicians are more likely to see mothers who do offer protection to their daughters than was indicated in the earlier literature. Of the 24 women in the third group, 13 protected their daughters without ambivalence and most were involved in long-term treatment. The other 11 were initially ambivalent but eventually sided with their daughters, and the majority of them sought treatment. Most women in this group were classified as having Dependent Personality Disorders, indicating a passive style of interacting and a lack of self-confidence.

As recommended earlier, the clinician must conduct a thorough evaluation to effectively design a treatment program for all family members when child sexual abuse has occurred. Parents may need to be involved in individual, group, parent-child dyad, and family therapy to address issues of self-esteem, depression, assertiveness, parenting skills, and communication (Mayer, 1983; Sgroi, 1982b).

Although data on treatment of mothers in incestuous families is limited, Landis & Wyre (1984) briefly describe a step-by-step approach to group treatment. The issues typically addressed in the group are the fear of intimate relationships with men, distrust and anger toward men, and poor communication with daughters. The authors describe a 10-session format that addresses the dynamics of incestuous families, focuses on values clarification, and encourages more assertive behavior.

Mayer (1983) discusses the therapeutic needs of mothers in incestuous families and recommends both individual and group therapy. She suggests using a cognitive-behavioral approach to increase the women's self-esteem and improve their coping skills. Although Mayer's assumption that all mothers consciously or unconsciously know about the abuse has not been clearly established, clinicians may find her treatment suggestions useful. (For additional information on mothers in incestuous families, see Sgroi, 1982b.)

Little has been written about parents whose children were abused by nonfamily members. In the authors' experience, these children are frequently from families that fail to offer sufficient supervision or protection for their children. A significant number of the children come from single-parent homes where, because of economic and personal stresses, the child may be left with numerous sitters. As the children become older, they may be left at home unsupervised, thus increasing the risk for abuse. If the parent is unmarried, the child may be exposed to a number of adult males who may be friends of the father or dating the mother.

The nonabusing parent most often seen by the authors is an unmarried mother whose child has been abused by an adult male acquaintance of the mother's or by an adolescent in a babysitting situation. Therapy in these cases has focused on educating the mother to provide more adequate protection for the child, assisting the mother in stabilizing her work and living arrangements, and increasing the mother's ability to form more supportive interpersonal relationships with both men and women.

At the other end of the continuum are nonabusing parents who are well-adjusted and who functioned as effective, appropriate parents before the abusive incident. When the abuse was disclosed, the parents believed the child and took appropriate action to protect the child from further abuse. If the perpetrator is a stranger or only slightly known to the family, the incident is more often reported to authorities (Finkelhor, 1984).

Parents in this category respond well to short-term crisis intervention and a supportive stance by the therapist. In our experience, the issues typically raised by the parents include: (a) guilt for their perceived lack of adequate protection of the child, (b) anger at the perpetrator, (c) ambivalence over decisions on the legal aspects of the incident, and (d) fear about the long-term consequences of the abuse for the child.

In their haste to protect the child and be supportive, well-meaning parents may become too restrictive of the child's activities or too indulgent toward the child. The parents may need help setting limits in areas that they handled effectively before the abuse, such as having the child follow his or her normal bedtime routine. If a child experiences nighttime fears following an incident of abuse, parents can be encouraged to read to the child at bedtime or to leave on an additional light. One helpful technique is to have the child listen to a relaxation tape at bedtime. The clinician can develop a tape with the child or use one of several that are available commercially (e.g., Lupin, 1981).

These parents generally are responsive to a supportive stance by the therapist. They need to be reassured that their child is developing normally and that their response to the abuse is an important factor in their child's successful coping with the incident. If the abuse was short-term and nonviolent, the chances of the child's having long-term psychological dysfunctions appear to be relatively small. However, the therapist can offer to be available to the parents in the future if they become concerned about the child's behavior or development.

TREATMENT FOR SIBLINGS OF VICTIMS

Although little has been written on siblings' reactions to their brother's or sister's abuse, it is recommended that clinicians spend some time assessing these children's responses (Sgroi, 1982b). In cases of intrafamilial abuse, all the children may be removed from the home and the perpetrator placed in jail. In these cases, the siblings may be angry and blame the victim for causing the disruption to the family. At other times, children may resent the attention paid to the victim, not understanding that their brother or sister may be frightened and upset rather than pleased with the extra attention.

A report of two cases of intrafamilial abuse by Lourie (1984) indicates that all members of incestuous families suffer harm, whether they were sexually involved or not. Reactions of the siblings in these two cases included withdrawal, extreme confusion and depression, a tendency to become asexual, and in one case, a psychotic episode. Although this report is based on two highly dysfunctional families, it is likely that the siblings do experience some degree of psychological distress in response to the abuse of their brother or sister.

Following an individual interview with each sibling, the clinician may recommend that these children be seen in individual, group, sibling, or family therapy. Depending on their ages and the circumstances of the abuse, these children may need training in assertiveness, personal safety, and social skills. Other issues that these children may need to clarify are: who was responsible for the abuse, what will happen to them as a result of the abuse, and what are the long-term consequences to the family unit.

Chapter 11

Intervention with Social and Situational Factors in Sexual Abuse

TREATMENT RELATED TO SOCIAL FACTORS

In planning a comprehensive treatment approach for families in which sexual abuse has occurred, certain social factors must be addressed. As described in previous chapters, the severity of these factors falls along a continuum, with the social factors in some families significantly contributing to the abusive situation while having only minimal relevance in other families. Based on a thorough evaluation, the structure and living style of some families will be seen as significantly dysfunctional. The families are often described as multiproblem families whose treatment and case management may involve personnel from several social service and mental health agencies (Sgroi, 1982b). These families will be viewed as high risk for abuse to recur, and it is likely that the children will be removed from the parents' custody. In such cases the parents often adamantly deny that the abuse occurred and refuse to enter treatment.

In the mid-range of severity are families who present with dysfunctions in social areas that can be productively addressed in therapy. These families may be lacking in appropriate social contacts and a supportive network or be a blended or reconstituted family (Finkelhor & Baron, 1986a; Russell, 1984). In working with families that are socially isolated, therapists need to assist the family as a whole and the individual members to increase their social networks. This may be done by reestablishing ties with members of the extended family, joining a support group such as Parents Anonymous or Parents Without Partners, or attending a church in the neighborhood.

In addition to family activities, the peer relationships of sexual abuse victims need to be carefully assessed as three studies have indicated that these children are isolated from their peers (e.g., Finkelhor & Baron, 1986a). Whether this isolation is a cause or a result of the abuse is not clear, but it does appear that victims need assistance in increasing their social contacts and peer relationships.

If the victim is young, therapists might recommend that he or she attend a nursery school, Headstart program, or other day-care facility on a regular basis. If the parents join a support group, the children often play in groups while the parents meet separately. For school-aged children, the therapist can assess their interests and recommend the child be involved in an after-school sports program, an organization such as the Blue Birds or Cub Scouts, or a church group such as the youth choir.

Adolescents who have not developed normal peer relationships may be more reluctant to join group activities initially. They may need training in social skills and how to establish friendships. It may be recommended that they form one or two friendships with peers and then move to group activites at a later date. (For information on social skills training, see Hops, Finch, & McConnell, 1985.)

An increasingly significant social factor that appears to be related to the incidence of child sexual abuse is the number of reconstituted or blended families. Although the degree of risk to the children in step-families has not been clearly established (Finkelhor & Baron, 1986a; Giles-Sims & Finkelhor, 1984), several studies have confirmed the increased risk for children with the absence of a biologically related father or the presence of a stepfather, or both (e.g., Finkelhor & Baron, 1986a; Gruber & Jones, 1983). A study by Russell (1984) surveyed adult women and found that 2.3% had been sexually abused by their natural fathers, whereas 17% had been abused by their stepfathers.

In working with blended families, therapists need to be aware of the parenting and marital issues that may differentially impact treatment planning, such as disciplining children, parental expectations, divided loyalties, and expression of affection between step-siblings (Visher & Visher, 1979). Parents in these families may benefit from joining groups that deal specifically with problems encountered by blended families, such as those sponsored by the Stepfamily Association of America, Inc. (900 Welch Road, Suite 400, Palo Alto, CA 94304). Therapists may also want to recommend that the family read and discuss books such as *The Boys and Girls Book About Stepfamilies* (Gardner, 1982).

At the other end of the continuum are families that have only minimal problems in the area of social functioning. These children and families will have adequate social support systems and will not be seen as isolated or socially dysfunctional. Although a child or adolescent in these families may tend to withdraw from friends or social activities following an incident of sexual abuse, they generally recover within a short period and are able to resume their normal activities.

TREATMENT FOR SITUATIONAL FACTORS

As in most of the literature on sexual abuse, there is little empirical data on situational factors that are consistently correlated with abuse. However, based on children's reports and surveys of adults who were abused as children, certain situations do appear to place a child at higher risk for initial abuse or for abuse to recur. These include factors related to the parental relationship, the supervision provided for the child, and the living arrangements within the home (Finkelhor & Baron 1986a; Gruber & Jones, 1983).

As outlined in the evaluation procedures in Figure 7.1, the therapist should carefully assess the home situation and living arrangements of the family. In certain families, numerous factors will be present that place a child at considerable risk for abuse. These factors include the frequent absence of parents for long periods of time, leaving the children in an unstructured, unsupervised condition, or a parental relationship that is so chaotic that little attention or care is extended to the children. Based on a thorough evaluation of the family situation, the therapist may decide to consult with the Child Protective Service worker involved regarding the temporary placement of the child or children in a more secure environment.

In other families, therapists can help parents to see the importance of providing more appropriate supervision for their child during outdoor play, after-school hours, or at family get-togethers. Children may need to check in more frequently with their parents during play times or parents may need to more closely monitor the children's activities. Additionally, parents may organize or ask that a neighborhood school, church, or youth facility offer an after-school program for children whose parents are employed.

Another factor that needs to be discussed with parents is the choice of babysitters. Reports from treatment programs for adolescent sex offenders indicate that boys frequently molest children in babysitting situations (Knopp, 1982). Additionally, the authors have worked with children molested by their female babysitter. There have also been widely publicized cases in which day-care staff have molested children in their care. To help prevent such abuse, parents should carefully interview potential caretakers for their children and be alert to any physical or behavioral signs in the child that problems may be occurring.

If both parents are working, it is possible that the children may be left alone with the perpetrator, usually the father, while the mother is working a different shift. Therapists need to assess this factor and make certain that the victim and other children in the family who may be potential victims are receiving adequate protection. It may be necessary for parents to change work shifts or for an additional adult to supervise the children while the nonabusing parent is at work. With older children, it may also be helpful for the victim to have a lock on the bedroom door that can be used when the nonabusing parent is away from home.

An additional factor in the family's living arrangements that should be evaluated is the sleeping arrangements of the family members. Because of lack of space or for convenience, children may have been allowed to sleep with their parents, in beds together, or with other family members, thus increasing the risk of abuse. This may be particularly problematic when friends or family members come for overnight visits. The therapist can assist the parents in planning the sleeping arrangements so that each child has a safe area that eliminates the risk of abuse. Younger children may feel more comfortable sleeping in the same room with an older sibling following an abusive incident. However, the therapist should discuss this with the sibling and make certain that the younger child will not be teased, resented, or subjected to further abuse.

Part IV
Prevention

Chapter 12

Prevention of Physical and Sexual Abuse of Children

Prevention efforts aimed at reducing the incidence of social problems tend to follow a relatively predictable course. The process begins when a social issue gradually becomes recognized as a problem and a few individuals organize to call public and professional attention to the situation. If the problem is life-threatening, as in cases of severe child abuse, aggressive prevention efforts are implemented. These efforts usually focus on protecting the victim and informing groups thought to be at risk so that protective measures can be taken.

Over time, funds are obtained to develop research projects and the problem area is further delineated. Based on the research findings, assumptions about causation are developed and empirically tested. The more clearly the causative factors can be isolated and identified, the more effective prevention efforts tend to be.

When the problem is a disease such as polio or tuberculosis, the progressive course of preventive efforts based on causation or contributory factors can be clearly followed. For example, the production and dissemination of an effective vaccine to prevent the occurrence of the disease may be the goal of the prevention process. However, when the problem is a complex social phenomenon such as the sexual or physical abuse of children, causative or contributory factors are much more difficult to delineate. As a result, prevention efforts are hampered by a lack of clearcut variables or etiologic factors on which to base effective intervention.

Primary prevention reflects those efforts directed towards ensuring that difficulties do not develop by having an impact on a large segment of the population independent of their level of risk for the particular difficulty. In the prevention of child abuse, primary prevention typically takes the form of approaches that strive either to enhance parental competencies, coping skills, and resources, or to reduce psychological difficulties that could potentially lead to an at-risk situation. Efforts to prevent physical abuse might include parent education classes for groups of expectant parents or programs to enhance parent-child bonding in the first days after delivery. Current primary prevention programs in sexual abuse include increasing the public's awareness of the problem, providing information to parents and professionals, and implementing personal safety programs for children.

Secondary prevention differs in that it focuses on the identification of high-risk groups and attempts to intervene with such individuals or groups so that the potential problem will be avoided. High-risk factors can be identified from a combination of conceptual and theoretical understanding of etiology and from empirical assessment studies. For example, in the area of physical abuse, some of the factors that are related to an increased probability of child maltreatment are high levels of stress, a lack of financial resources, unemployment, social isolation, and an adolescent parent.

Secondary prevention efforts might include screening parents using a pediatrics clinic to identify those who exhibit such factors and offering classes or services to reduce their level of risk.

Although less is known about risk factors in child sexual abuse, several factors have been delineated and studied (Finkelhor & Baron, 1986a, 1986b; Russell, 1984). Current findings indicate that girls are at higher risk than boys, and particularly girls who have lived without their natural fathers, whose mothers are employed outside the home, or who have witnessed conflict between their parents. Secondary efforts to prevent sexual abuse could include offering services or educational opportunities to girls and families considered to be at risk for sexual abuse.

Tertiary prevention represents after-the-fact attempts to ensure that abuse will not recur. The treatment sections of this book describe a variety of tertiary approaches for physical and sexual abuse.

A comprehensive approach to the prevention of child abuse has been developed by the National Committee for Prevention of Child Abuse (NCPCA), a nonprofit, volunteer-based organization with chapters in all 50 states. The NCPCA has provided national leadership in the areas of education and training activities, public awareness, research and evaluation projects, service programs, and advocacy. Focusing on primary and secondary prevention efforts, the NCPCA has identified various components that contribute to a comprehensive approach to child abuse prevention. The components include community-based projects such as education programs for parents, programs for abused children, self-help groups, life skills training for children and young adults, and continued public education on child abuse prevention. Other national organizations involved in the prevention of child abuse are the American Humane Association, the Child Welfare League of America, and the National Center for Child Abuse and Neglect.

Numerous programs to prevent child sexual abuse, physical abuse, and neglect have been developed and implemented throughout the United States. However, these programs are frequently lacking in adequate procedures to evaluate their impact. To establish the effectiveness of a program, a prevention project should include appropriate methodology (including comparison groups) and adequate measures of outcome. Additionally, a follow-up assessment of individuals who participated in the prevention program is necessary to assess the long-term effects of the intervention. Ultimately, the project must document a reduction in the incidence of child abuse and neglect.

The models presented in Figures 2.1 and 7.1 can be useful in understanding the necessity for a broad approach to prevention efforts. Interventions can be planned for each of the areas involved in an abusive situation: the offenders, nonabusing parents, the victims, and social and situational factors. The goal of prevention programs is to prevent offenders from their first act of abusive or neglectful behavior. During the period in which research studies are attempting to delineate causative and contributory factors involved in child abuse, prevention efforts may be targeted toward groups of at-risk victims. Based on empirical findings, later efforts are more likely to be geared towards interventions with at-risk offender groups.

When we examine the prevention of physical and sexual abuse from an historical perspective, an important discrepancy becomes apparent. Whereas research literature on physical abuse has been fairly abundant since the late 1960s, it has been only in the last 5 to 10 years that research in sexual abuse has come to the forefront. As a result, etiology and risk factors are better developed for physical abuse than for sexual abuse. Because preventive efforts depend on these two dimensions, current approaches to prevention are divergent.

This is particularly evident in the case of the perpetrator. Much is already known about the factors that increase the probability that an individual will physically abuse a child as well as the process by which this type of abuse most often occurs. In contrast, there is relatively little consistent data on at-risk factors associated with the perpetrator of sexual abuse. Although physical abuse prevention programs focus on the perpetrator, sexual abuse programs presently are unable to do so and therefore direct their efforts to the potential child victims. As research on the etiology of sexual abuse continues to grow, the possible prevention approaches will expand.

This chapter will briefly describe primary and secondary prevention programs designed for children, parents, offenders, professionals, and the general public. If available, research data related to the efficacy of the prevention approaches will be included.

PREVENTION OF PHYSICAL ABUSE

Over the past 10 years, the proliferation of literature examining causal factors in the occurrence of physical child abuse has provided a fertile basis for the development of preventive efforts. Despite the breadth of this literature, reports on programs intended to prevent physical abuse remain predominantly anecdotal. In fact, after surveying 400 articles, Helfer (1982) indicated that only 10 met the criteria for having both a prevention and a research focus. A more recent review by Rosenberg & Reppucci (1985) echoed this finding by stating that, "preventive approaches . . . will go no further until evaluation of prevention programs is taken as seriously as the ideas that formulate the programs" (p. 583). The discussion in the pages to follow will present representative efforts focused at reducing the incidence of abuse by targeting the victim of abuse, the perpetrator of abuse, and the general public, as well as significant professionals.

Prevention Efforts with Potential Victims

Programs directed towards potential victims represent the weakest area of efforts in the existing prevention literature. In part, this may reflect the persistent attitude of discipline as a private matter that should not be dealt with by persons outside the family. This difficulty is further complicated by varying definitions of appropriate versus inappropriate discipline practices. As a result, programs intended to educate children on what forms of parental discipline constitute physical abuse have been undertaken cautiously, out of concern that they might be perceived as inadvertently encouraging children to defy the appropriate authority of their parents. This is not to suggest that such programs are not in place, but rather that they are few in number and even fewer have been evaluated. The *Resource Book* distributed at the Seventh National Conference on Child Abuse and Neglect (1985) identified only three programs of this type.

Often programs take a broader "Personal Safety" approach. Children are taught a variety of skills that include what they should do in an emergency, how to reduce stress, decision-making, problem-solving, and assertiveness, as well as skills more directly related to reducing abuse (e.g., telling the difference between discipline and abuse, when to seek help and where, and how to avoid triggering abuse). Often skills are taught in preschool and elementary school classes. In many cases, programs use a multiple impact approach, with personal safety representing only one component. Typically, community awareness and parent education efforts complement personal safety programs.

Prevention Efforts Directed Towards the Perpetrator

Prevention programs for potential perpetrators have become very popular in the last 5 years. These approaches have been diverse in nature and have had both primary and secondary prevention goals. These programs have been developed from empirical studies that have identified skills deficits and risk factors that have been associated with an increased incidence of physical abuse. Related factors include inadequate early bonding, lack of social support, excessive stress, excessive child care demands, poor child management skills, and inappropriate developmental expectations. Programs can be characterized as having either a "Competency Enhancement" or "Support" emphasis.

Competency Enhancement. Competency enhancement programs strive to remediate key parental deficits (see Rosenberg & Reppucci, 1985). Such approaches have been used as both primary and secondary prevention initiatives. Live theater and televised skits modeling appropriate child management approaches to children's misbehavior represent an effective primary prevention approach. Gray (1983c) describes the use of live street theater to reach parents who do not typically come into contact with traditional service systems. Videotaped skits as well as live performances were offered in a variety of settings that included state fairs, well child clinics, community service offices, shopping centers, and a high school for teenage parents. Presentations offered alternative childrearing approaches to physical punishment, assertive problem-solving, and the use of natural support systems to reduce stress. Program evaluation data suggested that the skits that dealt directly with child behavior management issues had the greatest impact, with the demonstration of time-out being particularly potent.

Although this live theater was directed toward the general public, a number of efforts have appeared in the literature that were intended to have impact on particular high-risk groups. These groups included young adults who may be future parents (Morris, 1977), first-time parents (Cooper, Dreznick, & Rowe, 1982), and specific cultural groups (Alvy & Rosen, 1980). These programs focused on teaching parenting skills, offering developmental information, and teaching coping strategies to reduce stress. Gray (1983b) reported on successful programs of this nature with Hispanic and Asian parents.

A final intervention approach attempts to facilitate bonding by encouraging increased contact between parents and their child following delivery (Klaus & Kennell, 1976). The approach typically involves either rooming-in or increasing the number of hours that parents have contact with their child during the first days after delivery. To date, finding on the impact of this approach on bonding have been contradictory (O'Connor, Vietze, Sherrod, Sandler, & Altemeier, 1980; Cohen, Gray, & Wald, 1984; Gray, 1983a), suggesting the need for further research in this area.

Support. Support-oriented efforts entail bolstering parents' support networks and increasing their availability, enhancing parents' ability to use such supports, and reducing demands that result in overwhelming levels of stress. Such programs take on many forms and affect varying numbers of parents. These programs, however, are typically intended as secondary prevention efforts focusing on identified high-risk groups.

Parents Anonymous (PA) groups represent the most popular form of social support available to the abusive population. Local groups are part of a national network that is organized around a self-help charter. Group members use only their first names and attendance is on an as-needed basis. The size and activity level of local chapters can vary considerably and it is not uncommon for participants to informally exchange phone numbers and develop friendships. Many parents seem to benefit from their participation in PA, receiving necessary support and understanding from others who have experienced similar difficulties.

Crisis nurseries and relief nurseries represent another form of support-oriented service available in many communities to at-risk and abusive parents. (See Beezley & McQuiston, 1977, for an excellent discussion of practical considerations.) These programs typically offer day-care facilities for children as well as crisis intervention services for parents. In some cases, nurseries offer prearranged therapeutic preschool programs reflecting a set number of hours each week. For example, the "Lane County Relief Nursery" in Eugene, Oregon, provides a 6-hour program to low-income, at-risk, and abusive parents, which emphasizes building self-esteem, behavior management, and educational stimulation (NCCAN/NCPCA Resource Book, 1985). Other programs function strictly as a crisis nursery offering their services to parents when they can no longer cope with parental demands. In almost all cases, trained counselors are available to ensure that the nursery remains therapeutic and avoids facilitating a parent's abdication of his or her parental responsibility.

The efficacy of home visitation and parent aid programs with parents at risk for abuse was demonstrated in a series of studies conducted by Gray and associates (Gray, Cutler, Dean, & Kempe, 1976; Gray & Kaplan, 1980). These studies indicated that comprehensive pediatric follow-up by a health visitor significantly reduced the incidence of abuse in an at-risk group of parents when they were compared to parents receiving routine pediatric care. Positive results were also reported by Olds (1984) who began following teenage parents during the prenatal period. Olds (1984) made available free transportation to regular prenatal and well care visits, screening services, and nurse home visits through the pregnancy and the first 2 years of the child's life. Promising secondary prevention results have also been reported by DiAgustino (1980) with his "Parent to Parent" program. The Parent to Parent program trains volunteers who have been identified for their appropriate parenting skills and assigns them to a high-risk and abusive parents. Volunteers make weekly home visits and attempt to model appropriate parenting skills as well as offering support.

A final support-oriented approach which has received attention in the literature, involves providing support through the use of telephone hotlines and walk-in centers. Although most hotlines were conceptualized as preventive resources to reduce the incidence of abuse, findings indicate that a very small percentage of the contact are primary prevention-stress reduction calls (Boratynski, 1983). Such was the case when calls received by the Connecticut Child Welfare Association's (1978) "Care-Line" were examined. Less than 1% of the calls were found to be of a primary prevention nature, with 40% of the callers reporting abuse and neglect and the remaining 59% seeking information and referral. Because of the paucity of callers seeking preventive services, Michigan's "Warm-Line" reduced its program to an answering service (Gray, 1983b). This may be more of a generalized problem, suggesting that hotline approaches are not feasible unless prevention constitutes only one of a number of programmatic goals. Finally, a neighborhood walk-in center in England is described by Pillai, Collins, & Morgan (1982). The clients were primarily self-referred and the center was staffed by volunteers, a family case-worker, and a play therapist. Center staff provided mostly advice and counseling, with a secondary emphasis on informal networking. Results of an evaluation of the center's first 50 clients indicated improvements in child care and/or parent-child relationships for 37% of the clients.

Preventive Efforts with the General Public and Professionals

Many of the efforts directed toward the general public overlap those already mentioned with regard to the potential perpetrator. The purpose of prevention programs developed to affect the general public typically assume one of two directions. They are intended either as primary prevention programs to reduce the probability of persons in the "general public" becoming abusive or as attempts to facilitate the reporting of abuse by neighbors, friends, and family. To a lesser degree, programs are also available that represent secondary prevention goals.

Live theater and media campaigns (national and statewide) represent the most common approaches to primary prevention. As stated previously, modeling appropriate child management techniques and offering alternatives to physical punishment constitute much of the content conveyed in the live theater productions. Equally effective is the use of videotaped presentations or films to large community groups or school groups. Goals may be similar to those of live theater or may be oriented towards reducing risk factors that may later predispose a person to become abusive (e.g., increased stress). A national media campaign sponsored by the National Committee for Prevention of Child Abuse attempts to offer alternatives to abuse by using the theme of "ten things to do other than hitting your child." Similar programs are often sponsored by state and local groups. Although evaluation research has been inadequate to determine their relative effectiveness, these approaches reach a large segment of the population and seem to show considerable promise.

With the advent of a national hotline for anonymously reporting abuse in 1975, additional attention has been directed towards increasing reports of abuse. Some states have taken an active approach in facilitating abuse reporting through the use of local media campaigns. Florida, for example, used a series of posters and billboards urging the public to become involved in protecting children by reporting maltreatment. Although reports continue to increase in number, there remains the question of whether such efforts also increase the stigma associated with being an "abusive parent."

An often neglected focus of prevention programs is the professional. Given what we know about risk factors associated with physical abuse, we would expect many professionals to have contact with parents who either have the potential for or are actively abusing their children. Case workers administering "Aid to Families with Dependent Children" (AFDC), public health nurses, teachers, day-care workers, and mental health professionals constitute some of the logical targets of preventive efforts, yet physicians represent the vast majority of those who receive such information.

The focus on physicians may be attributed in part to the realization that physicians are likely to frequently be in a position to spot injuries that may have been caused by abuse and seem to underreport relative to their contact with such cases. (See Morris, Johnson, & Clasen, 1985, for a discussion of potential reasons for this phenomena.) Schmitt (1980) has suggested that physicians can stabilize dysfunctional families by providing anticipatory guidance, additional follow-up during difficult developmental stages or stressful acute illnesses, and helping parents feel successful in their role. Physicians also play an important role in early contract/bonding programs.

Because there remains some question as to the physician's awareness of issues associated with physical abuse, the most active approaches to prevention with professionals seem to have assumed the goal of increasing physicians' information and awareness. A "partnership" formed by the Medical Association of Georgia and the Georgia Department of Human Resources, called "It's OK to Tell," has designed and distributed a pamphlet entitled, "The Physician's Role in Preventing and Reporting Child Abuse." The pamphlet contains information on the incidence of abuse in Georgia, types of abuse and neglect, how to understand the parent, medical personnels' duty to report, how to make a report, the involvement of medical personnel following a report, and the role of medical personnel in preventing child abuse and neglect. The partnership has also distributed a handbook and slide show to medical societies throughout the state of Georgia to further inform physicians.

A self-instructional program, entitled "Diagnosis and Management of Physical Abuse of Children," has been developed by Charles F. Johnson, M. D., and Jacy Showers, Ed. D. (Child Abuse Program, Children's Hospital, Columbus, Ohio, 1985). A number of factors make this program unique, including the self-instructional format, the use of high quality color photographs, the inclusion of handbook evaluation forms, and the availability of Continuing Medical Education Credit (if pre-post questionnaires are completed and returned).

PREVENTION OF CHILD SEXUAL ABUSE

The prevention of child sexual abuse is a relatively new field that developed from a grassroots movement in the late 1970s. By 1980, federal funds from the National Center for Child Abuse and Neglect (NCCAN) were being funneled into local treatment projects begun by a variety of professionals such as rape crisis counselors, child advocates, district attorneys, police departments, physicians, and social service or mental health agencies. Although the establishment of treatment programs for victims and offenders continued to be a priority for professional efforts, the implementation of prevention programs is a major focus of the movement to deal with child sexual abuse. Articles reviewing prevention programs and bibliographies of child sexual abuse prevention resources are available that will be useful to those planning prevention programs

(Deitrich, 1981; Finkelhor, 1986; Finkelhor & Araji, 1983; Mayer, 1985; NCPCA, 1985; Schroeder, Gordon, & McConnell, 1986; Stuart & Stuart, 1983).

Prevention Efforts with the General Public and Professionals

A beginning step in any prevention program is to raise the general public's awareness of the problem and to increase professionals' knowledge in detecting and treating victims. The mass media plays a pivotal role in reaching the public with an accurate picture of a problematic situation. The nationwide showing on television of films such as "Something About Amelia," "Men Who Molest," and "One Terrific Guy," along with coverage on programs such as "60 Minutes" and "20/20" are effective in raising the general viewer's knowledge about child sexual abuse. In the last 3 years, most major magazines have carried feature articles on the sexual abuse of children (e.g., *Life* and *Time*). Although there has been no formal assessment of public knowledge on sexual abuse, it is generally assumed that the average person's awareness of child sexual abuse is greater today than it was 5 to 10 years ago.

Professionals who have contact with children, such as teachers, physicians, school counselors, clergy, day-care personnel, police, and mental health staff, can also have an important impact on prevention efforts. Although these professional groups as well as child protection workers have received training in child sexual abuse in recent years, the training has dealt mostly with detection and treatment rather than prevention. Increasing these professionals' knowledge in the area of prevention techniques could be an additional method of affecting the external factors that may prevent abuse (Mayer, 1985).

Prevention Efforts with Potential Victims

The current major effort in the prevention of child sexual abuse is to teach potential victims how to protect themselves from being abused. This focus reflects the current status of knowledge about preventing sexual abuse. As described earlier, the initial stages of preventive efforts frequently focus on populations thought to be at risk. This is to offer information about protection to potential victims while the cause of the problem is being studied. Because of the reported widespread prevalence of child sexual abuse (Peters, Wyatt, & Finkelhor, 1986), it is thought that most children, and particularly girls, are at substantial risk to be sexually abused. Therefore, one current priority is to educate large numbers of children and adolescents in self-protection techniques through school-based programs.

These programs address the third factor (child victim) in the model presented in Figure 7.1. Programs for children emphasize increasing the child's resistance, which is the fourth factor in Finkelhor's four preconditions of sexual abuse. Using a variety of media approaches, numerous films, plays, books, and school safety programs have been developed for both children and adolescents.

The basic theme of these materials is education: what sexual abuse is, who might be offenders, and what action a child should take if someone tries to sexually abuse him or her. The most widely used programs, such as "Talking About Touching: A Personal Safety Curriculum" (Harms & James, 1984), or "Child Sexual Abuse Prevention Project: An Educational Program for Children" (Kent, 1979), have several features in common. The programs generally use humor and an entertaining format, present milder forms of abuse to decrease the possibility of frightening children, incorporate analogies and metaphors, minimize specific sexual subject matter, emphasize reporting of abuse, and focus on learning concepts rather than behavioral skills.

The studies conducted to date on child sexual abuse prevention programs have assessed the program's effectiveness in conveying information to children, that is, are children more knowledgeable about sexual abuse and the appropriate action to take if they have participated in a personal safety or sexual abuse prevention program. These studies indicate that various approaches such as videotapes, plays, and personal safety curricula are effective in increasing children's knowledge about sexual abuse and appropriate preventive measures to take (Brassard, Tyler, & Kehle, 1983; Conte, Rosen, Saperstein, & Shermack, 1985; Garbarino, 1987; Saslawsky & Wurtele, 1986; Swan, Press, & Briggs, 1985; Wolfe, MacPherson, Blount, & Wolfe, 1986; Woods & Dean, 1985). A recent study compared the use of a filmed program with a Behavioral Skills Training (BST) program in which behavioral rehearsal, modeling, and social reinforcement were used to teach safety skills (Wurtele, Saslawsky, Miller, Marrs, & Britcher, 1986). The BST program was found to be more effective than the film alone, and the knowledge and skills learned by the children were maintained at a 3 month follow-up assessment.

However, although it is thought that children who are more knowledgeable about sexual abuse are less likely to be abused, this has not yet been empirically established. Little is known about the behavioral effects of prevention programs, that is, do children report abuse more frequently, and so forth. Future studies are needed to assess such issues as children's retention of information over time, prevention program effects

on reporting or disclosure rates, the comparative effectiveness of programs with different populations, and, ultimately, the effects of prevention programs on the incidence of child sexual abuse. (For a review of
prevention and research programs in child sexual abuse, see Finkelhor,
1986.)

Prevention Materials for Parents

Other materials have been developed to provide information to parents
on child sexual abuse. Parents are seen as an important factor in the
prevention effort as they can provide information to their children on an
ongoing basis, as opposed to what may be a one-time classroom presentation. Pamphlets and books, such as *A Better Safe Than Sorry Book: A
Family Guide for Sexual Assault Prevention* (Gordon & Gordon, 1984), or
Sanford's (1980) *The Silent Children: A Parent's Guide to the Prevention of
Sexual Abuse*, have been designed to help parents present prevention
information to their children on an individual basis. To date, no studies
have been conducted on the effectiveness of parental interventions in the
prevention of child sexual abuse.

Prevention efforts geared towards parents address the nonabusing parental factor in the model presented in Figure 7.1 and the third factor in
Finkelhor's model (1984), increasing external inhibitors to sexual abuse.
Through education and awareness of situations that may put their child
at higher risk for abuse, parents can become more effective in reducing
an offender's access to their child. They can, for example, increase their
supervision of the child during neighborhood play, rearrange sleeping or rooming conditions that might be conducive to inappropriate
sexual behavior between family members, and carefully check the child's
day-care and babysitting arrangements. (For additional materials developed for parents, see NCPCA, 1985.)

Prevention Materials for Offenders

Notably lacking are materials or programmatic approaches geared
towards preventing individuals from becoming sexual offenders. As
early as 1979, Swift recommended that prevention efforts be focused on
males who had been sexually abused themselves as children or who were
sexually uninformed and socially immature. However, as noted earlier,
recent prevention efforts have centered on teaching children about avoiding sexual abuse, and little research has dealt with primary or secondary
prevention efforts with potential offenders.

Programs to impact potential offenders could be designed to intervene
in the first two factors in Finkelhor's (1984) model: factors related to the

motivation to sexually abuse and factors related to the offender's internal inhibitors to abuse. Unfortunately, a great deal has yet to be learned about the etiology of sexually assaultive behavior and the internal and external factors that may contribute to its occurrence. Recently, however, professional attention has begun to focus more intently on developing prevention efforts for potential offenders. In 1985, NCPCA sponsored a Wingspread Conference entitled, "Preventing Child Sexual Abuse: A Focus on the Potential Perpetrator." Fifteen expert researchers and practitioners met to discuss and develop a comprehensive strategy designed to prevent potential molesters from sexually abusing children (Cohn, Finkelhor, & Holmes, 1985). The conference members suggested specific improvement in the areas of public awareness; education for parents, professionals, children, and adolescents; improved programs for victims and offenders; legal reforms; and a strong focus on research projects to assess prevention effectiveness.

One interesting suggestion for prevention efforts geared towards actual or potential offenders is a media campaign that would be similar to the current emphasis on drunk driving. The message would convey that: abuse is a crime; abuse is chronic unless you get help; children are hurt by sexual abuse; there is a number where you can get help; and so forth. Following up on this idea, Smith and Conte (1985) interviewed 175 male sexual offenders in a community-based clinic to assess the offenders' opinions about such an approach. This study indicated that:

1. 90% of the offenders thought such a message would have an effect on their abusive behavior, particularly just before or after their first offense;
2. 40% thought it might prevent them from molesting;
3. television was the recommended medium;
4. the message should come from an offender or victim rather than a celebrity or athlete;
5. the content should be direct and concrete;
6. the focus should be on consequences to the offender rather than on consequences to the victim;
7. the message should include a number where offenders can get help.

Some sample messages written by offenders were:

"I am a sex offender. I was discovered 2 years ago. My entire family has been hurt. I have been to jail and had to pay numerous fines and court costs. I am presently in treatment. That is not cheap either. I hope to be cured and to learn to control my problem. It hasn't been easy. I wish I never would have started. I knew what I was doing was wrong at the time and I should have stopped. Please don't go through what I've gone through. Seek help and stop. Believe me, it's just not worth it" (p. 5).

or

"You may be telling yourself that you need to be loved, that you are showing this child love, that you are teaching him or her about sex. You say that
this will be the last time because what you know is not right and you should
not be harming this child. But you know, as I do, that it won't be the last
time. This sexual deviancy is very strong and harmful and you are unable
to control it without the help of professional counseling. Just stop and think
back on the other times you have said it will be the last time" (p. 6).

FUTURE DIRECTIONS IN THE
PREVENTION OF CHILD ABUSE

Prevention efforts in the future should be tied closely to research efforts
that attempt to delineate causative and contributory factors of abusive
behavior (Garbarino, 1986). Explanatory models, such as Finkelhor's
(1984) in sexual abuse or Vasta's (1982) in physical abuse, are potentially
useful in directing the focus of intervention.

Although numerous prevention programs have been implemented
and are subjectively seen as helpful, more stringent evaluation procedures need to be implemented to assess program effectiveness. Several
methodological problems need to be corrected, such as the increased use
of carefully selected comparison groups and better selection of outcome
measures. Future studies should assess changes in behavior as well as
changes in attitudes or knowledge about abuse (Lorian, 1983). Additionally, studies should be designed to assess both short-term goals (acquired
knowledge) and long-term goals (reduced incidence of abuse).

Heller, Price, and Sher (1980) recommended that prevention programs
be designed to intervene on a variety of risk factors, such as age and
educational level of the parent, offender, and child; the level of stress in
the family; attendance at parent education classes; and previous victimization. Were this done, a well-designed study could then determine the
combination of factors predictive of abusive behavior. Obviously, this
would call for the commitment of substantial funding to a long-term
study with a relatively large sample. The benefits of such a commitment,
however, could be profound for future generations of potential victims
of abuse.

References

Abel, G. G., Becker, J. V., Cunningham-Rathner, J., Rouleau, J. L., Kaplan, M., & Reich, J. (1984). *The treatment of child molesters.* New York: Columbia University Press.

Abel, G. G., Becker, J. V., & Skinner, L. J. (1985). Behavioral approaches to treatment of the violent sex offender. In L. H. Roth (Ed.), *Clinical treatment of the violent person* (pp. 100–123). (DHHS Publication No. ADM 85–1396). National Institute of Mental Health. Rockville, MD: U.S. Department of Health and Human Services.

Abel, G. G., Blanchard, E. B., & Becker, J. V. (1978). An integrated treatment program for rapists. In R. T. Rada (Ed.), *Clinical aspects of the rapist* (pp. 161–214). New York: Grune & Stratton, Inc.

Abel, G. G., Mittelman, M., & Becker, J. V. (1985). Sex offenders: Results of assessment and recommendations for treatment. In H. H. Ben-Aron, S. I. Hucker, & C. D. Webster (Eds.), *Clinical criminology: Assessment and treatment of criminal behavior* (pp. 191–205). Toronto: M & M Graphics.

Abidin, R. R. (1983). *Parenting Stress Index,* Charlottesville, VA: Pediatric Psychology Press.

Adams, H. E., Tollison, C. D., & Carson, T. P. (1981). Behavior therapy with sexual deviations. In S. M. Turner, K. S. Calhoun, & H. E. Adams (Eds.), *Handbook of clinical behavior therapy* (pp. 318–346). New York: John Wiley & Sons.

Ageton, S. S. (1983). *Sexual assault among adolescents.* Lexington, MA: Lexington Books.

Aguilera, D. C., & Messick, J. M. (1978). *Crisis intervention* (3rd ed.). St. Louis, MO: C. V. Mosby Co.

Alberti, R. E., & Emmons, M. L. (1982). *Your perfect right* (4th ed.). San Luis Obispo, CA: Impact Publishers.

Allen, K., Hart, B., Buell, J., Harris, F., & Wolf, M. (1964). Effects of social reinforcement on isolate behavior of a nursery school child. *Child Development, 35,* 511–518.

Allen, R., & Wasserman, G. (1985). Origins of language delay in abused infants. *Child Abuse and Neglect, 9,* 335–340.

Alvy, K., & Rosen, L. (1980). *Personnel for parent development program. Report number Two. A controlled study of parent training effects with poverty-level Black and Mexican-American parents.* Studio City, CA: Center for the Improvement of Child Caring.

American Association for Protecting Children, Inc. (1985). *Highlights of official child neglect and abuse reporting 1983.* Denver, CO: The American Humane Association.

American Medical Association Council on Scientific Affairs (1985). Diagnostic and treatment guidelines concerning child abuse and neglect. *Journal of the American Medical Association, 254,* 796–800.

American Psychiatric Association. (1980). *Diagnostic and statistical manual of mental disorders* (3rd edition). Washington, D.C.: Author.

Amir, M. (1971). *Patterns of forcible rape.* Chicago: University of Chicago Press.

Anderson, E., & Burgess, R. (1977). *Interaction patterns between same-and-opposite gender parents and children in abusive and nonabusive families.* Paper presented at the annual meeting of the Association for the Advancement of Behavior Therapy, Atlanta, GA.

Annis, L. V. (1982). A residential treatment program for male sex offenders. *International Journal of Offender Therapy and Comparative Criminology, 26,* 223–234.

Araji, S., & Finkelhor, D. (1986). Abusers: A review of the research. In D. Finkelhor & Associates (Eds.), *A sourcebook on child sexual abuse* (pp. 89–118). Beverly Hills, CA: Sage Publications.

Arkowitz, H. (1977). Measurement and modification of minimal dating behavior. In M. Hersen, R. Eisler, & P. Miller (Eds.), *Progress in behavior modification,* (Vol. 5.) New York, Academic Press.

Asher, R. (1951). Munchausen's syndrome. *The Lancet,* Feb. 10, 339–341.

Awad, G. A., Saunders, E., & Levene, J. (1984). A clinical study of male adolescent sexual offenders. *International Journal of Offender Therapy and Comparative Criminology, 28,* 105–116.

Azar, S., Fantuzzo, J., & Twentyman, C. (1984). An applied behavioral approach to child maltreatment: Back to basics. *Advances in Behavior Research and Therapy, 6,* 56–62.

Azar, S., Robinson, D., Hekimian, E., & Twentyman, C. (1984). Unrealistic expectations and problem-solving ability in maltreating and comparison mothers. *Journal of Consulting and Clinical Psychology, 52,* 687–691.

Bagley, C., & Ramsay, R. (in press). Disrupted childhood and vulnerability to sexual assault: Long-term sequels with implications for counseling. *Social Work & Human Sexuality.*

Bakan, D. (1971). *Slaughter of the innocents: A study of the battered child phenomenon.* San Francisco, CA: Jossey-Bass, Inc.

Baldwin, J. A., & Oliver, J. E. (1975). Epidemiology and family characteristics of severely abused children. *British Journal of Preventive Social Medicine, 29,* 205–221.

Barahal, R., Waterman, J., & Martin, H. (1981). The social cognitive development of abused children. *Journal of Consulting and Clinical Psychology, 49,* 508–516.

Bard, L., Carter, D., Cerce, D., Knight, R., Rosenberg, R., & Schneider, B. (1983). *A descriptive study of rapists and child molesters: Developmental, clinical characteristics.* Bridgewater, MA: (Mimeo).

Bauer, W., & Twentyman, C.. (1985). Abusing, neglectful, and comparison mother's responses to child-related and non-child-related stressors. *Journal of Consulting and Clinical Psychology, 53,* 335–343.

Becker, J. V. (1985). *A model for the treatment of adolescent sexual perpetrators.* Paper presented at the 93rd Annual Meeting of the American Psychological Association, Los Angeles, CA.

Becker, J. V., & Abel, G. G. (1981). Behavioral treatment of victims of sexual assault. In S. M. Turner, K. S. Calhoun, & H. E. Adams (Eds.), *Handbook of clinical behavior therapy* (pp. 347–379). New York: John Wiley & Sons.

Becker, J. V., & Abel, G. G. (1984). Methodological and ethical issues in evaluating and treating adolescent sexual offenders. National Institute of Mental Health Monograph.

Becker, J. V., Cunningham-Rathner, J., & Kaplan, M. S. (1986). Adolescent sexual offenders: Demographics, criminal and sexual histories, and recommendations for reducing future offenses. *Journal of Interpersonal Violence, 1,* 431–445.

Becker, J. V., Kaplan, M. S., Cunningham-Rathner, J., & Kavoussi, R. (1986). Characteristics of adolescent incest sexual perpetrators: Preliminary findings. *Journal of Family Violence, 1,* 85–97.

Becker, J. V., & Skinner, L. J. (1984). Behavioral treatment of sexual dysfunctions in sexual assault survivors. In I. R. Stuart & J. G. Greer (Eds.), *Victims of sexual aggression: Treatment of children, women, and men* (pp. 211–233). New York: Van Nostrand Reinhold Co.

Becker, J. V., Skinner, L. J., & Abel, G. G. (1982). Treatment of a four-year-old victim of incest. *The American Journal of Family Therapy, 10*, 41–46.

Beezley, P., & McQuiston, M. (1977). *Crisis nurseries: Practical considerations.* Denver, CO: National Center for the Prevention of Child Abuse and Neglect.

Beland, K. (1985). *Talking about touching for parents and kids.* Seattle, WA: Committee for Children.

Bell, R., & Harper, L. (1977). *Child effects on adults.* Hillsdale, NJ: Erlbaum.

Berg, B. (1986). *The assertion game.* Dayton, OH: Cognitive-Behavioral Resources.

Berger, A. (1985). Characteristics of abusing families. In L. L'Abate (Ed.), *The handbook of family psychology and therapy* (pp. 900–936). Homewood, IL: Dorsey Press.

Berkowitz, B., & Graziano, A. (1972). Training parents as behavior therapists: A review. *Behavior Research and Therapy, 10*, 297–317.

Berkowitz, L. (1983). Aversively stimulated aggression: Some parallels and differences in research with animals and humans. *American Psychologist, 38*, 1135–1144.

Berlin, F. S. (1983). Sex offenders: A biomedical perspective and a status report on biomedical treatment. In J. G. Greer & I. R. Stuart (Eds.), *The sexual aggressor: Current perspectives on treatment* (pp. 83–123). New York: Van Nostrand Reinhold Co.

Berlin, F. S., & Meinecke, C. F. (1981). Treatment of sex offenders with antiandrogenic medication: Conceptualization, review of treatment modalities, and preliminary findings. *American Journal of Psychiatry, 138*, 601–607.

Berliner, L., & Ernst, E. (1984). Group work with preadolescent sexual assault victims. In I. R. Stuart & J. G. Greer (Eds.), *Victims of sexual aggression: Treatment of children, women, and men* (pp. 105–124). New York: Van Nostrand Reinhold Co.

Berliner, L., & MacQuivey, K. (1983). A therapy group for female adolescent victims of sexual abuse. In R. A. Rosenbaum (Ed.), *Varieties of short-term therapy groups* (pp. 101–116). New York: McGraw-Hill.

Bernstein, D., & Borkovec, T. (1973). *Progressive relaxation training: A manual for the helping professions.* Champaign, IL: Research Press.

Blumberg, M. (1974). Psychopathology of the abusing parent. *American Journal of Psychotherapy, 28*, 21–29.

Boat, B. W., & Everson, M. D. (1986). *Using anatomical dolls: Guidelines for interviewing young children in sexual abuse investigations.* Chapel Hill, NC: Authors.

Boratynski, M. (1983). *Final report. The child abuse primary prevention project.* New Haven, CT: Yale University, The Consultation Center.

Borgman, R. (1984). Problems of sexually abused girls and their treatment. *Social Casework: The Journal of Contemporary Social Work, 65*, 182–186.

Bornstein, P. H., & Kazdin, A. E. (Eds.). (1985). *Handbook of clinical behavior therapy with children.* Homewood, IL: The Dorsey Press.

Boszormenyi-Nagy, I., & Spark, C. (1973). *Invisible loyalties.* New York: Harper & Row.

Bousha, D. M., & Twentyman, C. T. (1984). Mother-child interactional style in abuse, neglect, and control groups: Naturalistic observations in the home. *Journal of Abnormal Psychology, 93*, 106–114.

Boyer, J. L., & Beckham, E. E. (in press). *A cognitive behavioral treatment of impulse control disorders: A naturalistic outcome study and follow-up.* National Institute of Mental Health Monograph.

Brassard, M. R., Tyler, A. H., & Kehle, T. J. (1983). School programs to prevent intrafamilial child sexual assault. *Child Abuse and Neglect, 7*, 241–245.

Bremner, R. H. (1970). *Children and youth in America: A documentary history* (Vol. I; 1600–1865). Cambridge, MA: Harvard University Press.

Bremner, R. H. (1971). *Children and youth in America: A documentary history (Vol. II: 1866–1932).* Cambridge, MA: Harvard University Press.

Briere, J. (1984). *The effects of childhood sexual abuse on later psychological functioning: Defining a "post-sexual-abuse syndrome"*. Paper presented at the Third National Conference on Sexual Victimization of Children, Washington, DC.

Briere, J., & Runtz, M. (1985). *Symptomatology associated with prior sexual abuse in a nonclinical sample*. Paper presented at the annual meeting of the American Psychological Association, Los Angeles, CA.

Browne, A., & Finkelhor, D. (1986a). Impact of child sexual abuse: A review of the research. *Psychological Bulletin, 99,* 66–77.

Browne, A., & Finkelhor, D. (1986b). Initial and long-term effects: A review of the research. In D. Finkelhor & Associates (Eds.), *A sourcebook on child sexual abuse* (pp. 143–179). Beverly Hills, CA: Sage Publications.

Brownell, K. D., Hayes, S. C., & Barlow, D. H. (1977). Patterns of appropriate and deviant sexual arousal: The behavioral treatment of multiple sexual deviations. *Journal of Consulting and Clinical Psychology, 45,* 1144–1155.

Burgess, A. W. (1984). *Child pornography and sex rings*. Lexington, MA: Lexington Books.

Burgess, A. W., Groth, A. N., & McCausland, M. P. (1981). Child sex initiation rings. *American Journal of Orthopsychiatry, 51,* 110–119.

Burgess, A. W., Hartman, C. R., McCausland, M. P., & Powers, P. (1984). Response patterns in children and adolescents exploited through sex rings and pornography. *American Journal of Psychiatry, 141,* 656–662.

Burgess, A. W., Holmstrom, L. L., & McCausland, M. P. (1978). Counseling young victims and their parents. In A. W. Burgess, A. N. Groth, & L. L. Holmstrom (Eds.), *Sexual assault of children and adolescents* (pp. 181–204). Lexington, MA: Lexington Books.

Burgess, R. L. (1979). Child abuse: A interactional analysis. In B. B. Lahey & A. E. Kazdin (Eds.), *Advances in clinical child psychology* (Vol 2, pp. 141–172), New York: Plenum Press.

Burgess, R. L., & Conger, R. D. (1977). Family interaction patterns related to child abuse and neglect: Some preliminary findings. *Child Abuse & Neglect, 1,* 269–277.

Burgess, R. L., & Conger, R. D. (1978). Family interaction in abusive, neglectful and normal families. *Child Development, 49,* 1163–1173.

Caffey, J. (1946). Multiple fractures in the long bones of infants suffering from chronic subdural hematoma. *American Journal of Roentgenology, 56,* 163–173.

Caffey, J. (1957). Some traumatic lesions in growing bones other than fractures and dislocations: Clinical and radiological features. *British Journal of Radiology, 30,* 225–238.

Carozza, P. M., & Heirsteiner, C. L. (1983). Young female incest victims in treatment: Stages of growth seen with a group art therapy model. *Clinical Social Work Journal, 10,* 165–175.

Cassell, R. (1962). *Child Behavior Rating Scale*. Los Angeles: Western Psychological Services.

Christophersen, E., Barnard, J., Ford, D., &, Wolf, M. (1976). The family training program: Improving parent-child interaction patterns. In E. Mash, L. Handy, & L. Hamerlynck (Eds.), *Behavior modification approaches to parenting*. New York: Brunner/Mazel.

Cohen, M., Raphling, D., & Green, P. (1966). Psychological aspects of the maltreatment syndrome of childhood. *Journal of Pediatrics, 69,* 279–284.

Cohen, S., Gray, E., & Wald, M. (1984) What do we really know from research about preventing child abuse and neglect. Chicago: National Committee for Prevention of Child Abuse.

Cohn, A., Finkelhor, D., & Holmes, C. (1985). *Preventing adults from becoming child sexual molesters*. Chicago, IL: National Committee for the Prevention of Child Abuse.

Cole, C. L. (1985). A group design for adult female survivors of childhood incest. *Women and Therapy, 4,* 71–82.

Combs, M., & Slaby, D. (1977). Social-skills training with children. In B. Lahey & A. Kazdin (Eds.), *Advances in clinical psychology* (Vol. 1, pp. 161–203). New York: Plenum.

Conger, R., Burgess, R., & Barrett, C. (1979). Child abuse related to life change and perceptions of illness: Some preliminary findings. *Family Coordinator, 28,* 73–78.

Connecticut Child Welfare Association, Inc. (1978). *Fitth annual report of the call-line, July 1, 1977–June 30, 1978.* Hartford, CT: Author.

Conners, C. K. (1970). Symptom patterns in hyperactive, neurotic, and normal children. *Child Development, 41,* 667–682.

Conners, C. K. (1969). A teacher rating scale for use in drug studies with children. *American Journal of Psychiatry, 126,* 884–888.

Constantine, L. (1977). *The sexual rights of children: Implications of a radical perspective.* Paper presented at the International Conference on Love and Attraction, Sevansee, Wales.

Conte, J. R. (1984). Progress in treating the sexual abuse of children. *Social Work,* May-June, 258–263.

Conte, J. R., Rosen, C., Saperstein, L., & Shermack, R. (1985). An evaluation of a program to prevent the sexual victimization of young children. *Child Abuse and Neglect, 9,* 319–328.

Cooper, H., Dreznick, J., & Rowe, B. (1982). Perinatal coaching: A new beginning. *Social Casework, 63,* 35–40.

Cordoba, O. A., & Chapel, J. L. (1983). Medroxyprogesterone acetate antiandrogen treatment of hypersexuality in a pedophiliac sex offender. *American Journal of Psychiatry, 140,* 1036–1039.

Courtois, C. (1979). The incest experience and its aftermath. *Victimology: An International Journal, 4,* 337–347.

Curran, J. (1975). An evaluation of a skills training program in reducing dating anxiety. *Behavior Research and Therapy, 13,* 65–68.

Curran, J. (1977). Skills training as an approach to the treatment of heterosexual anxiety: A review. *Psychological Bulletin, 84,* 140–157.

Curran, J., & Gilbert, F. (1975). A test of the relative effectiveness of a systemic desensitization program and an interpersonal skills training program with date anxious subjects. *Behavior Therapy, 16,* 510–521.

Curran, J., Gilbert, F., & Little, L. (1976). A comparison between behavioral training and sensitivity training approaches to heterosexual dating anxiety. *Journal of Counseling Psychology, 23,* 190–196.

Dahlstrom, W. G., Welsh, A. S., & Dahlstrom, L. E. (1972). *An MMPI handbook* (2 Vol, revised ed.). Minneapolis, MN: University of Minnesota Press.

Dale, P., & Davies, M. (1985). A model of intervention in child-abusing families: A wider systems view. *Child Abuse & Neglect, 9,* 449–455.

Dale, P., Morrison, T., Davies, M., Noyes, P., & Roberts, W. (1983). A family-therapy approach to child abuse: Countering resistance. *Journal of Family Therapy, 5,* 117–143.

Davidson, A. (1977). Child abuse: Causes and prevention. *Journal of the National Medical Association, 69,* 817–820.

Deisher, R. W., Wenet, G. A., Paperny, D. M., Clark, T. F., & Fehrenbach, P. A. (1982). Adolescent sexual offense behavior: The role of the physician. *Journal of Adolescent Health Care, 2,* 279–286.

Deitrich, G. (1981). Audiovisual materials with critique. In P. B. Mrazek & C. H. Kempe (Eds.), *Sexually abused children and their families* (pp. 257–259). New York: Pergamon Press.

Delson, N., & Clark, M. (1981). Group therapy with sexually molested children. *Child Welfare, 60,* 175–182.

De Mause, L. (1974). The evolution of childhood. In L. De Mause (Ed.), *The history of childhood* (pp. 1–73). New York: The Psychohistory Press.

Denney, D. R. (1983). Relaxation and stress management. In C. E. Walker (Ed.), *The handbook of clinical psychology: Theory, research and practice* (Vol. II, pp. 967–1008). Homewood, IL: Dow Jones-Irwin.

Department of Health and Human Services. (1981). *Study Findings: National Study of the Incidence and Severity of Child Abuse and Neglect.* No. (OHDS) 81–30325.

de Young, M. (1982). *The sexual victimization of children.* Jefferson, NC: McFarland & Co., Inc.

DiAugusti, P. (1980). *The family protection team: A multifaceted approach to child abuse.* Presented at the 5th annual Conference of the National Association of Social Workers, Florida Chapter, Miami, FL.

Dietrich, K., Starr, R., & Kaplan, M. (1980). Maternal stimulation and care of abused infants. In T. M. Field, S. Goldberg, D. Stern, & A. M. Sostek (Eds.), *High-risk infants and children: Adult and peer interactions* (pp. 25–41). New York: Academic Press.

Dietz, C. A., & Craft, J. L. (1980). Family dynamics of incest: A new perspective. *Social Casework: The Journal of Contemporary Social Work, 61,* 602–609.

Disbrow, M. A., Doerr, H., & Caulfield, C. (1977). Measuring the components of parents' potential for child abuse and neglect. *Child Abuse and Neglect, 1,* 279–296.

Doek, J. E. (1981). Sexual abuse of children: An examination of European criminal law. In P. B. Mrazek and C. H. Kempe (Eds.), *Sexually abused children and their families* (pp. 75–84). New York: Pergamon Press.

Donaldson, M. A., & Gardner, R., Jr. (1985). Diagnosis and treatment of traumatic stress among women after childhood incest. In C. R. Figley (Ed.), *Trauma and its wake: The study and treatment of post-traumatic stress disorder* (pp. 356–377). New York: Brunner/ Mazel.

Dubanoski, R. A., Evans, E. M., & Higuchi, A. A. (1978). Analysis and treatment of child abuse: A set of behavioral propositions. *Child Abuse and Neglect, 2,* 153–172.

Dumas, J. (1984). Indiscriminate mothering: Empirical findings and theoretical speculations. *Advances in Behavior Research and Therapy, 6,* 13–27.

Dumas, J. & Wahler, R. (1983). Predictors of treatment outcome in parent training: Mother insularity and socioeconomic disadvantage. *Behavioral Assessment, 5,* 301–313.

Ellerstein, N. S., & Canavan, J. W. (1980). Sexual abuse of boys. *American Journal of Diseases of Children, 134,* 255–257.

Elliott, C., & Ozolins, M. (1983). Use of imagery and imagination in treatment of children. In C. E. Walker, & M. C. Roberts (Eds.), *Handbook of clinical child psychology* (pp. 1026–1049). New York: John Wiley & Sons.

Elmer, E. (1965). *The fifty families study: Summary of Phase 1, neglected and abused children and their families.* Pittsburgh: Children's Hospital of Pittsburgh.

Elmer, E. (1967). *Children in jeopardy: A study of abused minors and their families.* Pittsburgh, PA: University of Pittsburgh Press

Elmer, E. (1977). *Fragile families, troubled children.* Pittsburgh, PA: University of Pittsburgh Press.

Elmer, E., & Gregg, G. S. (1967). Developmental characteristics of abused children. *Pediatrics, 40,* 596–602.

Exner, J. E. (1986). *The Rorschach: A comprehensive system* (2nd. ed.). New York: John Wiley & Sons.

Eyberg, S. M. (in press). Parents and children in therapy: Integration of traditional and behavioral concerns. *Journal of Child and Family Behavior Therapy.*

Eyberg, S. M., & Ross, A. W. (1978). Assessment of child behavior problems: The validation of a new inventory. *Journal of Clinical Child Psychology, 7*(2), 113–116.

Fantuzzo, J., & Twentyman, C. (1986). Child abuse and psychotherapy research: Merging social concerns and empirical investigation. *Professional Psychology: Research and Practice, 17*(5), 375–380.

Faranoff, A., Kennell, J., & Klaus, M. (1972). Follow-up of low birth weight infants: The predictive value of maternal visiting patterns. *Pediatrics, 49,* 287–290.

Fay, J., & Flerchinger, B. J. (1982). *Top secret: Sexual assault information for teenagers only.* Renton, WA: King County Rape Relief.

Fields, P. J. (1981). Parent-child relationships, childhood sexual abuse, and adult interpersonal behavior in female prostitutes. *Dissertation Abstracts International, 42,* No. 5. 20536–20546.

Finkelhor, D. (1979). *Sexually victimized children.* New York: The Free Press.

Finkelhor, D. (1984). *Child sexual abuse: New theory and research.* New York: The Free Press.

Finkelhor, D. (1985a). *Sexual abuse: Beyond the family systems approach.* Durham, NH: University of New Hampshire.

Finkelhor, D. (1985b). Sexual abuse of boys. In A. Burgess (Ed.), *Rape and sexual assault: A research handbook* (pp. 97–109). New York: Garland.

Finkelhor, D. (1985c). Sexual abuse and physical abuse: Some critical differences. In E. H. Newberger & R. Bourne (Eds.), *Unhappy families: Clinical and research perspectives on family violence* (pp. 21–30). Littleton, MA: PSG Publishing Co., Inc.

Finkelhor, D. (1986). Prevention: A review of programs and research. In D. Finkelhor & Associates (Eds.), *A sourcebook on child sexual abuse* (pp. 224–254). Beverly Hills, CA: Sage Publications.

Finkelhor, D., & Araji, S. (1983). *The prevention of child sexual abuse: A review of current approaches.* Durham, N.H.: University of Newhampshire.

Finkelhor, D., & Baron, L. (1986a). High risk children. In D. Finkelhor & Associates (Eds.), *A sourcebook on child sexual abuse* (pp. 60–88). Beverly Hills, CA: Sage Publications.

Finkelhor, D., & Baron, L. (1986b). Risk factors for child sexual abuse. *Journal of Interpersonal Violence, 1,* 43–71.

Finkelhor, D., & Browne, A. (1986). Initial and long-term effects: A conceptual framework. In D. Finkelhor & Associates (Eds.), *A sourcebook on child sexual abuse* (pp. 180–198). Beverly Hills, CA: Sage Publications.

Finkelhor, D., & Russell, D. (1984). Women as perpetrators: Review of the evidence. In D. Finkelhor (Ed.), *Child sexual abuse: New theory and research* (pp. 171–187). New York: Free Press.

Fisher, S. H. (1958). Skeletal manifestations of parent-induced trauma in infants and children. *Southern Medical Journal, 51,* 956–960.

Fitts, W. H. (1964), *Tennessee Self-Concept Scale.* Nashville, TN: Counselor Recordings and Tests.

Fomufod, A. K., Sinkford, S. M., & Louy, V. E. (1975). A mother-child separation at birth: A contributing factor in child abuse. *Lancet, 2,* 549–550.

Fontana, V. J., & Bernard, M. L. (1971). *The maltreated child.* Springfield, IL: Charles C Thomas.

Forehand, R., & King, H. E. (1977). Noncompliant children. *Behavior Modification, 1,* 93–108.

Forehand, R. L., & McMahon, R. J. (1981). *Helping the noncompliant child.* New York: Guilford Press.

Frankenburg, W., & Dodds, J. (1967). The Denver Developmental Screening Test. *The Journal of Pediatrics, 7,* 181–191.

Fraser, B. G. (1981). Sexual child abuse: The legislation and the law in the United States. In P. B. Mrazek & C. H. Kempe (Eds.), *Sexually abused children and their families* (pp. 55–74). New York: Pergamon Press.

Freeman-Longo, R. E. (1986). The impact of sexual victimization on males. *Child Abuse and Neglect, 10,* 411–414.

Freeman-Longo, R. E., & Wall, R. V. (1986). Changing a lifetime of sexual crime. *Psychology Today,* March, 58–64.

Freund, K. (1980). Therapeutic sex drive reduction. *Acta Psychiatrica Scandinavica Suppl: 287, 62,* 1–39.

Friedman, R., Sandler, J., Hernandez, M., & Wolfe, D. (1981). Behavioral assessment of child abuse. In E. Mash & L. Terdal (Eds.), *Behavioral assessment of childhood disorders*. New York: Guilford.

Friedemann, V. M., Morgan, M. K. (Authors), & Bosche, B. (Speaker). (1986). *Interviewing the young sex crime victim with the aid of dolls* (Audio Cassette). Eugene, OR: Migima Designs, Inc.

Friedrich, W. N., & Boriskin, S. A. (1976). The role of the child in abuse: A review of the literature. *American Journal of Orthopsychiatry, 46*, 580–590.

Friedrich, W. N., Urquiza, A. J., & Beilke, R. L. (1986). Behavior problems in sexually abused young children. *Journal of Pediatric Psychology, 11*, 47–57.

Fritz, G., Stoll, K., & Wagner, N. (1981). A comparison of males and females who were sexually molested as children. *Journal of Sex and Marital Therapy, 7*, 54–59.

Frodi, A. M. (1981). Contributions of infant characteristics to child abuse, *American Journal of Mental Deficiency, 85*, 341–349.

Frodi, A. M., & Lamb, M. E. (1980). Child abusers' responses to infant smiles and cries. *Child Development, 51*, 238–241.

Fromuth, M. E. (1983). *The long term psychological impact of childhood sexual abuse*. Unpublished doctoral dissertation, Auburn University, Auburn, AL.

Fromuth, M. E. (1986). The relationship of childhood sexual abuse with later psychological and sexual adjustment in a sample of college women. *Child Abuse and Neglect, 10*, 5–15.

Funk, J. B. (1981). Consultation in the management of sexual molestation, *Journal of Clinical Child Psychology, 10*, 83–85.

Furniss, T. (1983). Family process in the treatment of intrafamilial child sexual abuse. *Journal of Family Therapy, 5*, 263–278.

Gagne, P. (1981). Treatment of sex offenders with medroxyprogesterone acetate. *American Journal of Psychiatry, 138*, 644–646.

Galassi, J., Kosta, M., & Galassi, M. (1975). Assertive training: A one-year follow-up. *Journal of Counselling Psychology, 22*, 451–452.

Galdston, R. (1965). Observation on children who have been physically abused and their parents. *American Journal of Psychiatry, 122*, 440–443.

Garbarino, J. (1976). A preliminary study of some ecological correlates of child abuse: The impact of socioeconomic stress on mothers. *Child Development, 46*, 178–185.

Garbarino, J. (1977). The human ecology of child maltreatment: A conceptual model for research. *Journal of Marriage and the Family, 39*, 721–735.

Garbarino, J. (1986). Can we measure success in preventing child abuse: Issues in policy, programming and research. *Child Abuse and Neglect, 10*, 143–156.

Garbarino, J. (1987). Children's response to a sexual abuse prevention program: A study of the *Spiderman* comic. *Child Abuse and Neglect, 11*, 143–148.

Garbarino, J., & Shermen, D. (1980). High-risk neighborhoods and high-risk families: The human ecology of child maltreatment. *Child Development, 51*, 188–198.

Gardner, R. A. (1973). *The Thinking, Feeling, and Doing Game*. Cresskill, NJ: Creative Therapeutics.

Gardner, R. A. (1982). *The boys and girls book about step-families*. New York: Bantam Books.

Geer, J. H. (1980). Measurement of genital arousal in human males and females. In I. Martin & P. H. Venables (Eds.), *Techniques in psychophysiology* (pp. 431–458). New York: John Wiley & Sons.

Gelinas, D. J. (1983). The persisting negative effects of incest. *Psychiatry, 46*, 312–332.

Gelles, R. J. (1980). A profile of violence toward children in the United States. In G. Gerbner, C. J. Ross, & E. Zegler (Eds.), *Child abuse: An agenda for action* (pp. 82–105). New York: Oxford University Press.

Gelles, R. J. (1978). Violence toward children in the United States. *American Journal of Orthopsychiatry, 48*, 580–592.

Gelles, R. J. (1973). Child abuse as psychopathology: A Sociological critique and reformulation. *American Journal of Orthopsychiatry, 43*, 611–621.

George, C., & Main, M. (1979). Social interactions of young abused children: Approach, avoidance, & aggression. *Child Development, 50*, 306–318.

George, W. H., & Marlatt, G. A. (1986). *Relapse prevention with sex offenders: A treatment manual*. Tampa, FL: Florida Mental Health Institute.

Giarretto, H. (1982a). A comprehensive child sexual abuse treatment program. *Child Abuse and Neglect, 6*, 263–278.

Giarretto, H. (1982b). *Integrated treatment of child sexual abuse: A treatment and training manual*. Palo Alto, CA: Science and Behavior Books, Inc.

Gil, D. G., (1970). *Violence against children: Physical child abuse in the United States*. Cambridge, MA: Harvard University Press.

Gil, D. G. (1975). Unraveling child abuse. *American Journal of Orthopsychiatry, 45*, 346–356.

Giles-Sims, J., & Finkelhor, D. (1984). Child abuse in stepfamilies. *Family Relations, 33*, 407–413.

Giovannoni, J., & Billingsley, A. (1970). Child neglect among the poor: A study of parental inadequacy in families of three ethnic groups. *Child Welfare, 49*, 196–204.

Gitchel, S., & Foster, L. (1982). *Let's talk about . . . S-E-X*. Fresno, CA: Planned Parenthood of Fresno.

Goldberg, D. C. (1983). The treatment of sexual dysfunctions. In C. E. Walker (Ed.), *The handbook of clinical psychology: Theory, research and practice* (Vol II, pp. 666–712). Homewood, IL: Dow Jones-Irwin.

Goldstein, G., & Hersen, M. (Eds.). (1984). *Handbook of psychological assessment*. New York: Pergamon Press.

Gomes-Schwartz, B., Horowitz, J. M., & Sauzier, M. (1985). Severity of emotional distress among sexually abused preschool, school-age, and adolescent children. *Hospital and Community Psychiatry, 36*, 503–508.

Goodwin, J., (1982). The use of drawings in incest cases. In J. Goodwin (Ed.), *Sexual abuse: Incest victims and their families* (pp. 47–56). Boston: John Wright, PSG Inc.

Goodwin, J., & Flanagan, M. (1983). Incest: Treating child and family. *Physician and Patient, 2*, 59–68.

Goodwin, S., & Mahoney, M. (1975). Modification of aggression through modeling: An experimental probe. *Journal of Behavior Therapy and Experimental Psychiatry, 6*, 200–202.

Gordon, L. (1955). Incest as revenge against the preoedipal mother. *Psychoanalytical Review, 42*, 284–292.

Gordon, S., & Gordon, J. (1984). *A better safe than sorry book: A family guide for sexual assault prevention*. Fayetteville, NY: Ed-U-Press.

Gordy, P. L. (1983). Group work that supports adult victims of childhood incest. *Social Casework: The Journal of Contemporary Social Work*, May, 300–307.

Gottman, J., Gonso, J., & Shuler, P. (1976). Teaching social skills to isolated children. *Journal of Abnormal Child Psychology, 4*, 179–197.

Gray, E. (1983a). *Final report: Collaborative research of community and minority group action to prevent child abuse and neglect. Vol I: Perinatal interventions*. Chicago: National Committee for Prevention of Child Abuse.

Gray, E. (1983b). *Final report: Collaborative research of community and minority group action to prevent child abuse and neglect. Vol. II: Culture-based parent education programs*. Chicago: National Committee for Prevention of Child Abuse.

Gray, E. (1983c). *Final report: Collaborative group action to prevent child abuse and neglect. Vol.*

III: Public awareness and education using the creative arts. Chicago: National Committee for Prevention of Child Abuse.

Gray, J. (1979). Prediction and prevention of child abuse. *Seminars in perinatology, 3,* 85–90.

Gray, J. & Kaplan, B. (1980). The lay health visitor program: A eighteen-month experience. In C. Kempe & R. Helfer (Eds.), *The battered child* (pp. 373–378). Chicago: University of Chicago Press.

Gray, J., Cutler, C., Dean, J. & Kempe, C. (1976). Perinatal assessment of mother-baby interaction. In R. Helfer & C. Kempe (Eds.), *Child abuse and neglect: The family and the community* (pp. 377–392). Chicago: University of Chicago Press.

Green, A. H. (1976). A psychodynamic approach to the study and treatment of child-abusing parents. *Journal of the Academy of Child Psychiatry, 15,* 414–429.

Green, A. H. (1978). Psychopathology of abused children. *Journal of Child Psychiatry, 17,* 92–103.

Green, A. H. (1979). Child abusing fathers. *Journal of Child Psychiatry, 18,* 270–282.

Green, A. H., Gaines, R. W., & Sandgrund, A. (1974). Child abuse: Pathological syndrome of family interaction. *American Journal of Psychiatry, 131,* 882–886.

Gregg, G., & Elmer, E. (1969). Infant injuries: Accident or abuse? *Pediatrics, 44,* 434–439.

Groth, A. N., & Birnbaum, H. J. (1979). *Men who rape: The psychology of the offender.* New York: Plenum Press.

Groth, A. N., & Burgess, A. W. (1979). Sexual trauma in the life histories of rapists and child molesters. *Victimology, An International Journal, 4,* 10–16.

Groth, A. N., Hobson, W. F., & Gary, T. S. (1982). The child molester: Clinical observations. In J. R. Conte & D. A. Shore (Eds.), *Social work and child sexual abuse* (pp. 129–144). New York: Haworth Press.

Groth, A. N., Hobson, W. F., Lucey, K. P., & St. Pierre, J. (1981). Juvenile sexual offenders: Guidelines for treatment. *International Journal of Offender Therapy and Comparative Criminology, 25,* 265–272.

Groth, A. N., & Loredo, C. M. (1981). Juvenile sexual offenders: Guidelines for assessment. *International Journal of Offender Therapy and Comparative Criminology, 25,* 31–39.

Gruber, K. J., & Jones, R. I. (1983). Identifying determinants of risk of sexual victimization of youth: A multivariate approach. *Child Abuse & Neglect, 7,* 17–24.

Gurman, A., & Kniskern, D. (Eds.), (1981). *Handbook of family therapy.* New York: Brunner/Mazel.

Gutheil, T. G., & Avery, N. C. (1977). Multiple overt incest as family defense against loss. *Family Process, 16,* 105–116.

Hadden, D. V., & Gober Zimmerman, J. (1985). Directive group treatment of child sexual abuse victims. Unpublished manuscript.

Haley, J. (1984). *Ordeal therapy.* San Francisco: Jossey-Bass.

Harms, R., & James, D. (1984). *Talking about touching: A personal safety curriculum.* Seattle, WA: Committee for Children.

Hartman, C. R., Burgess, A. W., & Powers, P. (1984). Treatment issues with children involved in pornography and sex rings. In A. W. Burgess (Ed.), *Child pornography and sex rings* (pp. 177–185). Lexington, MA: Lexington Books.

Hayes, S. C., Brownell, K. D., & Barlow, D. H. (1983). Heterosocial-skills training and covert sensitization: Effects on social skills and sexual arousal in sexual deviants. *Behaviour Research and Therapy, 21,* 383–392.

Heim, N. (1981). Sexual behavior of castrated sex offenders. *Archives of Sexual Behavior, 10,* 11–19.

Heins, M. (1969). Child abuse: Analysis of a current epidemic. *Michigan Medicine, 68,* 887–891.

Helfer, R. E. (1973). The etiology of child abuse. *Pediatrics, 51,* 777.

Helfer, R. E. (1980). Developmental deficits which limit interpersonal skills. In C. H. Kempe & R. E. Helfer (Eds.), *The battered child* (3rd ed., pp. 36–48). Chicago: University of Chicago Press.

Helfer, R. E. (1982). A review of the literature on the prevention of child abuse and neglect. *Child Abuse and Neglect, 6,* 251–261.

Helfer, R. E., Hoffmeister, J. K., & Schneider, C., (1978). *A manual for use of the Michigan Screening Profile of Parenting.* Boulder, CO: Test Analysis and Development Corp.

Helfer, R., & Kempe, C. H. (1976). *Child abuse and neglect: The family and the community.* Cambridge, MA: Ballinger Publishing Co.

Heller, K., Price, R. H., & Sher, K. J. (1980). Research and evaluation in primary prevention. In R. H. Price, R. F. Kelterer, B. C. Bader, & J. Monahan (Eds.), *Prevention in mental health* (pp. 285–313). Beverly Hills, CA: Sage Publications.

Henderson, J. (1983). Is incest harmful? *Canadian Journal of Psychiatry, 28,* 34–39.

Hereford, C. F. (1963). *Changing parental attitudes through group discussion.* Austin, TX: University of Texas Press.

Herman, J. L. (1981). *Father-daughter incest.* Cambridge, MA: Harvard University Press.

Herman, J., & Schatzow, E. (1981). Time-limited group therapy for women with a history of incest. *International Journal of Group Psychotherapy, 34,* 605–616.

Herrenkohl, E. C., & Herrenkohl, R. C. (1979). A comparison of abused children and their nonabused siblings. *Journal of Child Psychiatry, 18,* 260–269.

Hersen, M., Kazdin, A., Bellack, A., & Turner, S. M. (1979). Effects of live modeling, covert modeling, psychiatric patients. *Behaviour Research and Therapy, 17,* 369–377.

Hoffman-Plotkin, D., & Twentyman, C. T. (1984). A multimodal assessment of behavioral and cognitive deficits in abused and neglected preschoolers. *Child Development, 55,* 794–802.

Holder, W. M., & Schene, P. (1981). *Understanding child neglect and abuse.* Denver, CO: The American Humane Association.

Holmes, T., & Rahe, R. (1967). The social readjustment rating scale. *Journal of Psychosomatic Research, 11,* 213–218.

Holter, J. C., & Friedman, S. B. (1968). Early case finding in the emergency department. *Pediatrics, 42,* 128.

Hoorwitz, A. N. (1983). Guidelines for treating father-daughter incest. *Social Casework: The Journal of Contemporary Social Work,* November, 515–524.

Howes, C., & Espinosa, M. (1985). The consequences of child abuse for the formation of relationships with peers. *Child Abuse and Neglect, 9,* 397–404.

Hunter, R. S., Kilstrom, N., Kraybill, E. N., & Loda, F. (1978). Antecedents of child abuse and neglect in premature infants: A prospective study in a newborn intensive care unit. *Pediatrics, 61,* 629–635.

Hunter, R. S., Kilstrom, N., & Loda, F. (1985). Sexually abused children: Identifying masked presentations in a medical setting. *Child Abuse and Neglect, 9,* 17–25.

Isaacs, C. (1982). Treatment of child abuse: A review of the behavioral interventions. *Journal of Applied Behavior Analysis, 15,* 505–520.

Jackson, T. L., & Ferguson, W. P. (1983). Attribution of blame in incest. *American Journal of Community Psychology, 11*(3), 313–322.

Jacobson, N., & Gurman, A. (1986). *Clinical handbook of marital therapy.* New York: Guilford Press.

Jacobson, N., & Margolin, G. (1979). *Marital therapy: Strategies based on social learning and behavior exchange principles.* New York: Brunner/Mazel.

James, J., & Megerding, J. (1977). Early sexual experiences and prostitution. *American Journal of Psychiatry, 134,* 1381–1385.

Jason, J., & Andereck, N. (1983). Fatal child abuse in Georgia: The epidemiology of severe physical child abuse. *Child Abuse and Neglect, 7,* 1–9.

Jason, J., Carpenter, M., & Tyler, C. (1983). Underrecording of infant homocide in the United States. *American Journal of Public Health, 73,* 195–197.

Johnson, B., & Morse, H. A. (1968). Injured children and their parents. *Children, 15,* 147–152.

Johnson, R. L., & Shrier, D. (1985). Sexual victimization of boys. *Journal of Adolescent Health Care, 6,* 372–376.

Johnson, S., & Christensen, A. (1975). Multiple criteria follow-up of behavior modification with families. *Journal of Abnormal Child Psychology, 3,* 135–154.

Johnson, W. R. (1981). Basic interviewing skills. In C. E. Walker (Ed.), *Clinical practice of psychology: A guide for mental health professionals* (pp. 83–128). New York: Pergamon Press.

Jones, D. P. H. (1986). Individual psychotherapy for the sexually abused child. *Child Abuse and Neglect, 10,* 377–385.

Jones, E. (1953). *The life and works of Sigmund Freud.* New York: Basic Books.

Justice, B., & Duncan, D. (1976). Life crisis as a precursor to child abuse. *Public Health Reports, 91,* 110–115.

Justice, B., & Justice, R. (1976). *The abusing family.* New York: Human Services Press.

Justice, B., & Justice, R. (1979). *The broken taboo: Sex in the family.* New York: Human Service Press.

Kanfer, F. (1980). Self-management methods. In F. Kanfer & A. Goldstein (Eds.), *Helping people change* (pp. 334–390). New York: Pergamon Press.

Kanner, A., Coyne, J., Schaefer, C., & Lazarus, R. (1981). Comparison of two modes of stress management: Daily hassles and uplifts versus major life events. *Journal of Behavioral Medicine, 4,* 1–39.

Karoly, P. (in press). *Handbook of child health assessment.* New York: John Wiley & Sons.

Kaufman, K. & Sandler, J. (1985). *A comparison of abusive and non-abusive mothers within a stress and coping framework: Support for Vasta's dual component model of child abuse.* Unpublished manuscript.

Kazdin, A. (1976). Effects of covert modeling, multiple models, and model reinforcement on assertive behavior. *Behavior Therapy, 7,* 211–222.

Keat, D. B., II. (1979). *Multimodal therapy with children.* New York: Pergamon Press.

Keinberger, P., & Diamond, L. (1985). The handicapped child and child abuse. *Child Abuse and Neglect, 9,* 341–347.

Kelley, S. J. (1984). The use of art therapy with sexually abused children. *Journal of Psychosocial Nursing, 22,* 12–18.

Kelly, J. (1983). *Treating child-abusive families.* New York: Plenum Press.

Kelly, R. J. (1982). Behavioral reorientation of pedophiliacs: Can it be done? *Clinical Psychology Review, 2,* 387–408.

Kempe, C. (1973). A practical approach to protection of the abused child and rehabilitation of the abusing parent. *Pediatrics, 51,* 804–812.

Kempe, C., & Helfer, R. (1972). *Helping the battered child and his family.* Philadelphia: J. B. Lippincott.

Kempe, R. S., & Kempe, C. H. (1978). *Child abuse.* Cambridge, MA: Harvard University Press.

Kempe, C. H., Silverman, F. N., Steele, B. F., Droegemuller, W., & Silver, H. K. (1962). The battered child syndrome. *Journal of the American Medical Association, 191,* 17–24.

Kendall, P., & Braswell, L. (1985). *Cognitive-behavioral therapy for impulsive children.* New York: Guilford Press.

Kendall, P., & Finch, A. (1979). Changes in verbal behavior following a cognitive-behavioral treatment for impulsivity. *Journal of Abnormal Child Psychology, 7,* 455–463.

Kennel, J., Voos, D., & Klaus, M. (1976). Parent-infant bonding. In R. E. Helfer & C. H. Kempe (Eds.), *Child abuse and neglect: The family and the community* (pp. 25–53). Cambridge, MA: Ballinger Publishing.

Kent, C. (1979). *Child sexual abuse prevention project: An educational program for children.* Minneapolis, MN: Hennepin County Attorney's Office, Sexual Assault Services.

Kent, J. (1976). A follow-up study of abused children. *Journal of Pediatric Psychology, 1,* 25–31.

Kerns, D. L. (1981). Medical assessment of child sexual abuse. In P. B. Mrazek & C. H. Kempe (Eds.), *Sexually abused children and their families* (pp. 129–142). New York: Pergamon Press.

Kilmann, P. R., Sabalis, R. F., Gearing, M. I.., II, Bukstel, L. H., & Scovern, A. W. (1982). The treatment of sexual paraphilias: A review of the outcome research. *The Journal of Sex Research, 18,* 193–252.

Kinard, E. (1980). Emotional development in physically abused children. *American Journal of Orthopsychiatry, 50,* 686–696.

Klaus, M., & Kennell, J. (1976) *Maternal-infant bonding.* St. Louis, MO: C. V. Mosby.

Klein, M., & Stern, L. (1971). Low birth weight and the battered child syndrome. *American Journal of Diseases of Children, 122,* 15–18.

Klien, D. (1981). Central nervous system injuries. In N. Ellerstein (Ed.)., *Child abuse and neglect: A medical reference* (pp. 73–99). New York: John Wiley & Sons.

Kluft, R. P., Braun, B. G., & Sachs, R. (1984). Multiple personality, intrafamilial abuse, and family psychiatry. *International Journal of Family Psychiatry, 5*(4), 283–301.

Knittle, B. J., & Tauna, S. J. (1980). Group therapy as primary treatment for adolescent victims of intrafamilial sexual abuse. *Clinical Social Work Journal, 8,* 236–242.

Knopp, F. H. (1982). *Remedial intervention in adolescent sex offenders: Nine program descriptions.* Syracuse, NY: Safer Society Press.

Knopp, F. H. (1984). *Retraining adult sex offenders: Methods and models.* Syracuse, NY: Safer Society Press.

Knopp, F. H. (1985). *The youthful sex offender: The rationale and goals of early intervention and treatment.* Syracuse, NY: Safer Society Press.

Knutson, J. F. (1978). Child abuse research as an area of aggression research. *Pediatric Psychology, 3,* 20–27.

Korsch, B. M., Christian, J. B., Gozzi, E. K., & Carlson, P. V. (1965). Infant care and punishment: A pilot study. *American Journal of Public Health, 55*(12), 1880–1888.

Kovacs, M. (1981). Rating scales to assess depression in school-aged children. *Acta Paedopsychiatry, 46,* 305–315.

Kramer, S. (1975). Effectiveness of behavior rehearsal and practice dating to increase heterosexual social interaction. *Dissertation Abstracts International, 36,* 913B–914B. (University Microfilms, No. 75–16, 693).

L'Abate, L. (1985). *The handbook of family psychology and therapy* (Vols. 1–2). Homewood, IL: Dorsey Press.

Lahey, B. B., Conger, R. D., Atkeson, B. M., & Treiber, F. A. (1984). Parenting behavior and emotional status of physically abusive mothers. *Journal of Consulting and Clinical Psychology, 52,* 1062–1071.

Lamphear, V., Stets, J., Whitaker, P., & Ross, A. (1985). Maladjustment in at-risk for physical abuse and behavior problem children: Differences in family environment and marital discord. Paper presented at the American Psychological Association National Convention, Los Angeles, CA.

Landis, L. L., & Wyre, C. H. (1984). Group treatment for mothers of incest victims: A step by step approach. *Journal of Counseling and Development, 63,* 115–116.

Langevin, R., Handy, L., Hook, H., Day, D., & Russon, A. (1983). Are incestuous fathers pedophilic and aggressive? In R. Langevin (Ed.), *Erotic preference, gender identity and aggression*. New York: Erlbaum Associates.

Lanyon, R. I. (1986). Theory and treatment in child molestation. *Journal of Consulting and Clinical Psychology, 54,* 176–182.

Larrance, D., & Twentyman, C. (1983). Maternal attributions in child abuse. *Journal of Abnormal Psychology, 92,* 449–457.

Lauer, B., Ten Broeck, E., & Grossman, M. (1974). Battered Child Syndrome: Review of 130 patients with controls. *Pediatrics, 54,* 67.

Lazarus, R. S., Speisman, J. C., Mordkof, A. M., & Davison, L. A. (1962). A laboratory study of psychological stress produced by a motion picture film. *Psychological Monographs, 76*(34, Whole No. 553).

Leiblum, S., & Pervin, L. (Eds.), 1980). *Principles and practices of sex therapy.* New York: Guilford Press.

Lewis, D. O., Moy, E., Jackson, L. D., Aaronson, R., Restifo, N., Serra, S., & Simos, A. (1985). Biopsychosocial characteristics of children who later murder: A prospective study. *American Journal of Psychiatry, 142,* 1161–1167.

Lewis, D. O., Shanok, S. S., Pincus, J. H., & Glaser, G. H. (1979). Violent juvenile delinquents: Psychiatric, neurological, psychological, and abuse factors. *Journal of the American Academy of Child Psychiatry, 18,* 307–319.

Light, R. J. (1973). Abused and neglected children in America: A study of alternative policies. *Harvard Educational Review, 43,* 556–598.

Lindberg, F. H., & Distad, L. J. (1985). Post-traumatic stress disorders in women who experienced childhood incest. *Child Abuse and Neglect, 9,* 329–334.

Liston, T. E., Levine, P. L., & Anderson, C. (1983). Polymicrobial bacteremia due to Polle syndrome: The child abuse variant of Munchausen by proxy. *Pediatrics, 72,* 211–213.

Locke, H. J., & Wallace, K. M. (1959). Short marital adjustment and prediction tests: Their reliability and validity. *Marriage and Family Living, 21,* 251–255.

Locke, H. J., & Williamson, R. C. (1958). Marital adjustment: A factor analysis study. *American Sociological Review, 23,* 562–569.

Longo, R. E. (1982). Sexual learning and experience among adolescent sexual offenders. *International Journal of Offender Therapy and Comparative Criminology, 26,* 235–241.

Longo, R. E., & Groth, A. N. (1983). Juvenile sexual offenses in the histories of adult rapists and child molesters. *International Journal of Offender Therapy and Comparative Criminology, 27,* 150–153.

Lorber, R., Felton, D. K., & Reid, J. B. (1984). A social learning approach to the reduction of coercive processes in child abusive families: A molecular analysis. *Advances in Behavior Research and Therapy, 6,* 29–45.

Lorber, R., Felton, D., & Reid, J. (1984). Coercive interactional processes in child abusive families: A social learning perspective. *Advances in Behavior Research and Therapy, 6,* 29–46.

Lorian, R. P. (1983). Evaluating preventive intervention: Guidelines for the serious social change agent. In R. D. Felner, L. A. Jason, J. N. Moritsugu, & S. S. Farber (Eds.), *Preventive psychology: Theory, research and practice* (pp. 251–268). New York: Pergamon Press.

Lourie, I. S. (1984). The locus of emotional harm in incest: The study of "non-victims" of incestuous families. *Clinical Proceedings, Children's Hospital National Medical Center, 40,* 46–54.

Lubell, D., & Soong, W.-T. (1982). Group therapy with sexually abused adolescents. *Canadian Journal of Psychiatry, 27,* 311–315.

Lupin, M. (1981). *The family relaxation and self-control program* (Vols. 1–2). Houston, TX: Biobehavioral Publishers & Distributors, Inc. (audio tapes).

Luria, A. R. (1966). *High cortical functions in man*. New York: Basic Books.

Lutzker, J., Welsch, D., & Rice, J. (1984). A review of project "12-Ways": An ecobehavioral approach to the treatment and prevention of child abuse and neglect. *Advances in Behavior Research and Therapy, 6*, 63–73.

Lynch, M. A., & Roberts, J. (1977). Predicting child abuse: Signs of bonding failure in the maternity hospital. *Child Abuse and Neglect, 1*, 491–492.

Lynch, M. A., & Roberts, J. (1982). *Consequences of child abuse*. New York: Academic Press.

MacFarlane, K., Waterman, J., Conerly, S., Damon, L., Durfee, M., & Long, S. (1986). *Sexual abuse of young children*. New York: The Guilford Press.

Madanes, C. (1981). *Strategic family therapy*. San Francisco: Jossey-Bass.

Madanes, C. (1984). *Behind the one-way mirror: Advances in the practice of strategic therapy*. San Francisco: Jossey-Bass Publishers.

Magrab, P. R. (Ed.). (1984). Child abuse. *Psychological and behavioral assessment: Impact on pediatric care* (337–363). New York: Plenum Press.

Maletzky, B. M. (1980). Self-referred versus court-referred sexually deviant patients: Success with assisted covert sensitization. *Behavior Therapy, 11*, 306–314.

Marshall, W. L., & McKnight, R. D. (1975). An integrated treatment program for sexual offenders. *Canadian Psychiatric Association Journal, 20*, 133–138.

Martin, H. (1976). *The abused child: A multidisciplinary approach to developmental issues and treatment*. Cambridge, MA: Ballinger Publishing Co.

Martin, H. P., & Beezeley, P. (1976). Personality of abused children. In H. P. Martin & H. Kempe (Eds.), *The abused child: A multidisciplinary approach to developmental issues and treatment* (pp. 105–111). Cambridge, MA: Ballinger Publishing Co.

Martin, H., & Beezley, P. (1977). Behavioral observations of abused children. *Developmental Medicine and Child Neurology, 19*, 373–387.

Martin, H. P., & Rodeheoffer, M.A. (1976). The psychological impact of abuse on children. *Journal of Pediatric Psychology, 1*, 12–15.

Marzillier, J., Lambert, C., & Kellet, J. (1976). A controlled evaluation of systematic desensitization and social skills for socially inadequate psychiatric patients. *Behavior Research and Therapy, 14*, 225–238.

Mash, E., Johnson, C., & Kovitz, K. (1983). A comparison of the mother-child interactions of physically abused and non-abused children during play and task situations. *Journal of Clinical Child Psychology, 12*, 337–346.

Masters, W. H., & Johnson, V. E. (1970). *Human sexual inadequacy*. Boston, MA: Little, Brown & Co.

Mayer, A. (1983). *Incest: A treatment manual for therapy with victims, spouses, and offenders*. Holmes Beach, FL: Learning Publications, Inc.

Mayer, A. (1985). *Sexual abuse: Causes, consequences and treatment of incestuous and pedophilic acts*. Holmes Beach, FL: Learning Publications, Inc.

Mayer, J., & Black, R. (1977). Child abuse and neglect in families with an alcoholic or opiate addicted parent. *Child Abuse and Neglect, 1*, 85–98.

Mayle, P. (1973). *Where did I come from?* Secaucus, NJ: Lyle Stuart Inc.

Mayle, P. (1975). *What's happening to me?* Secaucus, NJ: Lyle Stuart Inc.

McGovern, K. B. (1985). *Alice doesn't babysit anymore*. Portland, OR: McGovern & Mulbacker Books.

McIntyre, K. (1981). Role of mothers in father-daughter incest: A feminist analysis. *Social Work, 26*, 462–467.

Meadow, R., (1985). Management of Manchausen Syndrome by proxy. *Archives of Disease in Childhood, 60*, 385–393.

McRae, K. N., Ferguson, C. A., & Lederman, R. S. (1973). The battered child syndrome. *Canadian Medical Association Journal, 108,* 859–866.

Meichenbaum, D. (1977). *Cognitive-behavior modification: An integrative approach.* New York: Plenum Press.

Meichenbaum, D., & Goodman, J. (1971). Training impulsive children to talk to themselves: A means of developing self-control. *Journal of Abnormal Psychology, 77,* 115–126.

Meiselman, K. (1978). *Incest.* San Francisco: Jossey-Bass Publishers.

Melnick, B., & Hurley, J. R. (1969). Distinctive personality attributes of child-abusing mothers. *Journal of Consulting and Clinical Psychology, 33,* 746–749.

Merrill, E. J. (1962). Physical abuse of children. In: *Protecting the battered child,* pp. 1–15). Denver: American Humane Association, Children's Division.

Miller, L. K. (1980). *Principles of everyday behavior analysis.* Monterey, CA: Brooks/Cole Publishing Co.

Miller, L. C., Barrett, C. L. Hampe, E., & Noble, H. (1972). Factor structure of childhood fears. *Journal of Consulting and Clinical Psychology, 39,* 264–268.

Miller, J., Moeller, D., Kaufman, A., Divasto, P., Pather, D., & Christy, J. (1978). Recidivism among sexual assault victims. *American Journal of Psychiatry, 135,* 1103–1104.

Milner, J. S. (1986). *Child Abuse Potential Inventory: Manual.* Webster, NC: Psytech Inc.

Milner, J. S., & Wimberley, R. C. (1980). Prediction and explanation of child abuse. *Journal of Clinical Psychology, 36,* 875–884.

Minuchin, S., & Fishman, H. C. (1981). *Family therapy techniques.* Cambridge, MA: Harvard University Press.

Money, J., & Bennett, R. G. (1981). Postadolescent paraphilic sex offenders: Antiandrogenic and counseling therapy follow-up. *International Journal of Mental Health, 10,* 122–133.

Morris, J., Johnson, C., & Clasen, M. (1985). To report or not to report: Physicians' attitudes toward discipline and child abuse. *The American Journal of Diseases of Children, Feb. 1985, 139,* 194–197.

Morris, L. (1977). *Education for parenthood: A program, curriculum and evaluation guide.* Washington, D.C.: Department of Health, Education and Welfare.

Mrazek, P. B. (1981). The nature of incest: A review of contributing factors. In P. B. Mrazek & C. H. Kempe (Eds.), *Sexually abused children and their families* (pp. 97–108). New York: Pergamon Press.

Myer, M. H. (1985). A new look at mothers of incest victims. *The Journal of Social Work and Human Sexuality, 3* (213), 47–58.

National Center on Child Abuse and Neglect. (1981). *Study findings: National study of the incidence and severity of child abuse and neglect.* U.S. Department of Health and Human Services (Publication # OHDS 81–30325).

National Committee for Prevention of Child Abuse, (1985). *Child sexual abuse prevention resources.* Chicago, IL: National Committee for Prevention of Child Abuse.

Nelson, W., & Birkimer, J. (1978). Role of self-instruction and self-reinforcement in the modification of impulsivity. *Journal of Consulting and Clinical Psychology, 46,* 183.

Newberger, E. H., & Hyde, J. N. (1975). Child abuse: Principles and implications of current pediatric practice. *Pediatric Clinics of North America, 22,* 695–715.

Nielsen, T. (1983). Sexual abuse of boys: Current perspectives. *Personnel and Guidance Journal,* November, 139–142.

Novaco, R. W. (1978). Anger and coping with stress. In J. Foreyt & D. Rathjen (Eds.), *Cognitive behavior therapy: Research and applications* (pp. 135–173). New York: Plenum Press.

Nurse, S. M. (1964). Familial patterns of parents who abuse their children. *Smith College Studies in Social Work, 32,* 11–25.

Oates, R., Forrest, D., & Peacock, A. (1985). Self-esteem of abused children. *Child Abuse and Neglect, 9,* 159–163.

O'Connell, M. A. (1986). Reuniting incest offenders with their families. *Journal of Interpersonal Violence, 1,* 374–386.

O'Connor, S., Vietze, P., Sherrod, K., Sandler, H., & Altemeier, W. (1980). Reduced incidence of parenting inadequacy following rooming-in. *Pediatrics, 66,* 172–182.

O'Dell, S. (1974). Training parents in behavior modification: A review. *Psychological Bulletin, 81,* 418–433.

O'Dell, S., Blackwell, L., Larcen, S., & Hogan, J. (1977). Competency-based training for severely behaviorally handicapped children and their parents. *Journal of Autism and Childhood Schizophrenia,* 231–242.

O'Dell, S., Tarler-Benlolo, L., & Flynn, J. (1979). An instrument to measure knowledge of behavioral principles as applied to children. *Journal of Behavior Therapy and Experimental Psychiatry, 10,* 29–34.

Olds, D. (1984). *Final report: Prenatal early infancy project.* Washington, DC: Maternal and Child Health Research, National Institute of Health.

Oliver, J. E., & Taylor, A. (1971). Five generations of ill-treated children in one family pedigree. *British Journal of Psychiatry, 119,* 473–480.

Ollendick, T. H. (1983). Reliability and validity of the Revised Fear Survey for Children (FSSC-R). *Behavior Research and Therapy, 21,* 685–692.

Oppenheimer, R., Palmer, R. L., & Braden, S. (1984). *A clinical evaluation of early sexually abusive experiences in adult anorexic and bulimic females: Implications for preventive work in childhood.* Paper presented at the Fifth International Conferences on Child Abuse and Neglect, Montreal, Canada.

Orr, D. P. (1978). Limitations of emergency room evaluations of sexually abused children. *American Journal of Diseases of Children, 132,* 873–875.

Orten, J. D., & Rich, L. L. (Unpublished manuscript). *Ordering the chaos: Assessment of incestuous families.*

Ortmann, J. (1980). The treatment of sexual offenders: Castration and antihormone therapy. *International Journal of Law and Psychiatry, 3,* 443–451.

Otey, E. M., & Ryan, G. D. (Eds.). (1985). *Adolescent sex offenders: Issues in research and treatment* (DHHS Publication No. ADM 85–1396). A research monograph from the National Center for the Prevention and Control of Rape. Rockville, MD: U.S. Department of Health and Human Services.

Overholser, J. C., & Beck, S. (1986). Multimethod assessment of rapists, child molesters, and three control groups on behavioral and psychological measures. *Journal of Consulting and Clinical Psychology, 54,* 682–687.

Paperny, D., Hicks, R., & Hammar, S. L. (1980). Munchausen syndrome. *American Journal of Diseases of Children, 134,* 794–796.

Parish, R., Myers, P., Brandner, A., & Templin, K. (1985). Developmental milestones in abused children, and their improvement with a family oriented approach to the treatment of child abuse. *Child Abuse and Neglect, 9,* 245–250.

Parke, R., & Collmer, C. (1975). Child abuse: An interdisciplinary analysis. In E. M. Hetherington (Ed.), *Review of Child Development Research* (Vol. 5, pp. 509–590). Chicago: University of Chicago Press.

Parke, R., & Deur, J. (1972). Schedule of punishment and inhibition of aggression in children. *Developmental Psychology, 7,* 266–269.

Patterson, G. R. (1976). *Living with children: New methods for parents and teachers* (rev. ed.). Champaign, IL: Research Press.

Patterson, G., & Reid, J. (1970). Reciprocity and coercion: Two facets of social systems. In C. Newringer & J. L. Michael (Eds.), *Behavior Modification in Clinical Psychology* (pp. 133–177). New York: Appleton-Century-Crofts.

Patterson, G., Reid, J., Jones, R., & Conger, R. (1975). *A social learning approach to family intervention: Families with aggressive children.* Eugene, Oregon: Castalier Press.

Paulson, M. J., & Chaleff, A., (1973). Parent surrogate roles: A dynamic concept in understanding and treating abusive parents. *Journal of Clinical Child Psychology, 2,* 38–40.

Pelto, V. (1981). Male incest offenders and non-offenders: A comparison of early sexual history. *Dissertations, United States Internations University* (University Microfilms).

Pelton, L. (1978). Child abuse and neglect: The myth of classlessness. *American Journal of Orthopsychiatry, 48,* 608–617.

Perry, M., Doran, L., & Wells, E. (1983). Developmental and behavioral characteristics of the physically abused child. *Journal of Clinical Child Psychology, 12,* 320–324.

Peters, S. D. (1985). *Child sexual abuse and later psychological problems.* Paper presented at the 93rd Annual Meeting of the American Psychological Association, Los Angeles, CA.

Peters, S. D., Wyatt, G. E., & Finkelhor, D. (1986). Prevalence. In D. Finkelhor & Associates (Eds.), *A sourcebook on child sexual abuse* (pp. 15–59). Beverly Hills, CA: Sage Publications.

Pierce, R. L. (1984). Child pornography: A hidden dimension of child abuse. *Child Abuse and Neglect, 8,* 483–493.

Piers, E. V. (1969). *Manual for the Piers-Harris Children's Self-Concept Scale (The Way I Feel About Myself).* Nashville: Counselor Recordings and Tests.

Pillai, V., Collins, A., & Morgan, R. (1982). Family walk-in center—Eaton Socon: Evaluation of a project on preventive intervention based in the community. *Child Abuse and Neglect, 6,* 71–79.

Pithers, W. D., Marques, J. K., Gibat, C. C., & Marlatt, G. A. (1983). Relapse prevention with sexual aggressives: A self-control model of treatment and maintenance of change. In J. G. Greer & I. R. Stuart (Eds.), *The sexual aggressor: Current perspectives on treatment* (pp. 214–239). New York: Van Nostrand Reinhold Co.

Pithers, W. D., Marques, J. K., Gibat, C. C., & Marlatt, G. A. (1983). Relapse prevention with sexual aggressives: A self-control model of treatment and maintenance of change. In J. G. Greer & I. R. Stuart (Eds.), *The sexual aggressor: Current perspectives on treatment* (pp. 214–239). New York: Van Nostrand Reinhold Co.

Pitkanen, L. (1974). The effects of simulation exercises on the control of aggressive behavior in children. *Scandinavian Journal of Psychology, 15,* 169–177.

Pollock, C., & Steele, B. (1972). A therapeutic approach to the parents. In C. H. Kempe & R. E. Helfer (Eds.), *Helping the battered child and his family* (pp. 3–21), Philadelphia, PA: J. B. Lippincott Co.

Porter, E. (1986). *Treating the young male victim of sexual assault: Issues and intervention strategies.* Syracuse, NY: Safer Society Press.

Powers, R., & Osborne, J. (1976). *Fundamentals of behavior.* New York: West Pub Co.

Quinsey, V. L. (in press). Men who have sex with children. In D. Weisstub (Ed.), *Law and mental health: International perspective.* New York: Pergamon Press.

Quinsey, V. L. (1977). The assessment and treatment of child molesters: A review. *Canadian Psychological Review, 18,* 204–220.

Quinsey, V. L., Chaplin, T. C., & Carrigan, W. F. (1980). Biofeedback and signaled punishment in the modification of inappropriate sexual age preferences. *Behavior Therapy, 11,* 567–576.

Rambasek, P. E. (Producer), White, S., Strom, G., & Santilli, G. (Authors). (1985). *The young victims of sexual abuse* (film). Cleveland, OH: Child Guidance Center.

Ramey, J. (1979). Dealing with the last taboo. *Siccus Report 7,* 1–2, 6–7.

Reid, J. B., Taplin, P. S., & Lambert, R. (1981). A social interactional approach to the treatment of abusive families. In R. B. Stuart (Ed.), *Violent behavior: Social learning approaches to prediction, management, and treatment* (pp 83–101). New York: Brunner/Mazel.

Reidy, T. (1977). The aggressive characteristics of abused and neglected children. *Journal of Clinical Psychology, 33,* 1140–1145.

Reitan, R. M., & Davison, L. A. (Eds.). (1974). *Neuropsychology: Current status and applications.* Washington, DC: V. H. Winston & Sons.

Roberts, M., McMahon, R., Forehand, R., & Humphreys, L. (1978). The effects of parental instruction-giving on child compliance. *Behavior Therapy, 9,* 793–398.

Robin, A., & Schneider, M. (1974). *The turtle-technique: An approach to self-control in the classroom.* Unpublished manuscript. State University of New York at Stony Brook.

Robin, A., Schneider, M., & Dolnick, M. (1976). The turtle technique: An extended case study of self-control in the classroom. *Psychology in the Schools, 13,* 449–453.

Rogers, C. M., & Terry, T. (1984). Clinical intervention with boy victims of sexual abuse. In I. R. Stuart & J. G. Greer (Eds.), *Victims of sexual aggression: Treatment of children, women, and men* (pp. 91–104). New York: Van Nostrand Reinhold Co.

Rohrbeck, C., & Twentyman, C. (1983). *A multimodal assessment of impulsiveness in abusing, neglecting, and non-maltreating mothers and their preschool children.* Unpublished Masters Thesis, University of Rochester.

Romanczyk, R., Diament, C., Goren, E., Trunell, C., & Harris, S. (1975). Increasing isolate and social play in severely disturbed children: Intervention and post-intervention effectiveness. *Journal of Autism and Childhood Schizophrenia, 5,* 57–70.

Rosenberg, M. S., & Reppucci, N. D. (1985). Primary prevention of child abuse. *Journal of Consulting and Clinical Psychology, 53,* 576–585.

Rosenzweig, H. D. (1985). Sexual abuse: Some practical implications of our knowledge. In E. H. Newberger and R. Bourne (Eds.), *Unhappy families: Clinical and research perspectives on family violence* (pp. 47–66). Littleton, MA: PSG Publishing Co.

Ross, A. (1981). *Child behavior therapy,* New York: John Wiley & Sons.

Rule, B., & Nesdale, A. (1976). Emotional arousal and aggressive behavior. *Psychological Bulletin, 83,* 851–863.

Rush, F. (1980). *The best kept secret: Sexual abuse of children.* New York: McGraw-Hill.

Russell, A. B., & Trainor, C. M. (1984). *Trends in child abuse and neglect: A national perspective.* Denver, CO: The American Humane Association.

Russell, D. (1984). *Sexual exploitation: Rape, child sexual abuse, and sexual harassment.* Beverly Hills: Sage.

Russell, D. E. H. (1983). The incidence and prevalence of intrafamilial and extrafamilial sexual abuse of female children. *Child Abuse and Neglect, 7,* 133–146.

Russell, D. E. H. (1984). The prevalence and seriousness of incestuous abuse: Stepfathers vs. biological fathers. *Child Abuse and Neglect, 8,* 15–22.

Ryan, G. (1986). Annotated bibliography: Adolescent perpetrators of sexual molestation of children. *Child Abuse and Neglect, 10,* 125–131.

Ryan, T. S. (1986). Problems, errors, and opportunities in the treatment of father-daughter incest. *Journal of Interpersonal Violence, 1,* 113–124.

Rychtarik, R. G., Silverman, W. K., Van Landingham, W. P., & Prue, D. M. (1984). Treatment of an incest victim with implosive therapy: A case study. *Behavior Therapy, 15,* 410–420.

Salicrup, J. (1984). *Spiderman and powerpack: Secrets.* Chicago, IL: National Committee for Prevention of Child Abuse.

Sandler, J., Van Dercar, C., & Milhoan, M. (1978). Training child abusers in the use of positive reinforcement practices. *Behavior Research and Therapy, 16,* 169–175.

Sanford, L. (1980). *The silent children: A parent's guide to the prevention of child sexual abuse.* New York: Anchor Press/Doubleday.

Saslawsky, D. A., & Wurtele, S. K. (1986). Educating children about sexual abuse: Implications for pediatric intervention and possible prevention. *Journal of Pediatric Psychology, 11,* 235–245.

Scherer, M. W., & Nakamura, C. Y. (1968). A fear survey schedule for children (FSS-FC): A factor analytic comparison with manifest anxiety (CMAS). *Behaviour Research and Therapy, 6,* 173–182.

Schmitt, B. (1980). The prevention of child abuse and neglect: A review of the literature with recommendations for application. *Child Abuse and Neglect, 4,* 171–177.

Schneider, M., & Robin, A. (1976). The turtle technique: A method for the self-control of impulsive behavior. In J. D. Drumholtz & C. E. Thoresen (Eds.), *Counseling methods* (pp. 157–163). New York: Holt, Rinehart, & Winston.

Schoettle, U. C. (1980a). Child exploitation: A study of child pornography. *Journal of the American Academy of Child Psychiatry, 19,* 289–299.

Schoettle, U. C. (1980b). Treatment of the child pornography patient. *American Journal of Psychiatry, 137,* 1109–1110.

Schroeder, C. S., Gordon, B. N., & McConnell, P. (1986). Books for parents and children on sexual abuse prevention. *Journal of Clinical Child Psychology, 15,* 178–185.

Scott, W. J. (1980). Attachment and child abuse: A study of social history indicators among mothers of abused children. In G. J. Williams & J. Money (Eds.), *Traumatic abuse and neglect of children at home* (pp. 130–142). Baltimore: The Johns Hopkins Press.

Sedney, M. S., & Brooks, B. (1984). Factors associated with a history of childhood sexual experience in a nonclinical female population. *Journal of the American Academy of Child Psychiatry, 23,* 215, 218.

Seghorn, T. K., Prentky, R. A., & Boucher, R. J. (1987). Childhood sexual abuse in the lives of sexually aggressive offenders. *Journal of the American Academy of Child and Adolescent Psychiatry, 26,* 262–267.

Server, J. C., & Janzen, C. (1982). Contraindications of reconstitution of sexually abusive families. *Child Welfare, 61,* 279–288.

Sgroi, S. M. (1975). Sexual molestation of children. The last frontier of child abuse. *Children Today,* May–June, 18–21.

Sgroi, S. M. (1982a). Pediatric gonorrhea and child sexual abuse: The venereal disease connection. *Sexually Transmitted Diseases, 9,* 154–156.

Sgroi, S. M. (1982b). *Handbook of clinical intervention in child sexual abuse.* Lexington, ME: Lexington Books.

Sgroi, S. M., Porter, F. S., & Blick, L. C. (1982). Validation of child sexual abuse. In S. M. Sgroi (Ed.), *Handbook of clinical intervention in child sexual abuse* (pp. 39–79). Lexington, MA: D.C. Heath & Co.

Shapiro, D. (1984). *Psychological evaluation and expert testimony: A practical guide to forensic work.* New York: Van Nostrand Reinholt Co.

Shapiro, L. E. (1984). *The new short-term therapies for children.* Englewood Cliffs, NJ: Prentice-Hall.

Shaw, W. J., & Walker, C. E. (1979). Use of relaxation in the short-term treatment of fetishistic behavior: An exploratory case study. *Journal of Pediatric Psychology, 4,* 403–407.

Shnaps, Y., Frand, M., Rotem, Y., & Trosh, M. (1981). The chemically abused child. *Pediatrics, 68,* 119–121.

Showers, J., Farber, E. D., Joseph, J. A., Oshins, L., & Johnson, C. F. (1983). The sexual victimization of boys: A three-year survey. *Health Values: Achieving High Level Wellness, 7,* 15–18.

Shure, M., & Spivack, G. (1978). *Problem-solving techniques in childrearing*. San Francisco: Jossey-Bass.

Silbert, M. H., & Pines, A. M. (1981). Sexual child abuse as an antecedent to prostitution. *Child Abuse and Neglect, 5,* 407–411.

Silbert, M. H., & Pines, A. M. (1983). Early sexual exploitation as an influence in prostitution. *Social Work,* July-August, 285–289.

Silver, L. B., Dublin, C. C., & Lourie, R. S. (1969). Does violence breed violence? Contributions from study of the child abuse syndrome. *American Journal of Psychiatry, 126,* 404–407.

Silverman, F. N. (1953). The roentgen manifestations of unrecognized skeletal trauma in infants. *American Journal of Roentgenology, Radium Therapy and Nuclear Medicine, 69,* 413–427.

Silvern, L., Waterman, J., Sobesky, W., & Ryan, V. (1979). Effects of a developmental model of perspective taking training. *Child Development, 50,* 243–246.

Simpson, K. (1967). The battered baby problem. *Royal Society of Health Journal, 87,* 168–170.

Smith, S. M. (1975). *The battered child syndrome*. London: Butterworths.

Smith, S. M., & Hanson, R. (1975). Interpersonal relationships and child-rearing practices in 214 parents of battered children. *British Journal of Psychiatry, 125,* 513–525.

Smith, S. M., Hanson, R., & Noble, S. (1974). Social aspects of the battered baby syndrome. *British Journal of Psychiatry, 125,* 568–582.

Smith, T. A., & Conte, J. R. (1985). *Prevention messages for the perpetrator: What perpetrators have to say about prevention of child abuse*. Paper presented at the Seventh National Conference on Child Abuse and Neglect, Chicago, IL.

Soeffing, M. (1975). Abused children are exceptional children. *Exceptional Children, 142,* 126–133.

Solnit, A., & Stark, M. (1961). Mourning the birth of a defective child. *Psychoanalytic Study of the Child, 16,* 523.

Spielberger, C. D., Gorsuch, R. L., & Lushene, R. (1970). *State Trait Anxiety Inventory*. Palo Alto, CA: Consulting Psychologists Press.

Spinetta, J. J. (1978). Parental personality factors in child abuse. *Journal of Consulting and Clinical Psychology, 46,* 1409–1414.

Spinetta, J. J., & Rigler, D. (1972). The child abusing parent: A psychological review. *Psychological Bulletin, 77,* 296–304.

Spivack, G., Platt, J., & Shure, M. (1976). *The problem solving approach to adjustment*. San Francisco: Jossey-Bass, Inc.

Spivack, G., & Shure, M. (1974). *Social adjustment of young children. A cognitive approach to solving real-life problems*. San Francisco: Jossey-Bass, Inc.

Steele, B. (1980). Psychodynamic factors in child abuse. In C. H. Kempe & R. E. Helfer (Eds.), *The battered child* (3rd ed., pp. 49–85). Chicago: University of Chicago Press.

Steele, B. F. (1970). Parental abuse of infants and small children. In E. J. Anthony & T. Benedick (Eds.), *Parenthood: Its psychology and psychopathology* (pp. 449–477). Boston: Little, Brown.

Steele, B. F., & Alexander, H. (1981). Long-term effects of sexual abuse in childhood. In P. B. Mrazek & C. H. Kempe (Eds.), *Sexually abused children and their families* (pp. 223–233). New York: Pergamon Press.

Steele, B. F. (1976). Violence within the family. In R. E. Helfer & C. H. Kempe (Eds.), *Child abuse and neglect: The family and the community* (pp. 3–23). Cambridge, MA: Ballinger Publishers.

Steele, B., & Pollock, C. (1974). A psychiatric study of parents who abuse infants and small children. In R. E. Helfer and C. H. Kempe (Eds.), *The battered child* (2nd Edition), pp. 89–138). Chicago: University of Chicago Press.

Stein, R., & Jessop, D. (1984). Does pediatric home care make a difference for children with chronic illness? Findings from the Pediatric Ambulatory Care Treatment Study. *Pediatrics, 68,* 845.

Strain, P., Shores, R., & Timm, M. (1977). Effects of peer social initiation on the behavior of withdrawn preschool children. *Journal of Applied Behavior Analysis, 10,* 289–298.

Strong, B., Wilson, S., Robbins, M., & Johns, T. (1981). *Human sexuality: Essentials* (2nd ed.). St. Paul, MN: West Publishing Co.

Stuart, R. (1980). *Helping couples change: A social learning approach to marital therapy.* New York: Guilford Press.

Stuart, V., & Stuart, C. K. (1983). *Sexuality and sexual assault: Disabled perspective.* Marshall, MN: Southwest State University.

Sturkie, K. (1983). Structured group treatment for sexually abused children. *Health and Social Work, 8,* 299–308.

Summit, R., & Kryso, J. (1978). Sexual abuse of children: A clinical spectrum. *American Journal of Orthopsychiatry, 48,* 237–251.

Swan, H. L., Press, A. N., & Briggs, S. L. (1985). Child sexual abuse prevention: Does it work? *Child Welfare, 64,* 395–405.

Swensen, C. H., & Hartsough, D. M. (1983). Crisis intervention and brief psychotherapy. In C. E. Walker (Ed.), *The handbook of clinical psychology: Theory, research and practice* (Vol. II, pp. 713–744). Homewood, IL: Dow Jones-Irwin.

Swift, C. (1979). The prevention of sexual child abuse: Focus on the perpetrator. *Journal of Clinical Child Psychology, 8,* 133–136.

Tarter, R. E., Hegedus, A. M., Alterman, A. I., & Katz-Garris, L. (1983). Cognitive capacities of juvenile violent, nonviolent, and sexual offenders. *The Journal of Nervous and Mental Disease, 171,* 564–567.

Thomas, J. N., & Rogers, C. M. (1983). A treatment program for intrafamily juvenile sexual offenders. In J. G. Greer & I. R. Stuart (Eds.), *The sexual aggressor: Current perspectives in treatment* (pp. 127–143). New York: Van Nostrand Reinhold Co.

Thomson, J. A. K. (1953). *The ethics of Aristotle,* London: Allen & Unwin.

Thorne, F. C. (1965). *The Sex Inventory.* Brandon, Vermont: Psychology Research Associates.

Tilelli, J. A., Turek, D., & Jaffe, A. C. (1980). Sexual abuse of children: Clinical findings and implications for management. *New England Journal of Medicine, 302,* 319–323.

Tinklenberg, R. (1973). Alcohol and violence. In P. Bourne and R. Fox (Eds.), *Alcoholism: Progress in research and treatment* (pp. 195–210). New York: Academic Press.

Trower, P., Yardley, K., Bryant, B., & Shaw, P. (1978). The treatment of social failure: A comparison of anxiety-reduction and skills-acquisition procedures on two social problems. *Behavior Modification, 2,* 41–60.

Tsai, M., & Wagner, N. N. (1978). Therapy groups for women sexually molested as children. *Archives of Sexual Behavior, 7,* 417–427.

Turner, S. M., & Frank, E. (1981). Behavior therapy in the treatment of rape victims. In L. Michelson, M. Hersen, & S. M. Turner (Eds.), *Future perspectives in behavior therapy* (pp. 269–291). New York: Plenum.

Twentyman, C., & McFall, R. (1975). Behavioral training of social skills in shy males. *Journal of Consulting and Clinical Psychology, 43,* 384–395.

Tyler, R. P. T., & Stone, L. E. (1985). Child pornography: Perpetuating the sexual victimization of children. *Child Abuse and Neglect, 9,* 313–318.

Van Stolk, M. (1972). *The battered child in Canada.* Toronto: McClelland & Stewart.

Varley, C. K. (1984). Schizophreniform psychoses in mentally retarded adolescent girls following sexual assault. *American Journal of Psychiatry, 141,* 593–595.

Varni, J., & Henker, B. (1979). A self-regulation approach to the treatment of three hyperactive boys. *Child Behavior Therapy, 1,* 171–191.

Vasta, R. (1982). Physical child abuse: A dual-component analysis. *Developmental Review, 2,* 125–149.

Visher, E. B., & Visher, J. S. (1979). *Step-families: Myths and realities.* Secaucus, NJ: Citadel Press.

Wachter, O. (1983). *No more secrets for me.* Boston: Little Brown & Co.

Wahler, R. (1980). The insular mother: Her problem in parent-child treatment. *Journal of Applied Behavior Analysis, 13,* 207–219.

Wahler, R., Leske, G., & Rogers, E. (1979). The insular family: A deviance support system for oppositional children. In L. A. Hammerlynck (Ed.), *Behavioral systems for the developmentally disabled: I. School and family environments* (pp. 102–127). New York: Brunner/Mazel.

Walker, C. E. (1979). Behavioral intervention in a pediatric setting. In J. Regis McNamara (Ed.), *Behavior approaches to medicine: Application and analysis* (pp. 227–266). New York: Plenum Press.

Walker, C. E., Hedberg, A., Clement, P., & Wright, L. (1981). *Clinical procedures for behavior therapy.* Englewood Cliffs, NJ: Prentice Hall.

Walters, D. R. (1975). *Physical and sexual abuse of children: Causes and treatment.* Bloomington, IN: Indiana University Press.

Wasserman, S. (1968). The abused parent of the abused child. *Children, 14,* 175–179.

Watkins, J. T. (1973). Rational-emotive therapy and the treatment of behavioral excesses. *Rational Living, 8,* 29–31.

Watkins, J. T. (1977). The rational-emotive dynamics of impulsive disorders. In A. Ellis & R. Greiger (Eds.), *Handbook of rational-emotive therapy* (pp. 135–169). New York: Springer.

Watkins, J. T. (1983). Treatment of disorders of impulse control. In C. E. Walker (Ed.), *The handbook of clinical psychology: Theory, research and practice* (Vol. II, pp. 590–632). Homewood, IL: Dow Jones-Irwin.

Wechsler, D. (1981). *Manual for the Wechsler Adult Intelligence Scale—Revised.* New York: Psychological Corporation.

Weinrott, M., Carson, J., & Wilchesky, M. (1979). Teacher-mediated treatment of social withdrawal. *Behavior Therapy, 10,* 281–294.

Westerlund, E. (1983). Counseling women with histories of incest. *Women and Therapy, 2,* 17–31.

White, S., Strom, G. A. Santilli, G., & Halpin, B. M. (1986). Interviewing young sexual abuse victims with anatomically correct dolls. *Child Abuse and Neglect, 10,* 519–529.

Wickes, B. R., & Madigan, R. (1985, August). *Parental bonding, self-esteem, and sexual abuse: A retrospective study.* Paper presented at the annual meeting of the American Psychological Association, Los Angeles, CA.

Williams, G. J. (1978). Child-abuse. In P. R. Magrab (Ed.), *Psychological management of pediatric problems* (Vol. II, pp. 253–291). Baltimore: University Park Press.

Wilson, E. F. (1977). Estimation of the age of cutaneous contusions in child abuse. *Pediatrics, 60,* 750–752.

Wolf, S. C. (1985). Evaluation and treatment: Characteristics of adult sexual offenders. *Sexual Violence Quarterly, 1,* 7–10.

Wolfe, D. (1985). Child-abusive parents: An empirical review and analysis. *Psychological Bulletin, 97,* 462–482.

Wolfe, D., Kaufman, K., Aragona, J., & Sandler, J. (1981). *The child management program for abusive parents: Procedures for developing a child abuse intervention program.* Winter Park, FL: Anna Publishing Inc.

Wolfe, D., Fairbanks, J., Kelly, J., & Bradlyn, A. (1983). Child abusive parents: Physiological responses to stressful and nonstressful behavior in children. *Behavioral Assessment, 5,* 363–371.

Wolfe, D. A., MacPherson, T., Blount, R., & Wolfe, V. V. (1986). Evaluation of a brief intervention for educating school children in awareness of physical and sexual abuse. *Child Abuse and Neglect, 10,* 85–92.

Wolfe, D., & Mosk, M. (1983). Behavioral comparisons of children from abusive and distressed families. *Journal of Consulting and Clinical Psychology, 51,* 702–708.

Wolfe, D., Sandler, J., & Kaufman, K. (1981). A competency-based parent training program for abusive parents. *Journal of Consulting and Clinical Psychology, 49,* 633–640.

Wolfe, F. A. (1985). *Twelve female sexual offenders.* Paper presented at Next Steps in Research on the Assessment and Treatment of Sexually Aggressive Persons (Paraphiliacs), St. Louis, MO.

Wolff, R. (1977). Systematic desensitization and negative practice to alter the after-effects of a rape attempt. *Journal of Behavior Therapy and Experimental Psychiatry, 8,* 423–425.

Wolman, B., & Stricker, G. (Eds.), (1983). *Handbook of family and marital therapy.* New York: Pergamon Press.

Woods, S. C., & Dean, K. S. (1985). *Evaluating sexual abuse prevention strategies.* Paper presented at the Seventh National Conference on Child Abuse and Neglect, Chicago.

Woollcott, P., Aceto, T., Rutt, C., Bloom, M., & Glick, R. (1982). Doctor shopping with the child as proxy patient: A variant of child abuse. *Journal of Pediatrics, 101,* 297–301.

Woolley, P. V., & Evans, W. A. (1955). Significance of skeletal lesions in infants resembling those of traumatic origin. *Journal of the American Medical Association, 158,* 539–543.

Wurtele, S. K., Saslawsky, D. A., Miller, C. L., Marrs, S. R., & Britcher, J. C. (1986). Teaching personal safety skills for potential prevention of sexual abuse: A comparison of treatments. *Journal of Consulting and Clinical Psychology, 54,* 688–692.

Yorukoglu, A., & Kemph, J. P. (1966). Children not severely damaged by incest with a parent. *Journal of the American Academy of Child Psychiatry, 5,* 111–124.

Young, L. (1964). *Wednesday's children: A study of child neglect and abuse.* New York: McGraw-Hill Book Co.

Zalba, S. R. (1967). The abused child: II. A typology for classification and treatment. *Social Work, 12,* 70–79.

Zaphiris, A. G. (1986). The sexually abused boy. *Preventing Sexual Abuse, 1,* 1–4.

Author Index

205

Subject Index

About the Authors

C. Eugene Walker, Ph.D., is Professor and Director of Pediatric Psychology Training at the University of Oklahoma Medical School. He is also Associate Chief of Mental Health Services at Oklahoma Children's Memorial Hospital. Dr. Walker, who received his Ph.D. in Clinical Psychology from Purdue University in 1965, is a frequent lecturer at meetings and workshops on pediatric psychology and child psychotherapy. He has authored 10 books and approximately 200 articles. Dr. Walker is currently President of the Society of Pediatric Psychology. He is a Past-President of the Southwestern Psychological Association, Oklahoma Psychological Association, and the Section for Continuing Professional Development, Division 12, American Psychological Association.

Barbara L. Bonner, Ph.D., is an Assistant Professor in the Department of Psychiatry and Behavioral Sciences at the University of Oklahoma Health Sciences Center. She received her degree in Clinical Psychology from Oklahoma State University in 1984. She completed a 2-year Postdoctoral Fellowship in Pediatric Psychology and Adolescent Medicine at the University of Oklahoma Health Sciences Center. In 1986, she was awarded a grant from the Gannett Foundation to continue her work in the treatment and prevention of child abuse. Dr. Bonner is a Consultant to the Oklahoma Office of Child Abuse Prevention and is directing a project funded by the National Center on Child Abuse and Neglect to develop advanced training curricula in child sexual abuse for physicians, psychologists, nurses, and social workers. Dr. Bonner has authored several articles on psychotherapy outcome with children. She has lectured and presented workshops on child abuse both nationally and internationally.

Keith L. Kaufman, Ph.D, is Assistant Professor in the Department of

Pediatrics of Ohio State University, located at Columbus Children's Hospital. He serves as the Coordinator of Psychological Services for the Hospital's Child Abuse Program, providing both clinical and research consultation. He received his Ph.D. in Clinical/Community Psychology in 1985 from the University of South Florida. He has coauthored a number of articles in the area of child abuse as well as *The Child Management Program for Abusive Parents: Procedures for Developing a Child Abuse Intervention Program* (Anna Publishing, 1982).

Psychology Practitioner Guidebooks

Editors
Arnold P. Goldstein, Syracuse University
Leonard Krasner, Stanford University & SUNY at Stony Brook
Sol L. Garfield, Washington University

Elsie M. Pinkston & Nathan L. Linsk—CARE OF THE ELDERLY: A Family Approach

Donald Meichenbaum—STRESS INOCULATION TRAINING

Sebastiano Santostefano—COGNITIVE CONTROL THERAPY WITH CHILDREN AND ADOLESCENTS

Lillie Weiss, Melanie Katzman & Sharlene Wolchik—TREATING BULIMIA: A Psychoeducational Approach

Edward B. Blanchard & Frank Andrasik—MANAGEMENT OF CHRONIC HEADACHES: A Psychological Approach

Raymond G. Romanczyk—CLINICAL UTILIZATION OF MICROCOMPUTER TECHNOLOGY

Philip H. Bornstein & Marcy T. Bornstein—MARITAL THERAPY: A Behavioral-Communications Approach

Michael T. Nietzel & Ronald C. Dillehay—PSYCHOLOGICAL CONSULTATION IN THE COURTROOM

Elizabeth B. Yost, Larry E. Beutler, M. Anne Corbishley & James R. Allender—GROUP COGNITIVE THERAPY: A Treatment Method for Depressed Older Adults

Lillie Weiss—DREAM ANALYSIS IN PSYCHOTHERAPY

Edward A. Kirby & Liam K. Grimley—UNDERSTANDING AND TREATING ATTENTION DEFICIT DISORDER

Jon Eisenson—LANGUAGE AND SPEECH DISORDERS IN CHILDREN

Eva L. Feindler & Randolph B. Ecton—ADOLESCENT ANGER CONTROL: Cognitive-Behavioral Techniques

Michael C. Roberts—PEDIATRIC PSYCHOLOGY: Psychological Interventions and Strategies for Pediatric Problems

Daniel S. Kirschenbaum, William G. Johnson & Peter M. Stalonas, Jr.—TREATING CHILDHOOD AND ADOLESCENT OBESITY

W. Stewart Agras—EATING DISORDERS: Management of Obesity, Bulimia and Anorexia Nervosa

Ian H. Gotlib & Catherine A. Colby—TREATMENT OF DEPRESSION: An Interpersonal Systems Approach

Walter B. Pryzwansky & Robert N. Wendt—PSYCHOLOGY AS A
PROFESSION: Foundations of Practice

Cynthia D. Belar, William W. Deardorff & Karen E. Kelly—THE
PRACTICE OF CLINICAL HEALTH PSYCHOLOGY

Paul Karoly & Mark P. Jensen—MULTIMETHOD ASSESSMENT
OF CHRONIC PAIN

William L. Golden, E. Thomas Dowd & Fred Friedberg—
HYPNOTHERAPY: A Modern Approach

Patricia Lacks—BEHAVIORAL TREATMENT FOR PERSISTENT
INSOMNIA

Arnold P. Goldstein & Harold Keller—AGGRESSIVE BEHAVIOR:
Assessment and Intervention

C. Eugene Walker, Barbara L. Bonner & Keith L. Kaufman—THE
PHYSICALLY AND SEXUALLY ABUSED CHILD: Evaluation
and Treatment